D0394737

IRISH
america

IRISH
america

Coming into Clover

Maureen Dezell

THE EVOLUTION OF A PEOPLE AND A CULTURE

DOUBLEDAY
New York London Toronto Sydney Auckland

PUBLISHED BY DOUBLEDAY
a division of Random House, Inc.
1540 Broadway, New York, New York 10036

Book design by Fearn Cutler de Vicq de Cumptich

DOUBLEDAY and the portrayal of an anchor with a dolphin are
trademarks of Doubleday, a division of Random House, Inc.

Acknowledgment is made for the following artwork and photographs: emigrant's letter and envelope fragment, © 1988 by Geraldine O'Reilly; photograph of Maureen Dezell, by John Dezell; George Primrose, courtesy of Culver Pictures Inc.; James Cagney and Pat O'Brien in *Angels with Dirty Faces,* courtesy of Photofest; Donald O'Connor and Gene Kelly in *Singin' in the Rain,* courtesy of Photofest; Charles Coughlin photograph, courtesy of AP/Wide World Photos; Dr. Tom Dooley photograph, courtesy of St. Louis University Archives; Tom Hayden photograph, courtesy of Tom Hayden; photograph of Michael Harrington by John Blanding; Knights of the Red Branch, courtesy of the United Irish Cultural Center, San Francisco; John Callahan illustration, © 2000 John Callahan, distributed by Levin Represents; Margaret Tobin "Molly" Brown, courtesy of Library of Congress; Irish Repertory Theatre by Eric Baer, courtesy Irish Repertory Theatre; "The Ignorant Vote" of the Irish and African Americans, © 1876 by Corbis; photograph of Old St. Patrick's Church by Erin Jaeb; photograph of Helena Mulkerns by Mike Mandel; photograph of a scene from *Famine* by John Hyde, courtesy of Súgán Theatre; Eugene O'Neill and George M. Cohan photograph, courtesy of George Eastman House.

Acknowledgment is made for the following material: "You're Not Irish," © 1987 Robbie O'Connell, reprinted by permission of Slievenamor Music BMI; portions of text from *American Catholic: The Saints and Sinners Who Built America's Most Powerful Church,* © 1997 Charles R. Morris, by permission of Random House Inc.; lyrics from "Livin' in America" by Black 47.

Library of Congress Cataloging-in-Publication Data

Dezell, Maureen.
Irish America: coming into clover: the evolution of a people and a culture
Maureen Dezell.— 1st ed.
p. cm.
Includes bibliographical references and index.
1. Irish Americans—History. 2. Irish Americans—Social life and customs.
3. Irish Americans—Social conditions. 4. Irish American Catholics. I. Title.
E184.I6 D49 2001
973'.049162—dc21
00-063921

ISBN 0-385-49595-1

1   3   5   7   9   10   8   6   4   2

For John and Christopher

Acknowledgments

Thank you to Sean Clarkin for his wide-ranging interest and intellect; Caroline Knapp for her keen writer's eye and the comfort of knowing she was there; Tom McNaught both for editing and ebullience; Eileen Sullivan Shakespear for her inspiration and because when she liked what she read, I knew the rest was worth pursuing; and Sandra Shea for her wisdom.

I owe special thanks to Michael Patrick MacDonald for his insight and interest, and to Ciarán O'Reilly for his observations, enthusiasm, and generosity at so many junctures over the last three years. I didn't know Michael or Ciarán before I started this book, can't imagine having done it without either of them, and know I wouldn't have laughed as much if I had. As we Irish know, that counts for a lot.

Those who knew and miss the late John Brennan, as I do, will recognize his humor and acuity here.

Thomas Fleming offered excellent advice on the manuscript. I am indebted to Larry McCaffrey, whose teaching, books, and articles have illuminated the history of Ireland and Irish America for so many, and who shared his understanding with me in conversation, e-mails, and in reading and commenting on chapters in the book.

Thanks to savvy readers: Ellen Barry, James T. Fisher, Ruth-Ann Harris, Peter Keough, Kevin Mullen, Timothy Meagher, John Shea, and Mary Shea.

Thanks, too, to Beth Carney, Paul Colford, Ellen Denison, John King, Dick Lehr, Pamela McDermott, Bob McGrath, Tom O'Gorman, Orla O'Hanrahan, Maria O'Meara and the Bransfield O'Meara clan, Paul Shakespear, and Elizabeth Shannon.

My agent, John Taylor Williams, more than lived up to his reputation as "super-agent Ike Williams."

The *Boston Globe* gave me time off from my job in the Living/Arts department to write, and I am grateful to Mary Jane Wilkinson, deputy managing editor for features, for arranging the leave and easing the transition to it and from it.

Kathleen Hennrikus's exhaustive library research, Amy MacDonald's help with connections, and Anthony Savoie's patience and expertise in guiding me through a thicket of opinion polls and demographics are fundamental to this book. I truly could not have pulled together the vast details that went into this book without the help of Elizabeth Goodman, researcher extraordinaire, whose wide-ranging intelligence, skill, and resourcefulness wowed me with every phone call and e-mail (and there were a lot of phone calls and e-mails).

I have been blessed by the editing gods in Amy Scheibe at Doubleday, whose smarts and savvy in shaping the book were enhanced by a sense of humor and perspective about my subject that come from marrying into the Flynn family. Barbara Flanagan's line editing was superb and her perseverance admirable and essential during a few frantic fall weeks. Thanks also to the ever-resourceful Chris Litman.

I am thankful for my family, Dezells, Sheas, and Sullivans on both sides.

No one is more deserving of my gratitude and appreciation than John and Christopher Shea, my husband and son, who kept hearth, home, and me together with extraordinary patience, humor, and love.

Contents

Illustrations

Now, who do you think you are?

This is a book about an Irish America that isn't on parade on St.
Patrick's Day. It is a montage of reporting and history, observation and opinion—snapshots of a subculture taken at the turn of
the millennium, focused on people and experiences that are frequently left out of Irish American group portraits. Written by, for, and about
Irish Americans who have a more than sentimental interest in their heritage,
this is not a tale of saints and sinners, heroes and heroics. There is little in
the way of Kennedy family hagiography, hoary political legend, or nostalgia
for the days when most white-collar Irishmen were ordained.

The question that resounded in my mind while I researched this book
was "Who do you think you are?" The interrogative is tongue-in-cheek but
double-edged. It is a straightforward inquiry I posed to more than one
hundred people of Irish descent around the country in the past three years:
What, if anything, does Irish identity consist of in the United States today?
How does the Irish heritage shape sense of self; community; worldview?

The question also echoes the searing, sneering demand that reverberates in many an Irish Catholic psyche. "Who do you think you are?" is a
rhetorical question, asked incessantly by people whose intent is to hum-

ble. It demands a mute response, a swallowing of the dread sin of pride. The voices in this book answer back—in ways I hope readers will find refreshing and revealing, as I did.

Irish Catholics traditionally have been brought up not to think too highly of ourselves, and as a rule we do not. Overextended humility is, I think, to blame for the sorry way so much Irish culture presents itself in this country: the Eiresatz of plastic shamrocks and green beer; the pious intolerance that poses as Irish pride at the New York St. Patrick's Day parade and in ethnic enclaves; the notion that getting drunk is the same thing as being Irish.

Taught to underestimate our own achievements, we tend not to acknowledge the complexity of the Irish experience or our contribution to the American mix.

I interviewed college students, teachers, police officers, writers, nuns, priests, apostates, wealthy entrepreneurs, and impoverished artists, from age twenty to ninety-something. As a group, they were more affable and accommodating than most people I encounter as a journalist. They were an unusually voluble and quotable lot. Categorically, they had good senses of humor.

Yet most of them *apologized* at the end of interviews. At least three-quarters of the people I talked with felt compelled to say that what they'd told me probably didn't amount to much. ("Well, I hope some of this was a little helpful"; or "I don't think I've told you anything you'll be able to use, Maureen.") These were busy, accomplished men and women I had sought out because I suspected—usually with reason—that they had something of interest to say. They'd gone out of their way to talk to me about their families and their experiences.

Self-deprecation, I learned, is sine qua non in the Irish Catholic subculture. It is as ubiquitous as humor, fine talk, loyalty, and sympathy for the underdog, as characteristic as a tendency to drink too much, and to harbor trepidation that the light at the end of the tunnel is a train.

A trinity of sorts

Irish America: Coming into Clover was inspired by three St. Patrick's Days. Rather, I should say, it was inspired by the ambivalence and frustration I felt—first as an Irish American living in Boston, then as a mother, and shortly thereafter as a reporter and writer—about the way the Irish legacy is observed on March 17 in the United States.

Like many Americans who trace their ancestry to Eire, I grew up with limited knowledge and some fuzzy feeling about my heritage. Not begosh and begorrah fuzzy—I always knew that was nonsense—but benignly vague. I recall thinking it had to do with being Catholic but not Italian or Polish; that it involved a lot of joking, singing, and drinking, and an affinity for what was called Anglo-Irish literature. (For the record, Dezell is a derivation of an Irish surname.)

My middle-class, cold war Catholic upbringing notwithstanding, I was taken aback when I arrived as an undergraduate at Boston College to find that "Irish" was all too often a synonym for intolerance if not outright racism in Boston itself; a class-consciousness and defensiveness that occasionally devolves into pugilism, as it did in South Boston at the time of court-ordered public school integration in the mid-1970s. Like many others, I distanced myself as far and as fast as I could from Irishness in the city that likes to think of itself as the capital of Irish America.

I might never have paid much heed to this particular ethnic identity if I hadn't unwittingly become a cultural emissary of sorts when I was in my twenties and fell into, then out of, a career teaching English to people from other countries. I taught in a program at Boston University that emphasized writing and academic skills along with "cultural orientation." My classes might include a Japanese businessman, a Senegalese engineer, a few Europeans on extended vacation, and a bevy of South American and Middle Eastern undergraduates. We talked a lot about culture (it's safer than religion and politics) in class.

Occasionally I had students who were interested not just in my American way of doing and assuming, but in my Irish background. In their decades of teaching, preaching, and doing international relief work around the globe, the people of Ireland have become among the better liked of world citizens, and my students were curious about Ireland's national holiday and why it was such a big deal for the Irish in America.

One year, a group of students I was particularly fond of asked me to take them on a field trip to the St. Patrick's Day parade in South Boston. Not only would this be a good chance to speak English and learn about American customs, they said; it would give everyone a chance to celebrate *my* culture.

Readers who don't know Boston might reasonably assume this was a fine idea. Those who do will know why I was aghast at the very idea of bringing a group of young, sophisticated adults from Africa, Asia, and the Middle East to South Boston in the late 1970s. For all its decent and admirable qualities, this is not a community that has embraced cultural exchange. Exclusivity is a tradition, a point of "Southie pride" for some. That was particularly true at the time, a few years after forced integration, when the presence of people with black, brown, or beige faces, much less a group of them, speaking halting English, would be seen not only as an intrusion but as a provocation.

If my gaggle of internationals ventured into this God-, family-, and country-loving community, chances were very good that some would be verbally taunted. ("Hey, raghead!"; "Look, it's a yellow horde!") It was entirely possible that one of the Africans or Arabs would get beaten up. After all, many locals were sure to be celebrating the glories of their Celtic inheritance by throwing fists and throwing up on their shoes, emblems of Irish "pride" all over America.

It was at that point that I realized how far removed American St.

Patrick's Day was from the Irish culture my students and I admired. This behavior was boorish, obnoxious; it was not Irish, I explained. It was the first of many times I explained that the Boston Irish are *different* from the rest of the American Irish.

The power of kitsch

In 1996, some well-intended soul pinned a "Kiss Me I'm Irish" button on my then seven-and-a-half-year-old son on St. Patrick's Day.

I felt an irrational loathing for this little piece of kitsch that had less to do with the thing itself than with my frustration in telling him: "There is so much more to your background than that!"—and not having much more to say.

I realized that Christopher Dezell Shea was—and is—growing up in multi-culti America, celebrating diversity at school, forming friendships with kids who spend their Sundays at black evangelical churches or weekday afternoons at Hebrew school. With a single exception (one of my great-grandfathers was a Swamp Yankee), every one of his forebears (at least those born in the past two centuries) is Irish. When John Shea and I tied the knot, four women named Eileen Sullivan were at the wedding. Surely Christopher, who could blend in with any kid crowd in County Kerry, should have more to represent his heritage than a button with a silly slogan based on God knows what—and green beer when he gets a little older.

When John and I were his age, Catholicism was both a religion and a cultural identity. That isn't the case anymore—certainly not for those of us who gravitate to the fringes of the Roman Catholic fold or leave it. Some of our peers have turned to Celtic or Irish culture as a substitute for or enhancement to religion, and the recent surge of enthusiasm for all things green has spawned a spate of Celtophilia in the United States in the past few years. I love Irish literature and theater and enjoy Irish music, but I find Celtophiles almost as absurd as Anglophiles. (Only Americans could completely forget about historic details like human sacrifice.) I am not a Celt, nor am I of Ireland. I'm an American. An Irish American.

The following green season, I wrote an article about American St. Patrick's Day for the Living/Arts section of the *Boston Globe*. The piece bemoaned the booze, blarney, and stage Irish strutting that stands for Irish culture in mid-March in America and included an array of pithy quotes from people like Pete Hamill, Mary Gordon, the psychiatrist Garrett O'Connor (who called the celebrations pathological), and Frank McCourt, who at that point was a retired schoolteacher with a new surprise bestseller.

As a rule, readers call reporters when they're angry or upset, so I was pleasantly surprised when I got to work the morning the article appeared to find my voice mailbox filled with messages, all but one laudatory. More than half the callers had Irish accents. Like a lot of Irish Americans, I have an atavistic fondness for warm words spoken with a brogue ("Sure, Maureen, isn't it about time someone said this"). But theirs was not an unexpected response. Anyone who's spent any time at all around the native Irish knows how much they hate what we've done to their national holiday.

More striking, the calls from Irish Americans kept up all day. A few were belligerent. (One woman actually sputtered: "Just who do you think you are?") There were the inevitable letters accusing me of bigotry and racism. (Please.) But the response from people who felt much the same way I did continued. And I felt I had more to learn and say.

Living in American time

Teaching in an international setting for six years had stimulated my interest in culture—not my own, necessarily (I didn't think I had one at that point). I was fascinated by the unspoken assumptions about family and friendship, space and time, that make people from, say, North Africa different from those in Japan.

That cultural distinctions were quite real and not soon to disappear in a shrinking world was driven home to me each time I threw a party for a class at the end of the semester. If it started at 8 P.M., the Japanese students would almost invariably arrive at my apartment at about 6:30, laden with fish, vegetables, flour, and oil with which they'd make elaborate platters of tempura that were ready to serve at 8 on the dot.

No one else would be there. Typically, Europeans started drifting in with bottles of wine within the next half hour. Latin Americans most often showed up between 9 and 10, ready to dance, not nibble. The Middle Easterners came even later, as did the Africans. Everyone came at what he or she assumed was the right or polite time to arrive. Culture has less to do with what we say and do than with our assumptions about how to say and do it.

But it was another American teacher who first pointed out to me that I lived life with my own discreet set of assumptions. A native New Yorker of upper-class WASP mien (she said "to-mah-to"), she told me she found the Irish *fascinating*. She explained that she had a dear friend of Irish extraction in graduate school—I'll assume her name was Mary—whose home my friend adored going to for Sunday dinner. For one thing, the political arguments at the table were fierce. "Why, it was just like the beginning of *Portrait of the Artist*—the passion, and the way people would yell at one another, even old people." For another, Mary had a pair of colorful maiden aunts who were often in attendance.

The two were career women at a time when few middle-class women worked. They were great conversationalists, readers, theatergoers. One of the things that impressed my friend was that they commanded more respect in their family than many unmarried American women, whose opinions tend to be ignored. None of that for these two, who, of course, had plenty of observations to which they expected attention would be paid. When my friend had last seen the duo, they had been quite pleased to observe that Mary had broken up with her last boyfriend. They didn't like him, my friend said, guffawing, because he didn't speak well. That was *exceedingly* important. "Can you imagine?"

Well, of course I could imagine. Nothing I'd heard about Mary's family struck me as unusual at all. I was in my twenties then and assumed that impassioned political arguments at the dinner table were normal. I'd met any number of women like the aunts—didn't most families have them? As for their reservations about inarticulate men: I, like any number of my female forebears, could only wonder: What woman would want anything to do with a man who didn't speak well?

At the edge

I am not a military brat, the child of diplomats, or a scion of adventurers. My father was in the insurance business and worked for a while for corporations that transferred employees from city to city on a regular basis. Between the time I was born and my sixteenth birthday, we moved eight times in and around New York, Cleveland, southern New Jersey, and suburban Baltimore, where, for reasons never entirely clear to me, my parents stopped moving. My three younger brothers and sister, who hadn't entered high school at the time, grew up in what's known as "Balmermerlin." I went off to college two years later and would return only for visits.

Like many people who move a lot as children, I spent many formative hours in a temporal zone at the edge of schoolyards, in the corners of playgrounds, and anyplace else where "new kids" hang out alone, doing things like playing tic-tac-toe in the dirt against ourselves. What many of us are really doing as we feign independence is watching; learning the differences between the kid culture we came from and the one we're about to experience.

Observing the nuances of different cold war Catholic youth cultures in the 1960s made me an observant outsider-insider of Irish America's unwritten assumptions and unspoken rules. It also honed my skepticism about received wisdoms and the credibility of social conventions, many of which struck me as arbitrary and silly (and still do). My experience also contradicted a fundamental premise of parochial school education: that all rules exist for sound reasons (girlhood behavior that drove one order of nuns to frenzy hardly fazed sisters at another school).

Like a lot of girls who grow up to be writers, I also spent many childhood hours eavesdropping on adult conversations. I realize now that, each time we moved, my parents also were newcomers or outsiders. But my mother is an incredibly gregarious person who organizes dinner parties and large get-togethers with the frequency and skill many others put into hobbies like golf or tennis, so we always had company. There were plenty of opportunities to huddle on staircases or pretend to read while the grownups got exercised about the Cuban Missile Crisis or Vatican II.

The liveliest talk and the loudest laughter could usually be heard when the people who came to dinner had names like Murphy or Walsh or O'Connor. I remember noticing that what made those people different from other adults, but familiar to me, was that they were more like my parents. The men were funnier, the women more energetic, independent, and ambitious (if not overtly) than their peers. Politics were important to them, as was the Catholic Church. Alcohol abuse and reckless male behavior were unfortunate but not sinful, as sex was.

I think I sensed then what I know now, which is that education and accomplishment were respected, though creativity and introspection were not to be encouraged; a belligerent anti-intellectualism often coexisted with a deference toward the "well read" in Irish American settings.

Likewise, there was considerable concern that people should "do well" and things should "look right," but less importance placed on money and social status than in many middle-class milieus. Successful Irish Catholics tend to know that they're fortunate, and that they owe something to those who are less so. American baby boomers are famously malcontented, but I feel a sense of enormous gratitude for what I have in life that comes from repeatedly hearing such Irish Catholic verities as: "This could all be gone tomorrow. I've seen it happen."

What if it isn't there?

Shortly before I took a leave from my job at the *Boston Globe* to begin this book, I wrote a Sunday feature story on the Irish arts explosion that took place in the late 1990s. A friend put me in touch with the director Jim Sheridan, one of the dynamiters in said boom. Having run the Irish Arts Center in New York in the 1980s, Sheridan knew the territory upon which I was about to embark. And so I was given pause when, in the course of a phone interview, he said offhandedly: "I'm not sure there is such a thing as Irish America."

I took a breath, laughed a little, and said, "Oh, God, I hope you're wrong."

By any number of measures, he isn't. There is no Irish American voting bloc or ethnic group or community. That would be impossible. In the United States today, 44 million, or approximately one in seven, people claim *some* Irish ancestry. Of that number, more than half are Protestant, many of them Scotch-Irish descendants of Presbyterians from what is now Northern Ireland. The other 45 percent—approximately 20 million—are of Roman Catholic lineage. They are the people most Americans are talking about when they say "Irish American," and the subject of my book.

A note on nomenclature: Although I realize and acknowledge that the term "Irish American" is not truly a semantic equivalent for "Irish Catholic," I've followed the lead of historians and social scientists who've written on the subject and use the terms interchangeably. I also use "Irish" as an abbreviation for American Irish Catholic when the context is the United States (the South Boston Irish, for example, or the Irish legacy in Butte, Montana). That is how the term is used in American parlance—to the consternation of some born in Ireland, whom I distinguish as "native Irish" or "Irish-born."

Wondering if there was such a thing as Irish America, I went forward, braced for journalistic disappointment and disaster. Within a few months, I realized that such trepidation is as much a part of my cultural inheritance as fair skin and hazel eyes.

I had gleaned enough history, sociology, and statistical data from several dozen broken-spined texts and dog-eared articles to debunk stereotypes and expose myths for what they are. Contrary to the dearly held biases of America's chattering class, for example, most Irish in the United States are not blue-collar social conservative: As the sociologist and priest Andrew Greeley first pointed out thirty years ago, the Irish as a group are better educated, better off, and more liberal than all white ethnics other than Jews when it comes to affirmative action, gay rights, and women's rights.

But that's not what makes them interesting.

A separate realm

I came to realize that Irish America is indeed a culture. But beyond demographics, politics, and beliefs, it's defined by a complex of characteristics and a sensibility that has endured for generations.

First, as Monica McGoldrick suggests, the Irish in the United States had to assimilate less to fit in than a lot of other immigrants. They looked like the establishment, spoke the same language, and could keep up appearances without giving up fundamental "old world" ways. Hence the sometimes remarkably similar worldviews of a nineteenth-century tenant farmer in Mayo and his great-grandson on Wall Street. ("It could all be gone tomorrow. I've seen it happen.")

Second, the Irish are phenomenal doers and organizers, who built, maintained, and existed in a parallel Catholic culture for generations. The values and assumptions many grew up with were identified not so much as Irish as "the way things were."

Third—and I find this to be the most intriguing—the Irish don't know what makes us different from other Americans because we don't talk about most of what does. For all the faux blarney and bravado of institutional Irishness, most of us know next to nothing about our collective past, don't recognize our strengths (that would be showing off) or analyze our weaknesses (that would mean revealing ourselves). That is the reason so many people I interviewed apologized because they assumed they weren't good/interesting/helpful enough.

I didn't assume at the outset that *most* of the people I'd talk to would have good senses of humor, that they'd be unusually articulate, or that they'd drink more than other people, though I was hardly astonished that that turned out to be the case. Nor was it all too surprising when I found that the people I spent time with were gregarious, read newspapers and books, seemed more likely than most people to like poetry or drama, and considered politics a spectator sport.

The people I met in San Francisco, New York, Philadelphia, Chicago, and Boston, where I did most of my research, were more devoutly Catholic than I thought they would be, and more interested in and informed about things Irish. To be sure, they were a self-selecting group. But what impressed me more than their interest in heritage was that they were so generous, in so many ways. They were accommodating because they are naturally hospitable, it seemed—but also because I was writing a *book*.

For all the assimilation, the emphasis on brawn instead of brain and pragmatism rather than creativity, Irish America remains a place in which books still matter and independent learning is thought to be a worthwhile pursuit. Because I was doing research, I gravitated to people who "know things" and was delighted to discover a subset of a subculture I've dubbed the autodidact society.

For much of the latter half of the last century, the Irish heritage was kept alive in this country largely by male, orthodox Catholic, traditionalist interest groups. Much of what we know about ourselves as a subculture reflects that, which is why the story of Irish men in American politics is taken to represent an entire people's experience, even though it leaves out vast aspects of it, beginning with the lives of most women. Yet every historian I consulted while doing my research told me that women were the pioneers—the true forgers of Irish success in America. Those maiden aunts I mention are part of a phenomenal legacy in this country that almost no one knows about.

Among reasons we delve into our backgrounds is to understand ourselves: how we fit into a legacy. It is a truism that women, as Eavan Boland has said, are "outside history." But I am astonished that so little is known about Irish American women, particularly since there has been so much exploration of feminist and labor history in recent years. I was involved in getting the Women's Resource Center at Boston College off the ground in the mid-1970s, and I recall researching and ordering books for the center's library. But the material available then barely mentioned Irish women (not that I thought to ask). The Schlesinger Library at Radcliffe College has next to nothing on Irish women, even now.

As I learned what I now know about people like Leonora O'Reilly, Dr. Gertrude Kelly, the actress and activist Eileen Curran and their involvement in the struggle for Ireland's independence, I experienced the first shock of recognition I've ever felt reading American history. I was sure I would have known women like them; joined their cause. Why don't I know anything about this, I kept asking myself.

My mother, Eileen Sullivan Dezell, uncovered dozens of untold Irish immigrant and ethnic stories that would be familiar to many other Irish families when she was writing a family biography for an Elderhostel course. My favorite: Family lore has it that her father, Raymond F. Sullivan, and his brothers took over Eugene O'Neill's paper route in New London, Connecticut. My grandfather went on to become a very successful advertising entrepreneur; O'Neill did all right for himself too. Their stories are every bit as Irish American as the biographies of Al Smith or James Michael Curley—O'Neill's plays even more so. They are part of my story; the Irish American story.

What the recent Irish American culture revival has done is to open up new ways to understand and get involved with a very rich culture and to understand the essence of ourselves.

The way we live now

I think of Irish identity in the United States as the cultural equivalent of a regional accent. It's a variation on standard American, a characteristic rooted in history, and developed over time, that reveals something about attitudes, assumptions, and where we come from. You can get rid of a cultural sensibility or an accent, of course, but they tend to come back when you're with people who are like you, or when you're excited, or when your defenses are down. And while some variations of accent and culture can seem excessive or grating, they more often add nuance, distinction, flavor to the American mix.

In the United States, white ethnicity is optional, and culture is surely not definitive. Like many of my ethnic heritage, I probably share at least as many assumptions about family, gender, ways of relating, money, sex, and children with Jewish or Italian Americans as I do with native Irish people of my age and background. And some of what I have in common with my forebears are characteristics I'd rather not pass on.

But there are splendid aspects of the Irish inheritance I didn't recognize as such five years ago, and I feel privileged to know them.

Christopher now knows a lot more about Irish culture in the United States than most twelve-year-olds would care to. He enjoyed the research trips he, John, and I took together—particularly to Dingle and San Francisco (who wouldn't?). But it's his preadolescent prerogative to roll his eyes about the omnipresence and preoccupation with things Irish in our household—the books, the conversations, the cable package that includes Celticvision.

At the same time, he loves to read. He started a children's book award because there are no kids on panels that give prizes to young adult books. He is amused, as I am, at the seeming ubiquity on Celticvision of people talking about literature or poetry. Around St. Patrick's Day 2000, I pointed out that he comes from a lineage of people who've always loved books and who made their mark in America by organizing endeavors and entities the new world lacked. He beamed. Now, that's Irish pride.

CHAPTER ONE

Selling the Songs in Their Hearts

The Irish American Image in Popular Culture

E ach year in early March, the mud thaws, the days lengthen, and advertisers roll out images of shamrocks, party-hearty leprechauns, and freckle-faced inebriates. St. Patrick's Day is fast approaching, and competition is keen to sell beer and spirits by suggesting an Irish brand endorsement—a seal of approval of sorts from the ethnic group "known" to overimbibe.

St. Patrick's Day advertising is *sui generis* in the realm of niche marketing, and a slogan the Leo Burnett Company came up with to sell beer one year—*"Irish I had a Schlitz"*—explains why. The logo was the exception that proves the rule that unflattering ethnic images are far too offensive to use in the serious American business of selling. No sane advertiser would create a commercial for Florida condominiums suggesting: *"Jewish it cost less?"* None would put together a promotion for a white-shoe financial services house urging: *"Take the sting out of investing. Have WASPs watch your money."*

Obnoxious caricatures of the "clever Jew," "penny-pinching Protestant," or "inscrutable Asian" have mercifully disappeared from the American mainstream. The Irish boozer still bobs about in media flotsam, not

because some pernicious prejudice keeps the cliché afloat, but because Irish Americans endorse it. Drinking to wretched excess is a time-honored tradition on St. Patrick's Day in the United States, an annual occasion in which a splendid heritage is reduced to Eiresatz: a sentimental slur of imagined memories, fine feeling, and faux Irish talismans and traditions.

On the American day when everyone is Irish, lovely lasses and pugilistic Paddies parade on urban avenues carrying lucky clovers and silent harps; leering leprechauns serve as symbols of Irish wit and cunning; mawkish music and fight songs pay "tribute" to the Irish spirit; public drunkenness passes for Irish pride.

"No other ethnic group demeans itself this way," the Irish-born Los Angeles psychiatrist Garrett O'Connor has noted. "The Irish character becomes caricature" around St. Patrick's Day, "when being drunk is supposed to be the same thing as being Irish."

The New York St. Patrick's Day parade, which has long made a concerted effort to counter cultural clowning, is a caricature in its own right. A solemn, quasimilitaristic display of staunch Roman Catholicism, self-righteousness, and Irish republicanism, the event is recognized around the world as a symbol of Irish culture, when, in fact, it is not. The pageant reflects nothing so much as the membership and mind-set of the Ancient Order of Hibernians, the all-male fraternal society who organize the parade, and who once led an unsuccessful campaign to keep America safe from the Abbey Theatre. Today, they bar the equally insidious and threatening Irish Lesbian and Gay Organization from the line of march.

The essence and ethos of the New York parade were vividly expressed on a gusty, sun-warmed March 17 morning of 1999, when the late John Cardinal O'Connor greeted Irish screen actress Maureen O'Hara, grand marshal of the parade, on the steps of St. Patrick's Cathedral: conservative Catholicism meets *The Quiet Man*.

As the country's oldest, largest ethnic group, the Irish have been secure enough for long enough to shrug off anachronisms and hackneyed stereotypes that might raise hackles among others. Reasonable people of Celtic heritage figure that St. Patrick's Day displays are silly; life is too short to get exercised over a parade or a fifteen-second TV spot of a winking leprechaun swilling a Budweiser. Why get upset?

Why indeed.

Self-lampooning, a St. Patrick's Day staple, dates at least to vaudeville days, when struggling immigrants and their children realized that their comic sense and the songs in their hearts would sell. The stage Irishman's blarney-imbued "Don't mind me, I'm just a funny Irish guy" renditions of shuffle-alongs and happy drunks were officially hooted out of music halls and theaters in the 1900s—in a campaign led by the Ancient Order of Hibernians. But American popular culture by that time had embraced the idea that the Irish were a genial, down-to-earth, self-effacing people with a romantic past and a weakness for drink. For better and for worse, so had the Irish—which is why those notions define Irish America's image and self-image to this day.

A stage Irish story

Descendants of dreamers and tale-tellers in the land of money, myth, and Disney, the American Irish early on developed a capacity for romanticizing their heritage and sentimentalizing themselves.

The throngs who fled Ireland's Great Hunger and their children had little choice but to reinvent who they were. Famine immigrants spilled out of coffin ships into American cities "dressed in rags, weak with hunger, and numb with the fresh memory of corpse-filled workhouses, skeletal children, and tales of cannibalism," in Dennis Clark's words. They were premodern peasants, "homeless, nationless, and all but hopeless after a grim sea passage to an unwelcoming land."

Like immigrants who would later take their place on the bottom rung of the socioeconomic ladder, they represented much of what upstanding American society abhorred. The Irish were Celts, not Anglo-Saxons; Papists, not Protestants; rebels fighting to expel America's Motherland from their homeland. They were communal in a land of vaunted individualist achievers; drinkers at the dawn of the American temperance movement; a gregarious and boisterous people who showed little interest in serious American enterprise but loved politics.

Newspaper and magazine illustrators who provided visual definition for the pre-tabloid, pre-television age borrowed from British newspaper pages and vaudeville stages to reflect prevailing opinion with drawings of apelike Irish, drunken Paddys, menacing Micks, and surly Biddies. The influential cartoonist Thomas Nast "regarded the politicized Irish Celt as a menace to a good society," L. Perry Curtis Jr. writes in *Apes and Angels:*

The Irishman in Victorian Caricature. Anytime he "drew an Irish-American, he invariably produced a . . . cross between a professional boxer and an orangutan" (see illustration, page 142).

The Irishman onstage was Sambo with a shillelagh. Actor, producer, and writer Tyrone Power (forebear of a theatrical family that would include his namesake, the movie actor, and the director Tyrone Guthrie) made himself a star in the role of "Paddy Power," a re-creation of a blabbing, blundering Irish peasant who was such a hit in London. The Paddy stage schtick called for Irish props—pigs in the parlor, whiskey—and almost always featured a fight that turned into a melee. Brawls were a trademark of Irish immigrants, who gave name to the police vehicle, the paddy wagon.

Paddys played themselves as well as Sambos in minstrel shows, dancing and shuffling in blackface to a blend of Irish fiddle music and African American songs. Both Paddy and Sambo were childlike, musical, hapless, exuberant, and irrationally loyal to their employers, the music historian William H. Williams observes in his insightful, delightful study of Irish image in popular song lyrics, *'Twas only an Irishman's Dream.*

Vaudeville helped turn Paddy, Mick, and Biddie into Pat, Mike, and Bridget. "In vaudeville, to be Irish was to dance. Irish immigrants brought traditional step dancing to America, where it became part of theatrical dancing," writes Williams. "Irish step dancing provided the start for more than one twentieth-century tap dancer. George M. Cohan began his career with the same Irish steps his father had used when he started in the theater."

While stage Irishmen were entertaining the masses, Irish community leaders were doing their best to soften and sanitize the tough urban Irish image. The Ancient Order of Hibernians seized control of New York's St. Patrick's Day celebration in the late 1850s and turned it into a prototype public relations campaign "to send a favorable message about the Irish at their best to the rest of the city." Each year, they assembled thousands of "impeccably dressed Irish" to march in a solemn display of probity and patriotism through Manhattan's wealthiest neighborhoods.

Irish apologists like Thomas D'Arcy McGee propagandized on behalf of the Irish, portraying "the Celt [as] a being spiritually superior to the materialistic Saxon," according to Thomas N. Brown. "The Celt, he argued, is 'naturally aristocratic and full of veneration. . . .' Duty, Death, Eternity, are more congenial subjects to the Irish mind than Wealth, Liberty, or Fame." The myth of elevated Celtic spirituality would capture the imagination of people of influence, from the poet and critic Matthew Arnold in the Victorian era to the singer Enya a century later. But most Americans, Brown points out, preferred to emphasize "not uniqueness and magic, but the earthy ability to get along with people of diverse origins," and Irish secular democratic traditions.

Irish stereotypes gradually began to take on new dimensions in the latter half of the nineteenth century, as Catholic Church and political organizations established themselves, and Irish communities became less impoverished and more stable. The Civil War Draft Riots and the Orange Riots of 1870 and 1871 underscored the extent to which the Irish of New York remained an enemy within (see Chapter 6). But the tens of thousands who enlisted and fought bravely in regiments like the 69th New York militia, which became known as the Civil War Irish Brigade, for example, lent salutary connotations to the "fighting Irish" caricature.

––––––––

The arrival of the celebrated actor/director/producer Dion Boucicault, a talented sensationalist and pioneer of melodrama, was cause for applause among the nascent Irish middle classes in the 1860s. Boucicault managed to couch Irish nationalist sentiment with broad audience appeal. There is a heroic British soldier, for example, in *The Shaughraun*, which he used to propagandize on behalf of Fenian prisoners.

To be sure, Boucicault brought with him new casts of Celtic caricatures: His Irish plays *The Shaughraun, The Colleen Bawn*, and *Arrah na Pogue* are wild romps through spectacular countrysides, where the peasants are wily and self-sufficient, and daredevil rogues outwit their British overlords with blarney and outmaneuver them with brawn. At the time, no less a light than Henry James, reviewing *The Shaughraun* in *The Nation,* compared it favorably to standard Irish fare, calling it a portrayal of "love, devotion, self-sacrifice, humble but heroic bravery, and brimming with Irish *bonhomie* and irony."

It was those characteristics, mixed with stage Irish slap-happiness and tippling, that came to define a consummate Irish American persona: the self-effacing regular guy. The theatrical origins of this enduring type owe much to writer, producer, and actor Edward "Ned" Harrigan and performer Tony Hart, the wildly popular vaudeville and theater team whose shows, including *The Mulligan Guards, Reilly and the Four Hundred*, have been hailed as precursors of at least three American art forms: the musical, the knockabout comedy, and the sitcom. Harrigan, whose renderings of urban life were compared to those of Charles Dickens, did some of his writing while perched on a New York park bench, leaping to his feet and following characters he found interesting, listening and scribbling. His shows sold out for weeks on end in Manhattan from the mid-1870s to the early 1890s. Harrigan and Hart productions teemed with ethnic stereotypes of all sorts, but a star among them was Dan Mulligan, hero of at least eight shows. A ward heeler, Civil War hero, American patriot, and Irish nationalist who was convinced Lafayette was really an Irishman named Lafferty, Dan was good-hearted if a bit of a rogue; a devoted son both of Erin and America who loved his glass; a hopeless beneficiary of his wife Cordelia's civilizing ambitions.

A hardworking, home-and-family-loving Irish girl in the early Mulligan shows, Cordelia lost her heart and humor as she evolved into a social climber, and she and Dan moved from their shanty digs on Mulligan Alley (a stage re-creation of slums like Five Points) to a nice place uptown. There, she dressed him in suits and ensconced him in parlors where he was such a fish out of water, he drank out of a goldfish bowl. "Cordelia, I know you saved my money, and I know you're trying to elevate me, but I can't forget me neighbors," said Dan. "There's no one up here to sit out on the front stoop and have a glass of beer wid me. There's no barber shop open of a Sunday morning where you could hear the news of the week."

The social implications in this comedy of working-class urban manners are as subtle as slapstick. Irish women at the time tended to be better educated, more gainfully employed, and, like Cordelia, more socially aspirant than their men (see Chapter 4). All for the better, many might assume. But that would be a Protestant assumption. For the Mulligans and their friends and family in New York, the move into the middle classes suggested selling out or getting "above yourself"—and that is a hell-bent place in Irish culture.

Defining sentimental style

Early in the American Century, the Ancient Order of Hibernians launched an all-out effort to rid theaters of the likes of Dan Mulligan, Pat, and Mike, and other renderings they deemed demeaning to the Irish image. That included productions by the Abbey Theatre, who sent a troupe touring under the name the Irish Players to the United States in 1911–12. The Hibernians—who had passed a resolution assailing "Yeats, Synge, and other so-called Irish dramatists"—tried to organize boycotts of John Millington Synge's *Playboy of the Western World* in major cities. (*Playboy* had already provoked nationalist rioting in Dublin.)

The Irish Players boycotts were not successful—which is not to say the Hibernians were alone in taking offense at, or at least in feeling unease with, Synge's dramatic realism. The Irish press, the clergy, and many among the nascent "lace curtain" class had long been grumbling about Irish caricature that was too close for middle-class comfort to the demeaning Irish representations of Thomas Nast and Paddy Power.

On the night *Playboy* opened in Boston, a young Rose Fitzgerald Kennedy sat "blushing and squirming" in her seat. Years later, she told the historian Doris Kearns Goodwin that "no matter how hard she tried, she could not help but feel embarrassed by the coarse dialogue and the sordid portrayal of the Irish people as 'drunken sods and quarreling fools.' " For it was those "qualities of poverty, dirt and sloth" that the Yankees maintained were characteristic of the Boston Irish. But as offended as she was by the play—which she knew was "indeed a work of art"— Kennedy was "far more embarrassed by the tasteless response of many of her kinsmen in the audience, who, in their anger, began throwing tomatoes and eggs at the stage and hissing and booing loudly."

John Devoy, Fenian editor of *The Gaelic American,* railed against Synge's play from the time of its debut in Dublin, as Terry Golway recounts in his biography of the influential Irish nationalist.

> Devoy called it "a vile libel on Irish womanhood and a gross misinterpretation of their religious feelings." When William Butler Yeats, who had met with Devoy while passing through New York in 1903, and shared a platform with him in early 1904, defended Synge, Devoy denounced him as "foul, gross and vulgar." Various Irish societies were encouraged to pass sharply worded resolutions condemning the play, the author, and their supporters.
>
> When the play opened in New York in late 1911, Devoy . . .

stood up at one point in the performance and shouted, "Son of a bitch, that's not Irish." He, of course, had not been in Ireland in more than thirty years.

The notion that nonidealized portrayals of the Irish were not just offensive but in fact "not Irish," touted by Irish nationalists, held considerable appeal for upwardly mobile Irish Americans. As historian Thomas Brown explains it, much of the support for Irish nationalism in this country was motivated not so much by an interest in Ireland's political future as by a desire for respectability. Ireland's servitude to Britain was seen as a stigma of inferiority—a rationale for Irish second-class social standing in the New World.

Historians have noted an intense nostalgia in Irish American communities among Famine immigrants who were forced out of Ireland, and later arrivals, many of whom were economic refugees. The Irish, as James Carroll has written, came to regard the defeated land from which they came as a mythic motherland. "They remembered a land of extraordinary beauty . . . the sod when it had been theirs, and not the landlord's. They remembered an Ireland blessed with rare human virtues—the courage of the Irish patriots, the conviviality of the pubs, the holiness of saints, and the friendliness of strangers were always featured. The Catholic faith in this memory was salvation pure, and not also a shackling to that other great colonial power in the Irish story: Rome."

Remarkably, mythical Mother Ireland became institutionalized on Tin Pan Alley in early twentieth-century America. The prodigiously popular tenor and poet of disconnect, Chauncey Olcott, Buffalo born and brought up on the minstrel stage, made a career out of writing and starring in musicals like *The Heart of Paddy Whack* and *Isle o' Dreams*, whose evocations of Erin were jarringly juxtaposed to the place itself. When Olcott was warbling "Toora-Lural-Lura, That's an Irish Lullaby," in the musical *Shameen Dhu,* in 1914, the " Isle o' Dreams" was an impoverished colonial outpost on the brink of revolution. Another popular song stateside was "A Little Bit o' Heaven (Sure, They Call It Ireland)."

During the Easter Rising in Dublin two years later, hundreds were killed and thousands wounded. Dublin was devastated. Tom Clarke, Thomas MacDonagh, Patrick Pearse, Willie Pearse, Joseph Plunkett, Edward Daly, Michael O'Hanrahan, John MacBride, Con Colbert, Eamon Ceannt, Michael Mallin, Sean Heuston, Thomas Kent, Sean MacDermott, and James Connolly were executed. Connolly was wounded, shot propped in a chair. Eamon De Valera escaped execution because he was a U.S. citizen. Meanwhile, Americans were singing and whistling "Ireland Must Be Heaven for My Mother Came from There."

Numerous Irish Americans were, of course, actively supporting the fight for independence in Ireland (see Chapter 8) and were involved in serious causes and endeavors. But a strong element of irony defines the era. It is worth noting that, for example, at a peak time of musical mother worship, Margaret Higgins Sanger was indicted for circulating the magazine *The Woman Rebel*, coined the term "birth control," and opened the first family planning clinic.

Nonetheless, sentimentality became Irish America's signature style, as the famed Irish tenor John McCormack's recordings of Olcott's celebrations of Irish mothers and home spilled out of middle-class parlors, theaters, and music halls. The meeting of two stereotypes—the affable Irish American and the Emerald Isle of Enchantment—represented a welcome change for the socially ascendant Irish middle class, Williams observes: "Hard-working, disciplined, sober, competitive, Protestant America of the early twentieth century [bought] into the image of the light-hearted, home-loving, quick-tempered but genial, sentimental, loyal, extravagant, hard-drinking Irish who dared to love Ireland as much as America."

At the dawn of the twentieth century, "Irish" meant something very different than it had in the United States fifty years before. Paddy, who traversed urban terrain in the eponymous wagon, had evolved into Pat the driver (a fine fellow if kept away from the bottle), who begot the back-slapping, glad-handing, ever-smiling, professional Irishman. Biddie was Bridget, and her household was becoming a respectable place—distant enough from tenements and shanties that a song like "Who Put the Overalls in Mistress Murphy's Chowder?" could comically recall the habits of the bad old days, when there was only one kettle in the kitchen for the washing and cooking.

Step dancing across the silver screen

Professional Irish America's poster boy was George M. Cohan, the great American song and dance man, who is probably known today more for his tribute to Ned Harrigan ("Proud of all the Irish blood that's in me/ Divil a man can say a word agin me") and anthems ("Over There," "Yankee Doodle Dandy," "Give My Regards to Broadway") than for his many plays and musicals.

James Cagney won an Oscar for playing Cohan in *Yankee Doodle Dandy,* an adulatory 1942 biopic of the great American performer, which is famous for Cagney's hoofing (he too got his start in vaudeville) and for a splendid episode in American ethnic screen history: A black butler escorts Cohan into Franklin D. Roosevelt's office, where the President will award Cohan the Medal of Honor. At FDR's behest, the performer tells the story of how he and the Four Cohans (né Keohane) sang and danced their way from the vaudeville circuit, to Broadway, and through the doors of the White House, albeit briefly. (Lest we forget, Al Smith was resoundingly defeated as the Democratic presidential candidate in 1928.)

"That's one thing I've always admired about you Irish Americans," Roosevelt tells Cohan/Cagney. "You carry your love of country like a flag, right out in the open. It's a great quality." Irish exuberance and patriotism set Cohan and his kind apart from both the patrician Roosevelt and the butler, who applauds when the Great George M. tap-dances joyfully down the steps of a White House staircase near the end of the film, to join a parade of soldiers outside.

By the time this movie melding the careers of two great entertainers was released, Cohan was an American performer and impresario, Cagney an American movie icon in the making. The significance of their ethnicity had diminished. In the 1920s and 1930s, the traits associated with Irish American character—street-smart, tough-talking, funny, irreverent—increasingly became identified as urban American characteristics, as Daniel Patrick Moynihan and Peter Quinn have pointed out.

American pop culture absorbed the sunshine in Irish identity—the humor, the wit, the musicality and dance. It left the shadows and slack. The Irish in movies gradually came to be identified with what were seen as American virtues: humor, bravery, loyalty, dedication to the greater good. The avatar of all these qualities was the Irish movie priest.

Pat O'Brien played a priest opposite Cagney's bad boy Rocky Sullivan (who may or may not have died yellow) in the 1938 classic *Angels with Dirty Faces.* Cagney was nominated for an Oscar for the role, but

lost to Spencer Tracy, who won that year for his Father Flanagan in *Boys Town*.

Cagney and O'Brien took on the roles of sinner and saint two years later in *The Fighting 69th*, a hokey if wholly likable rendering of the famed Irish regiment led by William "Wild Bill" Donovan (George Brent), war hero and founder of the OSS, the predecessor to the CIA. Cagney plays cowardly and cynical soldier Jerry Plunkett opposite O'Brien's benevolent chaplain, Fighting Father Duffy (a monument to whom today stands near George M. Cohan's in Times Square).

The Irish Great War movie features one of the more splendid examples of that central-casting standard, the American army platoon as melting pot: As a Jewish soldier (who has claimed his name was Murphy so

he could join the famed regiment) lies dying, O'Brien reads to him portions of the *Kaddish*—and recites a line in Hebrew, no less. Here is American courage and tolerance, beating loudly out in the great big heart of an
Irish priest.

In *his* deathbed scene with O'Brien, Cagney—who has given in to Father Duffy's urging, returned to the front, shown his bravery, and taken a
fatal hit—looks up at his savior here on earth, and quips, "I've just been
talkin' to your boss." The movie moment captures a cultural sensibility in
a one-liner; tragedy leavened with humor—thoroughly in the Irish tradition—is distilled in a wisecrack, delivered in a New York accent.

Movies that functioned on a certain level as superordinary public relations campaigns for American Catholicism were a byproduct of Hollywood's Production Code, an industry self-regulation measure written by
a Jesuit, Daniel Lord, and enforced from the early 1930s through the early
1950s largely by a wheeling-dealing Irish Catholic, Joseph Breen. Breen
brokered a meeting of minds—or, at least, of pragmatic interests—between Hollywood producers, many of whom were Jewish, and Catholic
bishops, who forged their unlikely alliance because neither could live
with the other's unchecked influence over the populace. The Church
feared Hollywood hedonism almost as much as movie moguls dreaded
the power of Catholic boycotts at the box office. And neither Hollywood
nor the Catholic hierarchy wanted the federal government to regulate
what was seen on screen.

The code—and the movies—reflected Church concerns: censoring
sex, often to an absurd degree (married movie couples slept in twin
beds); deglamorizing violence; anticommunism. They also helped de-
mystify the Church, presenting genial, down-to-earth, and duty-bound
priest personas like Tracy, O'Brien, and Bing Crosby in *Going My Way*—
professional Irishmen who were a bit better than the rest.

Assimilation Valhalla

In 1952, a century after their fleet-footed forebears were dancing in blackface, wielding Paddy props, Gene Kelly and Donald O'Connor starred in
the musical tour de force *Singin' in the Rain*. Their Irishness was inci-
dental. Kelly at that point was an utterly American success story. So was
Grace Kelly, the golden girl who became a princess. So, for that matter,

were Jackie Gleason, who introduced the world to Ralph, Ed Norton, Alice, and Trixie on his CBS variety show the year Eisenhower was elected, and TV personality and archbishop Fulton J. Sheen. Sheen's popular TV show *Life Is Worth Living* debuted on the DuMont network that year. (When the cool, collected, and charismatic prelate was awarded an Emmy for the show, he thanked his writers: Matthew, Mark, Luke, and John.)

What *was* recognizably Irish in America in the early 1950s was *The Quiet Man* (1952), John Ford's tall tale in Technicolor, starring John Wayne, Maureen O'Hara, and Barry Fitzgerald. Ford constructed a Potemkin Village in one of the more depressed reaches of a depressed country to film the movie, set in the Emerald Land of Enchantment, where eyes smile, and purer, wiser folk live in thatched cottages, seemingly sustained by Irish mist and turf fires, the local pub, the routine brawl, and the wisdom of the parish priest.

Ford was a son of Irish immigrants, whose life's work etched John Wayne and Monument Valley in the memories of the moviegoing world. But with such notable exceptions as his haunting, expressionistic film version of Liam O'Flaherty's *The Informer* (1935), the director often seemed to lose his sense of subtlety and complexity when his subject was Ireland or the American Irish.

Ford Westerns frequently feature episodes of Idiot Irish relief, usually with Victor McLaglen, boozing, brawling, and singing with a gaggle of good-ole-boys with brogues who could have upstaged Paddy Power. Ford's *The Last Hurrah* gives treacly treatment to Edwin O'Connor's gossamer-veiled novelization of the life and times of Boston's notorious mayor and political scoundrel James Michael Curley.

If O'Connor "transmuted the dab of bad in Skeffington into a lump of good," as Curley biographer Jack Beatty put it, Ford performed alchemy in the movie version. Spencer Tracy plays Skeffington as benign paterfamilias to a motley but lovable clan of political operatives; his murkiest motivation is his will to make miserable the powerful family of Yankee tightwads who fired his mother from her servant's job for a trifling offense.

The Last Hurrah, which combines the conceit of Irish American nobility of spirit with stage Irish roguery, underscores how tedious those notions had become.

What's Irish?

Late in his life, Eugene O'Neill lamented to his son that "the critics have missed the most important thing about me and my work, the fact that I am Irish."

The country's first modern dramatist, and arguably its best, O'Neill discovered "the existence of real theatre" in the work of the Irish Players, a troupe he saw first during their embattled run in New York. He spent much of his writing life rebelling against the "unreal, artificial, and irrelevant" American stage Irish tradition, which had defined the careers of his father and George M. Cohan (who, ironically, starred in O'Neill's only upbeat play, *Ah, Wilderness!*).

O'Neill's autobiographical *Long Day's Journey into Night* has been called the quintessential Irish American text for its exploration of the bitterness and loss of immigration, assimilation, delusion, addiction, and "selling out." His Irishness might have been more evident if he had had more peers. He didn't.

Writers of Irish descent have produced some of the best in American literature: Flannery O'Connor; William Faulkner, who was of half Ulster Stock; John Steinbeck. Edmund Wilson wrote once of F. Scott Fitzgerald, "He is vain, a little malicious, of quick intelligence and wit, and has an Irish gift for turning language into something iridescent and surprising."

Unlike his socially (W)aspirant contemporary, John O'Hara, Fitzgerald didn't wholly loathe his background or himself for being of Irish descent. But he set his stories in the Jazz Age, on the Riviera, among the nouveau riche of West Egg, not in the lace-curtain Irish St. Paul where he grew up. For some time, only select aspects of the Irish experience were rendered by better-known writers: Mr. Dooley's barroom; James T. Farrell's Chicago; Frank Skeffington's red-brick city.

There were good reasons for ambitious Irish American authors not to emphasize their background. Catholicism was looked down on in intellectual circles, and hyphenated Americanism was not something many aspired to until the last third of the last century—at which point, writers risked being pigeonholed if they explored ethnic characters and themes.

What is more, there was a decided anti-intellectualism in Irish America. "Derision of the hifalutin all too easily shaded into contempt for intelligence and learning, particularly on the lace-curtain fringe," Daniel Patrick Moynihan has written. In the early 1900s, "John Quinn, a New York lawyer, and important patron of Irish writers, showed an early copy of [*Playboy of the Western World*] to John Devoy, the Fenian journalist so dedicated to a dynamite and blood solution" to Irish land ownership. Quinn marveled later that Devoy railed in his newspaper at the bad language in Synge's drama as "foul, un-Irish, indecent, blasphemous, and so on."

Narrow-minded nationalism and cultural conservatism provoked "a steady emigration from the Irish 'community' of many of the strongest and best of the young," according to Moynihan. "Excepting those with a strong religious vocation, the sensitive, perceptive children of the American Irish born in the early twentieth century found little to commend itself in the culture to which they were born."

"There were no Irish museums, no centers of learning" built in the United States, noted Niall O'Dowd, founding publisher of the *Irish Voice* and its sister publication, *Irish America* magazine. "A lot of Irish Catholics in the United States were Catholic first and Irish second, and this was a peasant church. They built an education system. They built a stairway to heaven. But there was a huge failure of the imagination in terms of history and culture. A sense of inferiority."

That sense has encouraged a defensiveness about the way Irish life is portrayed in literature among the small cadre of academics and scribes who pay attention to Irish American culture; an unfortunate tendency to treat literature as sociology, and to pass judgment on the basis of its "sympathy" for Irish subjects.

It is an article of faith among certain academicians, for example, that Mary Gordon's writing is unsympathetic and "angry" (a sexist descriptive not typically applied to male writers). The respected critic and professor of Irish American literature Charles Fanning has railed repeatedly against Gordon, in one instance claiming that she "perceives Irishness as a genetic defect and cultural curse." Fanning suggests that the critical success of *Final Payments*, a groundbreaking bestseller he dismisses as a "collection of clever stereotypes," owes something to liberal anti-Irish bias.

This sort of received wisdom filters down and into popular writing, such as the coffee table book that accompanied the PBS series *The Irish in America*, which tsk-tsks the work of Farrell, Jimmy Breslin, Mary Gordon, and Anna Quindlen for their "pictures of Irish America that are either disturbing, openly hostile, or decidedly ambiguous," while allowing that Breslin "at least seems a great deal more comfortable with tradition and heritage than his female counterparts."

Breslin, of course, writes about boyos and cops and other aspects of tough-talking, blue-collar Irish America, where the traditional Church looms large, the guys are regular and roguish, and most of the long-suffering women are at home or somewhere else on the sidelines of the story. That world, an anachronism now, was not a comfortable place for many women (as Breslin's novel *Table Money*, for one, makes clear). Any complex Irish American literature is bound to show that.

It is worth noting, too, that Eugene O'Neill, who was extremely proud of his background, was nevertheless accused of being hostile to it throughout a brilliant career.

Renderings dark, but not deep

In the late nineteenth and early twentieth centuries, the Irish turned stereotypes that were used to stigmatize them into cultural currency, said Timothy Meagher, a historian who is head of Irish Studies at Catholic University. "They turned them into virtues: It was 'We're not lazy, we're generous; we're romantics, not drunks.' Not only that, we're better because we're this way."

The Irish image in popular culture went through a reversal of fortunes in the 1960s. In the 1940s and 1950s in the movies, "the Irish were riding high," said Meagher. But in the early 1960s, "the police and the priests became the bad guys. They were seen as symbols of the old order—corrupt cops, racists, and nutty anti-Communists. They became representatives of white, ethnic conservatives, starting with the cops in *The Godfather* and *Serpico*."

The assumption that the Irish represented the "old order" was not without premise. Irish Catholic anticommunism, given virulent voice by Joe McCarthy, was expounded by Irish leaders of the American Church, notably New York's Francis Cardinal Spellman, who trumpeted what he saw as inseparability of conservative American interests and Irish Catholicism.

Then, in the early 1970s, an angry, ugly, race-hating Irish image came to the fore as the battle over forced public school desegregation began in Boston (see Chapter 6). The Irish were not about to lose the conservative, ethnic label anytime soon.

On television, Archie Bunker wasn't supposed to be Irish, even though he was. (Was there anyone in the country who looked at and listened to Carroll O'Connor and thought: "That guy reminds me of a Methodist from Minneapolis I used to know"?) Robert DeNiro played a conflicted, semicorrupt Irish monsignor in *True Confessions*. The ultimate hard-hat reactionary so infuriated by peace, love, and tie-dye that he massacres a bunch of hippies was a New York Irishman in the 1970 independent film *Joe*. The people of Eire were portrayed as cartoons, who were either fanciful (*Darby O'Gill and the Little People* [1959]; *Ryan's Daughter* [1970]; or fearsome (*Patriot Games* [1982]). IRA members became standard Hollywood villains in the 1980s; only Arab terrorists were more crudely portrayed.

Somehow, Irish "humor" books have always found publishers. The 1999 *How to Be Irish (Even If You Already Are)*, which typifies the genre, features an irreverent guide to Irish figures of speech ("Irish coat of arms: two black eyes and a bloody nose") and a chapter called "How to Eat Irish," which is illustrated with a picture of a potato sitting on top of a six-pack, and opens with the witticism: "The Great Hunger is not only the name given to the agony of the Irish population during the potato famine, but to the condition of many a tourist in Ireland to this day." Readers who don't find the Famine jokes funny enough might get a bigger kick out of the tongue-in-cheek treatment of the hunger strikers Terence MacSwiney and Bobby Sands in the same chapter.

Villard published the extended bad joke *How to Be Irish* in early 1999, and reputable booksellers displayed it during the St. Patrick's Day sales season in March that year. Passover was coming up in a few weeks, and some merchants exhibited Jewish books alongside the Irish titles. Not surprisingly, there were no jokey tomes about tourism in Israel filled with anti-Semitic stereotypes and lambastes of Jewish martyrs to be found among those.

Goodwill for the future

It is no small irony that *Good Will Hunting*, the upbeat and enormously popular Oscar-winning movie, is set in South Boston. Because there are no white-haired mothers, misty-eyed monsignors, happy drunks, or other standard allusions to Irishness in it, the film wasn't widely recognized as an Irish story. But high school students who lived in Southie at the time were thrilled to see themselves portrayed, and some who knew the neighborhood saw the film as a paean to Irish strengths like loyalty and humor, set against a backdrop of dysfunction: alcoholism, missing parents, and ambivalence about love and work.

The actor and moviemaker Edward Burns set *The Brothers McMullen* in a middle-class Irish American enclave because, like most Americans born after the Vietnam War, he is too young to have seen Cagney, Tracy, or Crosby, even on late-night TV. "My friends and I always wondered why movies were never made that took a look at our lives and the people we grew up with," Burns has said. "Any Irish American can tell you what a colorful bunch we are. We saw that Italian Americans had Scorsese and Coppola, Jewish Americans had Woody Allen and Barry Levinson, and African Americans had Spike Lee and later John Singleton and the Hughes brothers."

By the late 1990s, Irish Americans had Burns and the Quinn brothers (*This Is My Father*); they had Frank McCourt (*Angela's Ashes*); Alice McDermott (*Charming Billy*); Colin Quinn (*Colin Quinn's An Irish Wake*). There was even a spate of expression out of and about South Boston, including John Shea's *Southie*, written by David McLaughlin, whose play *God Willing* was produced in Boston and New York; Michael Patrick MacDonald's memoir *All Souls*; and Dick Lehr and Gerard O'Neill's *Black Mass*.

Much in the way Tom Wolfe incorporated savvy, hilarious Irish American cops and lawyers into his sprawling novel of New York, *Bonfire of the Vanities*, a few of TV's savvier producers and directors have created Irish characters who are not in the standard mold into their programs: Maggie O'Connell in *Northern Exposure*; David Kelley's Bobby Donnell, defender of the underdog, on *The Practice*; Leo McGarry on *West Wing*.

But American television networks continue to turn out shows and specials that are firmly in the Emerald Land of Enchantment and stage Irish traditions. NBC produced an entire miniseries, *The Magical Legend of the Leprechauns*, for the 1999 November sweeps. Recent shows include *Costello*, which was set in a South Boston bar (where else?); CBS's *To Have and to Hold*, about a family of civil servants who drink too much (of course) and their domineering mother; *Madigan Men*, about three generations of winsome but winning Irish stereotypes starring the actors Gabriel Byrne and Roy Dotrice.

The ambitious and serious 1998 *Trinity* presented a parade of sibling caricatures: a priest, a policeman, a labor-union representative, a ne'er-do-well alcoholic, and a sister whose career is a success and emotional life a mess. As Mike Flaherty wrote in *Entertainment Weekly*, "Allusion is also made to a brother who overdosed at the age of fifteen (what was he, a leprechaun?)."

Meanwhile, the New York St. Patrick's Day parade marches on. For much of the twentieth century, the pageant offered its organizers and rank and file a once-a-year opportunity to demonstrate to New York's established orders that "Despite your religious and racial prejudice against us, this is what we Irish have accomplished: We are good citizens and proud of it."

In turn-of-the-millennium America, Frank Skeffington's private-sector heirs hobnob with the American President, the Irish Prime Minister, and an assortment of heavyweights of Celtic heritage at the annual White House St. Patrick's Day party, and the American Ireland Fund raises millions for peace, culture, and charity in Eire each year at cocktail party fundraisers held in majestic homes in Nantucket, Massachusetts, and Pacific Heights, California. It seems safe to say the Irish have arrived in America's black-tie-and-brie meritocracy—in any number of arenas, they *are* the established orders.

But the safeguarding of Irish culture as the New York Hibernians define it—male, blue-collar, religious, republican—persists at the parade that is metaphor for an Irish America it does not represent. The majority of Americans of Irish Catholic heritage are college-educated suburbanites who disagree with Church teachings on social issues. As a group, they are more liberal than most Americans in their thinking on gay rights and race. And many if not most of them, when they hear "IRA," think first and foremost of individual retirement accounts.

In Ireland, March 17 has traditionally been observed as a religious feast and family holiday. Secular celebrations that have sprung into existence in Ireland in recent years are distant kin to the New York pageant. In the mid-1990s, Dublin launched a four-day St. Patrick's Day festival, a government-funded, $1.2 million extravaganza overseen by Michael Colgan, the artistic director of Dublin's Gate Theatre, and directed by Rupert Murray, the lighting director for *Riverdance*. The grand marshal at the first, pointedly cosmopolitan St. Patrick's Day pageant was an Irish soccer star, Paul McGrath, who is black; Irish pop singer and teen idol

Ronan Keating would preside a few years later. Gays and lesbians are welcome in Dublin as well as in places like Galway and Cork, where gay floats regularly garner prizes.

The American parade has become an open embarrassment to many. "It's like the drunken uncle at the family get-together," writer and publisher Michael Quinlin complained to a room full of nodding Irish American heads at a late-1990s book signing. "You wish it would go away—or get some help."

But even beer ads are begging for mercy from the self-parodic traditions of American St. Patrick's Day. A turn-of-the-twenty-first-century campaign for Murphy's Irish Stout showed a formidable-looking foursome looking wryly into a camera, registering comment: "Yeah, green beer is the national drink of Ireland," reads the caption. "And we've all got pet leprechauns that love to drink it."

CHAPTER TWO

Terrains and Textures of a Diaspora

F irst, a smattering of facts.

In 1900, one of the most Irish towns in the United States was Butte, Montana. A higher percentage of residents in that copper mining capital traced their ancestry to Erin than in Boston, New York, Philadelphia, Chicago, or San Francisco.

One of the first monuments in the United States built to commemorate a woman, a statue of Cavan-born nineteenth-century activist and philanthropist Margaret Gaffney, stands today in the area called the Irish Channel in New Orleans.

The Irish American Cultural Institute was founded and based for thirty-three years not in New York, Boston, or even Chicago, but in St. Paul, Minnesota.

The second-largest St. Patrick's Day parade in the United States takes place in Savannah, Georgia, each year.

Tidbits such as these and the tales they tell are missing from the familiar, if truncated, story of the Irish in America that is told most often and that takes place almost entirely to the east of the Hudson River and north of the Mason-Dixon Line. It is in large part because of that yarn

that Irishness in Boston and the heritage on display at the New York St. Patrick's Day parade are taken as representative of the rest of Irish America. They are not.

"The Irishman of the stereotype is the hard-drinking, brawling, embittered product of the New York and Boston slums," the late socialist visionary Michael Harrington wrote. But he, like many Irish Americans, grew up in places where "Irish did not necessarily mean poor or even working class." In the "Midwest, there was a different, much less frantic ethnic experience, particularly for those of us whose parents had fought their way into the middle class."

Harrington's grandfather lived in a large three-story house in St. Louis, where he grew roses in the backyard; his father was a patent lawyer and his mother a former schoolteacher. His family practiced a "much more relaxed and less embattled Catholicism that produced an extremely innovating Church in places like St. Louis and Chicago." Only two generations removed from steerage, "I was welcome at debutante balls," he recalls. Among his classmates at St. Louis University High School was Thomas A. Dooley, the charismatic navy doctor whose much-publicized medical missions in Laos and Vietnam in the 1950s helped ease the way toward American intervention in Southeast Asia (see Chapter 6).

That the same enclave in the same year produced Harrington—Catholic Worker, conscientious objector during the Korean War, and founder of the Democratic Socialist Organizing Committee—and Dooley—the cold war hero described by his biographer as a Madison Avenue Schweitzer and mid-century "secular saint"—attests to the seldom acknowledged diversity within the Irish Catholic subculture, even in mid-century middle America.

"Senator Eugene McCarthy, the ironic poet and ideologist, is as authentically Irish-American as Al Smith (who wasn't really that Irish after all)," Harrington points out. The same might be said of antiwar activist turned California state senator (now retired) Tom Hayden, who, just a few years after Harrington and Dooley were double-dating in St. Louis, was serving Mass as an altar boy at the Shrine of the Little Flower in suburban Detroit—the parish of the infamous radio priest and ideologue Father Charles Coughlin in the 1920s.

The majority of the three million people who made their way from Ireland to the United States from the time of the Great Famine to the end of Ireland's civil war settled in industrial cities in the East. But tens of thousands went west, and in 1880 more than one-third of the Irish born in the United States lived someplace other than the East Coast. The Irish who moved away from the Atlantic seaboard tended to be "young, skilled, literate, and generally more resourceful newcomers" than those who stayed, and "the likelihood of encountering a white-collar Irishman during the 19th century increased as one moved west across the continent." That trend has continued. For much of the twentieth century, Midwesterners and Westerners in general were better educated, better employed—and, some would say, better off—than their counterparts on the East Coast.

————

To be sure, Boston is America's most Irish city. Almost 130,000, or approximately one-fifth of all residents of the city proper, are of Irish ancestry. New York has the largest number of Irish Americans and the densest populations of recent Irish immigrants in places like Norwood in the Bronx and Sunnyside, Queens. But there are significant numbers of people of Irish inheritance throughout the United States, in metropolitan Philadelphia, Chicago, and San Francisco, as well as Kansas City, St. Louis, and Dallas—even Seattle, where at the time of the 1990 census, 14 percent of the residents were of Irish descent.

Immigrants from Ireland who had the misfortune to debark in Boston, the so-called Athens of America, faced more hardship than those who went elsewhere. They suffered longer from discrimination and lack of economic and social opportunity. What's more, they have never gotten over it.

"The world's most oppressed majority," as the late historian William Shannon described descendants of those immigrants, have run politics in the city for a century and a half and dominated its private sector in recent decades. The American Ireland Fund dinner held annually in "the Hub" is that very flush organization's biggest moneymaker. Yet in many places where politicians and self-conscious "professional Irish" of the city gather, whether they're wearing blue collars or black ties, there's a palpable undercurrent of resentment, an overweening need to prove something, a defensive exclusivity.

It isn't just that the annual St. Patrick's Day celebration of "family, Irish tradition, and Southie pride" in South Boston is off-limits to gays and, for all intents and purposes, minorities. Boston's Clover Club, a charitable organization that throws a thrice-yearly dinner for the politically powerful and important, is not open to *women*.

When the *Boston Globe* pointed out in 1999 that the Irish consul, Orla O'Hanrahan, could not attend St. Patrick's Day at the Clover Club, the observation apparently provoked more scorn than embarrassment among the black-tied, prosperous men at the gathering. William Bulger, president of the University of Massachusetts, longtime leader of the

Massachusetts Senate, and brother of the Irish mob boss and career criminal Whitey Bulger, reportedly joked to an appreciative audience that Ireland's consul was "in the kitchen." The *Globe* report, someone said and
several agreed, was yet another instance of the "elite" and "Yankee" paper
picking on the poor Irish.

"There is a sense of grievance built into the history of the Boston Irish
that doesn't exist elsewhere," explained the historian Thomas N. Brown.
"The Irish in Los Angeles or San Francisco, for example, have almost no
grievances to speak of." They are surprised that "the Boston experience
gets adapted as representative of their experience on some literal level
and a level of the imagination."

Put another way, "Every time I've gone to Boston, I've gotten into an
argument about something ridiculous that supposedly has something to
do with being Irish," said San Francisco judge James McBride. "The last
time I was there, it was about women in the priesthood. You couldn't pick
a fight like that in San Francisco."

Gold Coast greenery

San Francisco isn't usually thought of as an Irish city. But Erin's heirs
have been making their way there since James Wilson Marshall struck
gold near Sacramento in 1848. "The first Irishman joined the Boston police force in 1851—and that was only under court order," said Kevin
Mullen, retired San Francisco deputy chief of police and an amateur historian, as he meandered through Mission Dolores, burial place of many
of San Francisco's Irish settlers. Athlone-born "Malachi Fallon became
the first Irish chief of police in San Francisco in 1849." Tombstones of
Irish victims of vigilante murders dot the graveyard. Make no mistake:
Irish Catholics faced some fierce prejudice because of their religion in the
Bay Area. "But they weren't so embattled" as in Boston, said Mullen.
"There weren't the enclaves. And that affects the ways the communities
are different today."

In 1870, half of the 150,000 residents of San Francisco and its suburbs
were foreign-born, the majority of them from Ireland. San Francisco
elected its first Irish mayor, Frank McCoppin, in 1867, nearly two decades
before Boston achieved that milestone with Hugh O'Brien. David C.
Broderick, the first Irish Catholic elected to the U.S. Senate, was a San
Francisco politician. Irish immigration to the West Coast ebbed and

flowed as it did in the East: Steady from the time of the Famine exodus through the early 1920s, it subsided almost entirely during the Depression, surged again in the 1950s and the 1960s, then retreated until the influx in the 1980s and early 1990s of tens of thousands of "New Irish" immigrants. At the turn of the twenty-first century, approximately 10 percent of San Francisco's population were of Irish extraction.

East Coast immigrants often had to fight to establish a toehold in communities where power and status had been entrenched among a few prosperous families, often for as long as two hundred years. California in the 1850s, however, had no establishment to speak of; opportunity abounded for any white English speaker with the wherewithal to take advantage of it. The early San Francisco Irish made their mark in worlds besides politics, and the city bears their imprint. O'Farrell Street, a major thoroughfare, is named for Dublin-born Jasper O'Farrell, the city planner and engineer who designed the streets in what would become America's favorite tourist city. Irish-born Peter Donahue, founder of the gasworks company that designed and constructed San Francisco's streetlights and the street railway system on which San Francisco's cable cars would run, was related by marriage to Edward Martin, who started San Francisco's Hibernia Bank.

The Phelan Building in San Francisco is named for banker and entrepreneur James Phelan, and the James Flood Mansion, which houses the Pacific Union Club, was the home of one of "the Irish Four"—James Flood, James Fair, William O'Brien, and John Mackay—who made their fortunes in California and Nevada silver. San Francisco Irish society mixed and mingled with a gaggle of wealthy Chicago and East Coast Irish, among them the McDonnells, who may have been the first Irish Americans to get rich in the stock market; the Murrays, heirs of inventor Thomas E. Murray, who made a fortune in electric lighting; and the Cuddihys of *Literary Digest* fame. When Edward VII toured America in the Roaring Twenties, he dined at one of Mackay's estates on Long Island, where he danced with the multimillionaire's daughter, the writer Elin Mackay, who, to the consternation of her family, married a young Russian-Jewish composer named Irving Berlin.

Not all Irish San Franciscans were plutocrats, of course. Late-nineteenth-century San Francisco was home to some notable Irish social agitators, from Father Peter Yorke, the Galway-born "labor priest" and newspaper editor; to Kate Kennedy, the union organizer and Irish Land League advocate who won the first "equal pay for equal work" state supreme court ruling; to Denis Kearney, famed for railing against both the "Nabob" rich of Nob Hill and the Chinese immigrant laborers.

There is a tradition of political and cultural dissent that has made Baghdad on the Bay an appealing destination for like-minded Irish since the turn of the last century, pointed out Clare-born Eddie Stack, artistic director of the city's Irish Arts Foundation. "The old Irish came because they knew forty-niners here; it was a Gold Rush city." Many among the New Irish "came because of the sixties: the left. Timothy Leary. Ken Kesey. Jerry Garcia; he was half Irish, you know. His first instrument was the accordion."

———

San Francisco Controller Ed Harrington grew up thinking that all Irish families migrated from Cork to Butte, Montana, and then to San Francisco. That was true of his family, and "everyone else" in the Mission district in the 1950s and 1960s, when "it was an Irish neighborhood. The kids took Irish dancing, and we had regular parties at the Knights of the Red Branch Hall or people's houses, where we'd pull up the rugs," he recalled.

"People had pictures of the pope and JFK on the wall, everyone's father worked for the government, and the goal was to have a cabin at Russian River." Any number of San Francisco Irish couples met at the Harrison Street home of Elizabeth and Pat Piggott, who hosted regular social gatherings "and had benefits—if you were going to go back to Ireland or needed help for some reason, they had benefits." The Irish community in the Mission dispersed in the '60s and '70s, "because there was a sense that cities were getting more dangerous," Harrington said. "But you didn't get the racist stuff here you had in Chicago or the East . . . if only because nobody has lived in San Francisco for generations."

Harrington's early-life impression of a Cork–Butte–San Francisco axis was not entirely a figment of a child's imagination. Butte in 1900 was home to twelve thousand people of Irish descent, a disproportionate number of whose families came from Cork (where there were, in fact, copper mines). They lived in the mineral-rich settlement on a mountainside that built up around the Anaconda Copper Company, an enterprise owned and operated by Cavan-born Marcus Daly. After twenty-odd years eking out a living as a laborer in New York and on the Comstock Lode in Nevada, Daly struck silver, then copper in Butte. By the 1890s, he was supplying one-third of the copper used in the United States and had accumulated one of the largest fortunes made in the country to date.

The first four chief executive officers of Anaconda—Daly, William Scallon, John D. Ryan, and Cornelius Kelly—were each "Irish, Catholic, and a member of one or both of Butte's major Irish societies, the Ancient Order of Hibernians, with three divisions, or the Robert Emmet Literary Society. Butte's chapter of the Clan-na-Gael was the second largest behind Chicago's in the United States," according to historian David M. Emmons, an authority on the Montana Irish.

Daly paid miners $3.50 for an eight-hour day—almost twice the going rate for industrial workers at the time—and Butte led the country in per capita income and union membership. More than a mineral baron, Daly was "Himself" in Butte. "He took care of people, and he won their loyalty because of it," said the historian and author Peter Quinn. He built irrigation systems, railroads, and banks. He was an organizer of the state's Democratic Party. He loved horses and raised them on the grounds of his lavish home.

"If the Irish had ever had the numbers, the strength, and the power to re-create the world, it probably would have looked a lot like Butte," said Quinn. Irish organizations functioned as "self-help fraternities" for newcomers. Unions and the Hibernians maintained flush funds for widows and orphans and paid off the mortgages of family breadwinners who died. "Old-timers" were kept on at union wages even though little was expected of them. The mines were closed and celebrations held for St. Patrick's Day, the anniversary of the Manchester Martyrs, Miners' Union Day, and the Fourth of July. The Robert Emmet Society hosted a gala ball every New Year's Eve for seventy years. Saloons were open every day, round the clock.

Icons and other influences

Beyond San Francisco, there is an array of monuments to the Irish legacy in California: the William Mulholland Memorial Fountain and Mulholland Drive (a tribute to the water engineer) and Doheny Mansion (now owned by the Sisters of St. Joseph Carandolet, originally by Edward L. Doheny, the oil magnate made infamous in the Teapot Dome scandal) in Los Angeles; the Concannon Winery (California's oldest continuously operating winery) in Livermore; and the Daniel O'Connell memorial bench in Sausalito. The perch is named not for Ireland's Great Emancipator, but for his nephew and namesake, a poet, raconteur, and founder of the Bohemian Club, which is famed less for its legacy in letters than for Bohemian Grove, its summer camp for presidents, plutocrats, and other men who run the world. The presidential libraries of two "Bohemians" of Irish descent, Richard Nixon and Ronald Reagan, are in Southern California.

Irish Americans have figured prominently in the creation of the American West's landscape and larger-than-life legends. The director John Ford, a son of Irish immigrants, defined the region for generations of Americans in films like *Stagecoach, Fort Apache,* and *The Searchers.* Georgia O'Keeffe's landscapes and paintings of bleached bones and desert flowers evoke abstract, now-familiar images of her adopted home, New Mexico.

And then there was Billy the Kid. The infamous Lincoln County War of 1878 in which the mythological outlaw (also known in his short lifetime as William H. Bonney, Henry McCarty, and Kid Antrim) took part is "usually described as a fight between whites and Indians, but was just as surely an orange-green battle," Fintan O'Toole wrote in *The New Yorker*. The infamous Kid was a hired gun of an "urgently Protestant and insistently British" paramilitary group called the Regulators, who sought revenge for the murder of one of their leaders on the local Murphy-Dolan syndicate, a group of Catholic, Irish-born thugs and gunslingers who ran local law and all important Lincoln County business out of a place called the House, which O'Toole likened to "Tammany Hall with Stetsons and six-shooters."

Margaret Tobin "Maggie" Brown, better known as "the Unsinkable Molly," made her mark in the Atlantic Ocean, where she won her name and fame by commandeering a lifeboat full of people who survived the sinking of the *Titanic*. Brown is often described as an eccentric, nouveau riche Denver socialite. But she had the gift of gab in spades and spoke several languages, which helped her to communicate with the ad hoc international crew in her lifeboat. She was a fundraiser extraordinaire: Before the *Titanic* rescue boat docked, she had collected $10,000 from wealthier passengers to benefit families whose loved ones had drowned. Later, she lent her fame and fortune to a variety of causes, from woman suffrage to Catholic charities. She also ran unsuccessfully for the U.S. Senate in 1914, before women had the vote in national elections.

Molly Brown's Denver home has been turned into a museum, one of several historic houses and landmarks that memorialize the diversity and success of Irish men and women in the American West. Silver king Thomas Kearns's lavish digs are now the Utah State Governor's Mansion in Salt Lake City. There is a Mackay Museum of Mines and Mackay Memorial in Reno, and the Mackay Mansion is among tourist attractions in Virginia City, Nevada.

Thomas Burke, "the man who built Seattle," defended the rights of Chinese to live in that city (a feat that nearly got him lynched), helped establish the Great Northern Railroad, led diplomatic missions to the Far

East for Teddy Roosevelt, *and* endowed Seattle's Burke Museum of Natural History. Spokane, Washington, is home to the rather less assuming Crosby Library at Gonzaga University, where Bing Crosby's letters, photos, records, and Academy Award for *Going My Way* are on display.

The Walworth Library in Greenville, Texas, pays homage to the most decorated United States soldier to serve in the Second World War, Audie Murphy, one of the few Americans who actually did star in a movie of his own life, *To Hell and Back.*

There is no monument at the border of Texas and Mexico at the site of one of the more infamous Irish American military episodes, the defection of the San Patricios, or St. Patrick's Battalion, from the United States Army during the Mexican War. Some three hundred recent immigrants—largely Irish, but also German and American—who had joined the U.S. Army, mostly for a meal ticket and $7 a month, abandoned General Zachary Taylor's troops when they arrived at the Mexican border. The enemy, emphasizing their shared Catholicism, offered them $10 bonuses and large tracts of land if they switched sides. They formed a battalion that fought under a green flag with an image of St. Patrick on one side and the Mexican eagle on the other.

Fifty of the San Patricios were captured and hanged by the U.S. Army at the end of the war, in 1847. Most legend and lore characterized them as drunks and traitors until the one-hundredth anniversary of the conflict. Revisionist historians, looking into what had gone on before the San Patricio defection, have discovered that the Irish had been grossly mistreated by Protestant army officers and that they had fought with extraordinary bravery for the Mexican side. Longtime heroes in Mexico, the San Patricios have recently been revisited in American books and film documentaries.

It is among the grimmer ironies of the Irish American heritage that a people who were subjugated and treated as inferior savages in their native land played a vital part in the destruction and containment of Native Americans.

General Philip H. Sheridan is memorialized in statues around the country, most impressively in Sheridan Circle, Washington, D.C., site of a monument to him by Gutzon Borglum, the sculptor who designed Mt. Rushmore. A hero in the Union Army, Sheridan became a ruthless commander when he was sent to the Great Plains after the Civil War. Today he is remembered as much for his claim that "the only good Indian I ever saw was dead" as for Civil War valor.

Northern Territories

An equestrian monument to the many achievements of Thomas Meagher stands in Helena, Montana, erected with funds raised in Butte. An Irish patriot banished from his native land and imprisoned in a Tasmanian penal colony for his role in the 1848 Irish Rising, Meagher escaped from prison, made his way to the United States, and became a lawyer, editor, and champion of Irish independence. In 1861, he joined the Union Army and organized what became the 69th New York State Militia, known as the Civil War Irish Brigade, a unit renowned for its bravery in battle as well as some devastating losses. Meagher resigned his commission in 1863, and descriptions of how he spent the remainder of his military days differ. (Some accounts say his resignation was refused, others that he asked for and got it back again but behaved in so drunken and disorderly a fashion that he was relieved of his duties and resigned his commission.)

Regardless, Meagher won a presidential appointment as secretary to the governor of the Montana Territory and served as acting governor for a year. In 1867, he died in a steamboat accident on the Missouri River outside Fort Benton, Montana. According to historian Emmons, the man had a plan that may have been his undoing: He wanted to "be the representative and champion of the Irish race in the wild, great mountains" and put colonies of dispossessed East Coast Irish on Montana farmlands. That scheme did not sit well with Protestants, nativists, or vigilantes.

Few Irish had owned the land they tilled in Ireland, and their utter dependence on the soil had proven devastating during the Famine. They were loath to rely on it again, and not many of them became farmers. The enterprising Archbishop John Ireland of St. Paul, Minnesota (see Chapter 7), did organize some Irish farming colonies in southeastern Minnesota, some of which are owned and operated by the descendants of those first farmers today. But Ireland's efforts to bring impoverished Irish from Erin and the Eastern seaboard to the bounteous American Midwest faltered in a disastrous move of twenty-four families from mountainous, rain-drenched Connemara, Ireland, to farmland near Graceville, Minnesota, in 1880.

Mostly fishermen or people who worked small plots of land on rocky hillsides, the Connemarans were overwhelmed by the demands of wheat farming and could not cope with the bitter Minnesota winters. Stories of bewildered Irish freezing and floundering about in snow-blown farmhouses on the plains appeared first in the local press and then drew national media attention. The relocation plan ended as a public relations fiasco, and Ireland moved the Connemarans yet again, finding many of them railroad jobs in St. Paul.

The Twin Cities were home to a large number of upwardly mobile Irish. The year the Connemarans were suffering through the Midwestern winter, 36.8 percent of Minneapolis residents of Irish households worked as laborers. Twenty-five years later, it was 18.4 percent. Over the same period, the number of Irish employed as clerical workers in the city more than tripled.

Irish religious and cultural life in the cities on either side of the Mississippi River contrasted sharply with that in many East Coast cities. Archbishop Ireland was one of American Catholicism's more progressive leaders, and several of his successors have continued in that tradition. The foremost is the Rev. John A. Ryan, an intellectual and social advocate who in 1906 published *A Living Wage: Its Ethical and Economic Aspects,* a seminal book that put in a twentieth-century American context Pope Leo XIII's social encyclical *Rerum novarum.* Ryan also was dubbed the "Right Reverend New Dealer" when he provided articulate Catholic counterpoint to Father Charles Coughlin's airwave demagoguery in 1936. The following year, Ryan became the first Catholic priest to say benediction at a presidential inauguration.

While the Irish made their mark in local politics and the labor movement in the Twin Cities, several writers and intellectuals of note—F. Scott Fitzgerald, Mary McCarthy, Eugene McCarthy, and Kate Murray Millett among them—hail from the area. In a region more readily identified with German and Swedish than Irish inheritance, Celtic-inspired dramatic productions, literary societies, and parish festivals have flourished. In 1996, the Center for Irish Studies was established at the University of St. Thomas, with a gift from St. Paul philanthropist Lawrence

O'Shaughnessy. The Twin Cities have also been an American center of the traditional Irish music revival since the 1970s.

Tales of two cities

In *The Proper Bostonians*, Cleveland Amory tells a story of a letter of recommendation a Boston law firm sent to a Chicago bank that was considering an applicant from the city that calls itself "the Hub." The firm "Lee, Higginson could not say enough for the young man," Amory recounts. "His father, they wrote, was a Cabot, his mother a Lowell. Farther back his background was a happy blend of Saltonstalls, Appletons, Peabodys, and others of Boston's first families." The Chicago bank, acknowledging the letter, wrote back: "We were not contemplating using Mr. ——— for breeding purposes."

And therein lies a crucial difference between the Hub and the Second City.

E. Edward Burke, a longtime Chicago alderman and an avid student of local history, likes to point out that "the Yankees who came to Chicago came to leave things behind." They were Easterners, often "second sons," who lacked patience with the overly prescribed social order of the Northeast.

That is not to say Chicago's founding fathers eagerly embraced the Irish in their midst. "Scratch a convict or a pauper and the chances are that you tickle the skin of an Irish Catholic at the same time—an Irish Catholic made a criminal or a pauper by the priest and politicians who have deceived him and kept him in ignorance, in a word, a savage, as he was born," the *Chicago Evening Post* inveighed in 1868. Still, the Irish in Chicago had more to offer than the Boston Irish did.

The first large influx of immigrants came to the city in the 1830s, "armed with the familiar tools of Irish enterprise—the shovel and pick," to work on the building of the Illinois and Michigan Canal, Thomas J. O'Gorman wrote in the *World of Hibernia* magazine. They lived in shanties along the canal project, where life treated them roughly, and they did the same to each other. Famine immigrants in the 1840s made their way to Chicago, and by 1850 the Irish were 20 percent of the city's population. By 1870, some 49,000 native-born Irish lived and worked in the city.

Among their number were Patrick and Catherine O'Leary, residents of a wooden frame house with a small cow barn in back where, it is said, the Chicago fire started on October 8, 1871. No one knows for sure how the blaze began, according to Burke, who has investigated the common but mistaken assumption that it was started by Mrs. O'Leary's cow kicking over a kerosene lantern. In 1998, a resolution he promulgated exonerating Mrs. O'Leary and her cow passed the Chicago Board of Aldermen. Indisputably, the fire raged for two days, leaving three hundred dead, ninety thousand homeless, and most of the city in ashes.

The Chicago fire turned into an opportunity for Irish workers, who helped rebuild what is known as the nation's Second City (though it is now third in size, after Los Angeles). In the course of doing so, many moved away from the center of Chicago to neighborhoods in the North Side, West Side, and South Side. There were Irish-dominated neighborhoods, but the Irish ghettoized less in Chicago than ethnic groups like the Germans and Poles did, and their numbers and presence in neighborhoods around the city added to the political advantage they already enjoyed by virtue of language and experience with democratic politics. So did the understanding that "the Irish were willing to share with everyone, but they'd be the ones passing out the shares," as O'Gorman puts it.

They seized control of Chicago politics in the 1880s and have held it since. A disproportionate number of Chicago officials still have Irish surnames, and the politically savvy in the city say that the best assurance of winning a judgeship in Cook County is to be a woman with an Irish last name.

———

Chicago accents can be heard all over campus at what is arguably the most widely revered monument in the American heartland, the University of Notre Dame. Ever since Knute Rockne's Fighting Irish football team showed they had the stuff to beat Army in a New York stadium in 1923 and then go on to best Princeton, bastion of Ivy League Protestantism, the following year, the school in South Bend, Indiana, has been the sentimental alma mater of tens of thousands of football fans who started calling themselves "subway alumni" in the halcyon days when "the Irish" played Army in New York City. The loyalty of subway alums who have never set foot on campus—or, for that matter, in a subway—remains strong.

The estimable longtime president of Notre Dame, the Rev. Theodore Hesburgh, and the Rev. Michael Walsh of Boston College were among those in the 1960s who spearheaded the successful effort to bolster the academic standards and resources of Catholic colleges and universities so they could compete academically with secular institutions.

Notre Dame's character is more Midwestern and Catholic than it is Irish, despite its football legacy—and a mascot that is, curiously, a hybrid of two nineteenth-century Irish stereotypes, the fighter and the leprechaun. There was no concerted effort on campus to build and fund a department of Irish studies until former trustee Donald Keough and his wife, Marilyn, endowed an Irish studies chair in 1993. (*Sotto voce*, some Notre Dame officials wondered if the generous gift couldn't have gone to a broader field of study.)

Notre Dame evolved from a provincial institution, the school of choice for Catholic Chicagoans and sons of alumni, in the middle of the last century. Boston College, founded to educate the children of Famine immigrants, grew from a local commuter college to a financially flush university over a longer period. But in the last third of the last century, a number of newly rich graduates have given generously to their school, and BC's endowment expanded from $5 million to $1.1 billion (the thirty-fifth largest in the country).

Now number five in the country in applications received each year, BC with its leafy campus on the western border of Boston today exudes a buoyant air of prosperous meritocracy—one waggish alum compares it to "Morehouse—for the Irish." In recent years, BC has become aggressively green, extending its traditional rivalry with Notre Dame beyond the football field (where, truth be told, there has never been a contest) to Irish academic studies, special collections, business programs, and a satellite campus in Eire.

TV sportscasters refer to the "Catholic Super Bowl" when the Notre Dame and Boston College football teams compete, and the crowds at the games offer one of the best extant samplings of middle-class Irish American anthropology. On the field, Notre Dame is a national powerhouse; BC is not. The contrasts between the Boston Irish stronghold and the home of the Fighting Irish in the Midwest are in some ways most evident during pregame and halftime rituals.

A heavy concentration of Notre Dame grads lives in the Boston area. Many of those who turned out early to tailgate outside Alumni Stadium at the BC-ND match in November 1998 were readily distinguishable from the home team supporters. It wasn't only that they wore their emblematic blue and gold; they tended to be dressed in Land's End and Banana Republic weekend wear. The attire of choice among the BC crowd on Shea Field, by contrast, was white baseball caps and maroon and gold BC jackets. The Irish fans sipped wine with their sausages and salads; the Eagles drank beer with their chips and cold cuts. The Notre Dame contingent were in their seats in time for kickoff; the BC bunch drifted in throughout the first quarter.

At halftime, a message congratulating newly elected Massachusetts Governor Paul Cellucci (BC '74) appeared on the stadium's electronic display board, followed by salutations to the other graduates who had recently won local elections. BC has transformed itself into a competitive national university, but even in the late 1990s, many of its more prominent alumni were still local politicians.

———

Boston is a city riven with consciousness of ethnicity, class, and the past.

"Washington is a meritocracy. Chicago is a meritocracy. Boston is the only place in America where somebody will ask you 'Where did you go to school?'" said Matthew V. Storin, editor in chief of the *Boston Globe*, a former editor of both the *Chicago Sun-Times* and the *New York Daily News* (and a graduate of Notre Dame). "I've lived in New York, Chicago, Washington, and have never been asked [that], except in the latter parts of the conversation, when it came up in some germane way. In Boston, it may come up in the first conversation. In Washington, it doesn't mean that much. In New York, nobody ever gets around to it. It's 'How much money did you make—today?'" But in Boston until quite recently "it was 'How much money did your family make two centuries ago?'"

For generations in Boston, politics was the only career path open to a young Irishman who wanted to put on a blue serge suit without donning a chauffeur's cap, as Frank Skeffington told his nephew in *The Last Hurrah*.

The desperate, diseased, Gaelic-speaking swarm of refugees from the Great Famine who sought shelter and sustenance in Boston arrived in a metropolis that had no place for them. Upstanding citizens considered Roman Catholicism a dire threat to things Anglo-Saxon, American, and democratic. The Rev. Lyman Beecher, the father of both the avid abolitionist Henry Ward Beecher and the author of *Uncle Tom's Cabin*, Harriet Beecher Stowe, took to the pulpits of three Boston Protestant churches in 1834 calling for "decisive action" against the rise of Catholicism in America. The next night, a mob of nativist workingmen heeded his admonition and set fire to an Ursuline convent and boarding school in Charlestown.

Boston at the time of the Famine migration was the American capital of industry and intellect, a city, as William Shannon observes, that was dotted with hallowed halls attesting to its own history and high-minded accomplishment: the Old North Church, Faneuil Hall, Harvard College. It was also a metropolis that was beginning to turn inward. The days of the adventuresome Yankee merchants were over by the 1850s; the era of cautious, conservative Brahmin Boston ascendant.

The immigrant wave swamped the city. As Jack Beatty recounts, "During the entire year of 1840, fewer than 4,000 Irish arrived in Boston, whereas on the single day April 10, 1847, more than 1,000 landed on its shores. By 1850, the number of Irish had risen to 35,000 in a total population of 136,900." Between 1850 and 1855, the Irish population increased by 200 percent; the non-Irish presence grew by 15 percent.

"To the Yankee factory operatives and laborers and artisans of Massachusetts, the Irish were the class beneath and they feared to let the Irish rise," writes Beatty. " 'Our lower people hate the Irish,' the Rev. Lyman Beecher declaimed, 'because they keep the wages low, are good at a fight, and they despise them for their ignorance, poverty, and superstition.' Economic competitors for the native-born workingman, the Irish were also a burden on the native-born taxpayer." The cost of providing "poor relief" rose from $43,700 in 1845 to $137,000 in 1851. The number of foreign-born paupers tripled. Grog shops proliferated, as did violent crime.

Anglo-Boston was an abolitionist hotbed, and the antislavery activists were among America's first NIMBY (not in my back yard) liberals. Many were ardent supporters of the Know-Nothing Party, a "reform" movement that sanctioned government discrimination and harassment against Irish Catholics in Massachusetts.

The Know-Nothing legislature in the 1850s "enacted laws requiring reading of the King James, or Protestant Bible in the public schools, banning the teaching of foreign languages, disbanding Irish militia movements, and forcing the Irish off the state payroll." Laws were passed forbidding Roman Catholics from holding public office. A statute called the "pauper removal law" allowed authorities to round up more than 1,300 Irish living in state almshouses and asylums—"leeches upon our taxpayers"—and ship them to Liverpool, according to Beatty.

By the time Hugh O'Brien was elected mayor in 1885, Boston was well on its way to becoming a place where money was managed and conserved, not made. The shoe and textile industries that flourished on the outskirts of Boston in the decades after the Civil War—thanks in large part to cheap Irish labor—would soon relocate in the South and Midwest, where even lower wages could be paid. Local financiers failed to see the wisdom of linking transcontinental railroads to Boston, and so the city was eclipsed as a commercial center by cities on the rails.

The Irish were taking control of the public sector by the time John Francis Fitzgerald, better known as "Honey Fitz," took office as Boston's mayor in 1906. But the Brahmins kept their grip on private enterprise in Boston and had "built a wall of fashionable churches, clubs, and other institutions [the Boston Symphony Orchestra and the Museum of Fine Arts] as a barrier against invaders," writes Russell B. Adams in *The Boston Money Tree*.

A dearth of entrepreneurship among the descendants of Yankee merchants had made the Boston economy so stagnant that in the 1920s, when most of the country was going through an economic boom, Boston's unemployment rate was consistently between 12 and 15 percent. The Great Depression pushed the city further into doldrums. Absent private-sector opportunity, the Irish focused energy and ambition on protected jobs in the civil service.

When *Harper's* magazine dispatched a correspondent to the Massachusetts capital in 1928, he found a city in "social stasis, economic entropy, cultural decline" caused and exacerbated by a "racial antithesis" between the dwindling Yankee Protestant population and the Irish Catholic majority. Through World War II, Irish did not apply for jobs as officers at the city's premier financial institutions and Yankee preserves. As recently as the early 1970s, an Irish American employee in the trust department of a major Boston bank was told never to expect to hold an officer's title; Irish just didn't.

Honey Fitz's son-in-law Joe Kennedy packed up his family and moved to New York, saying Boston was "no place to bring up Irish Catholic children." As Stephen Birmingham writes in *Real Lace*, his rather breathless chronicle of the country's "first Irish families," the wealthy Irish of Boston "formed their own, often pathetically imitative, social institutions." Rose Kennedy was a member of the "Cecilian Guild, the Irish answer to the exclusive Junior League, and had helped organize the Ace of Clubs, a group of 'better' Irish girls (an ability to speak French was a requirement for admission)."

When Joseph P. Kennedy applied for membership in the Cohasset Country Club, he was blackballed, according to Birmingham. As ever-so-proper Bostonian Ralph Lowell explained it, "the women of Cohasset looked down on the daughter of 'Honey Fitz,' and who was Joe Kennedy but the son of Pat, the barkeeper?"

Years later, Rose Kennedy would ask a college friend of the future American President, "Tell me, when are the nice people of Boston going to accept us?"

The New York wealthy Irish did not immediately accept Joe Kennedy and his family, who were considered a little rowdy among the "real lace" Irish families who spent summers in the Hamptons—one of New York's many Irish enclaves.

In "the city" and its environs

The American metropolis that goes by the moniker "the city" has long been the nation's capital of Irish republicanism, publishing, and culture, and American Irish Catholicism. For some time, it was also the seat of Irish American political power. But for reasons Daniel Patrick Moynihan explored both memorably and famously in his ranging, dirge-like essay "The Irish" in *Beyond the Melting Pot*, those days are gone.

The Duke of York, later James II, appointed Thomas Dongan, an Irish Catholic, governor of New York in 1683. Dongan was a progressive, according to John Ridge's chronicle in *The Encyclopedia of the Irish in*

America. "He sponsored a Charter of Liberties and Privileges which guaranteed freedom of religion to all denominations and protected basic civil rights." He invited a group of English Jesuits to America, where they opened a small school and said the first public Mass in Manhattan. Dongan's term came to an end when William of Orange defeated King James II at the Battle of the Boyne in 1690.

In the eighteenth century, immigrants from the north of Ireland established Presbyterian congregations in Manhattan. The first Roman Catholic parish, St. Peter's on Barclay Street, was founded in 1785. The second, St. Patrick's, was built in 1815 in what is now Little Italy but was at the time a heavily Irish enclave.

A number of Irish political exiles made their way to Manhattan in the wake of the failure of the 1798 Rising of the United Irishmen. Among them were Thomas Addis Emmet, the brother of Robert Emmet, who was hanged after leading an insurrection in Dublin in 1803. A doctor, lawyer, and writer, Thomas Emmet, who had served jail time in Dublin for subversive political activity, became active in the Democratic Party, served as attorney general of New York, and was a leading advocate for Irish immigrants.

The 1798 exiles helped establish New York's first Irish weekly, *The Shamrock*, in 1810. It would be followed by a line of influential periodicals and books—the *Irish World*, the *Gaelic American*, the *Irish Echo*, and, most recently, the *Irish Voice*—that would help make Irish politics and culture a palpable presence in the city.

The emigration of Irish nationalist leaders after the failed insurgencies in 1848 and 1867 and of later exiles from Ireland's civil war also ensured that New York would be a hotbed of Irish nationalism. The Fenian Brotherhood, the Clan-na-Gael, both secret societies, and the Ancient Order of Hibernians were all founded there. So was the Irish Northern Aid Committee (Noraid) in 1970.

County Tyrone–born John Hughes, who became bishop of New York in 1842 and was appointed the city's first archbishop in 1850, was the first in a series of formidable diocesan heads, including Francis Cardinal Spellman and John Cardinal O'Connor, to exert powerful political as well as religious leadership. Hughes urged immigrants living in shantytowns and the slums of Five Points to vote; established the city's first parochial school system; laid the cornerstone for a new St. Patrick's Cathedral in

1858; encouraged the Jesuits and Christian Brothers to establish schools and colleges in the city; and supported the founding of new orphanages and relief organizations for immigrants from Ireland's Great Famine, which would serve as the basis of New York's extensive Catholic social services system.

He was also an autocrat and rhetorician of the first order, who opposed moves that would democratize the governing structure of the American Church. He told a friend with pride that he had reduced a group of prominent Catholic New Yorkers to tears by telling them that they would surely be disavowed and disowned by their forefathers in heaven if they "allowed pygmies among themselves to filch away rights of the church which their glorious ancestors would not yield but with their lives to the persecuting giant of the British empire."

The first "official" immigrant to enter the New World through Ellis Island in 1892 was Annie Moore, a fifteen-year-old Irish schoolgirl. In 1900, some 692,000 of the city's approximately 3 million residents were of Irish ancestry. The same was true of a half million residents in 1940. But by 1960 the presence had dwindled to 312,000, a decade later to 220,000. By the 1980s, the Irish made up less than 10 percent of New York's population.

What happened, of course, is that they moved to the suburbs. Harrigan and Hart's musicals (see Chapter 1), which poked fun at the preoccupations and pretenses of the lace curtain Irish, were solidly based in sociology and demography. In the late nineteenth century, the New York Irish started moving from lower Manhattan uptown to more respectable quarters. In the coming years, they followed the subway and bridge routes to the Bronx, Brooklyn, and Queens. After 1945, second- and third-generation Irish started migrating out of neighborhoods like Inwood in Manhattan or Fordham in the Bronx as increasing numbers of blacks and Hispanics began moving in.

Census figures in 1990 show that "approximately twice as many persons of Irish ancestry lived in New Jersey's Bergen County and New York's Rockland, Westchester, Nassau, and Suffolk counties than in New York City. The largest concentrations of Irish Americans were found in Nassau and Suffolk counties on Long Island."

"For a long time, the Irish felt it was their town. It is no longer, and they know it," Moynihan wrote in 1963. They lost political power not just because they no longer had the numbers to sustain it, but because they had done little with it when they had it, Moynihan maintains. Their church embraced a wrongheaded, fervent anti-intellectualism, exemplified by Francis Cardinal Spellman's public embrace of Joe McCarthy and the fact that "New York Catholics have been prone to think they have learned something when the leader of Tammany Hall informs a communion breakfast of the Sanitation Department Holy Name Society that 'there is no Mother's Day behind the Iron Curtain.' "

Lacking new vitality out of Ireland, Irish American culture in its capital city—which Moynihan considered a pale presence to begin with— had become moribund by the time John F. Kennedy was president. "Working toward a decline of Irish identity in America are the decline of immigration, the fading of Irish nationalism, and the relative absences of Irish cultural influence from abroad on the majority of American Irish," Moynihan wrote.

Even the Irish saloon was vanishing, "unable to compete with the attractions of television, and the fact that Italians can cook."

That Moynihan bemoaned Irish Catholic anti-intellectualism suggests things were not quite so vapid as they might have seemed in the early 1960s. In his essay, he speculated that a heightened consciousness of Irish heritage would emerge "in the next generation" among those "with the fewest conventional Irish attachments" to Irish nationalism or the church. Andrew Greeley would make much the same prediction some years later.

The country's preeminent Irish American social scientists appear to have been prescient. A new consciousness of Irish heritage unencumbered by traditional Catholicism or conventional notions of Irish nationalism has indeed emerged, and nowhere is the "New Irish" identity more vital than it is in New York.

The trends Moynihan described began reversing themselves beginning in the late 1960s, when the outbreak of "the Troubles" in Northern Ireland broadened interest in Irish identity and politics beyond the orbit of fervent American republican activists (some of whom had fought on the losing side in Ireland's civil war), who had kept the cause of a united Ireland alive, most visibly at the New York St. Patrick's Day parade. In the eighties and nineties, as thousands of "New Irish" immigrants started arriving in the United States, many of the younger and more sophisticated among them headed right for America's most cosmopolitan city, which, conveniently enough, was also its Irish culture capital (see Chapter 8).

Seemingly, there is every sort of Irish enterprise thriving today in New York, from four-star hotels in Manhattan to bakeshops in Queens; fleadhs on fairgrounds; readings and film series at the Glucksman Ireland House at New York University; theater at the Irish Arts Center and Irish Repertory Theatre; rock at Connolly's and "trad music" at the Blarney Star. And there is good food to be had at some "New Irish" bars.

Music and more

The resurgence of Irish culture in New York City reverberates up and down the Atlantic seaboard and north of the city, in and around Albany. As readers of William Kennedy's novels know, Albany has been an Irish city since immigrants arrived in 1818 to dig the Erie Canal. Nearby Greene County in the Catskills, a popular vacation spot for immigrant and first-generation Irish from New York in the mid-twentieth century, is once again an Irish summer resort and cultural destination, a favorite performing spot for "trad" musicians during July and August. The only Irish American museum is located in Greene County, in East Durham.

Traditional music is flourishing in Philadelphia and all over Pennsylvania, in bars, at fairs, and even in the academy, thanks in large part to the energetic efforts of Mick Moloney, a seminal figure in Irish music who teaches at Villanova University when he is not playing, writing, or leading tours for the Smithsonian through the west of Ireland.

The Irish experience in the Quaker State differed from what it was in the Northeast. Pennsylvania coal-mining country in the nineteenth century was the site of some of the nation's fiercest labor battles, the most infamous of them involving the secret society the Molly Maguires. (In Ireland, the "Mollys" were a violent agrarian society that dressed in women's clothes as they terrorized and avenged landlords and landowners.) According to historian Kevin Kenny, the Mollys took control of the labor movement in Pennsylvania and "assassinated a policeman, a justice of the peace, a miner, two mine foremen, and a mine superintendent in the summer of 1875."

Over the next two years, a witch-hunt-like investigation and arrests led to the indictment of more than fifty men, women, and *children* for crimes linked to the Mollys. According to Kenny, "the defendants were arrested by private policemen, and convicted on the evidence of an undercover detective who was accused of being an agent provocateur, along with a series of informers who turned state's evidence to save their necks. Irish Catholics were excluded from the juries as a matter of course. Most of the prosecuting attorneys worked for railroads and mining companies."

In 1877, twenty men, all Irish Catholic and accused on sometimes specious evidence as members of the Molly Maguires, were hanged in Pottsville and Mauch Chunk for murders dating to the Civil War. Families of miners have sought redress for false accusations and convictions over the years. In 1978, the family of miner Jack Kehoe won a reversal of his conviction that was signed by Governor Milton Sharp.

Out of Pennsylvania's pitched labor battles came leaders like John Siney, who organized the Miners National Association, a large industrial union that emphasized "solidarity among workers across ethnic divisions, and union discipline," and Terence Powderly, Grand Master Workman of the Knights of Labor. Powderly and the Knights were instrumental in fighting to end child labor and in instituting the eight-hour workday. Powderly also served three terms as mayor of Scranton and as a leader in Michael Davitt's Land League and finance chairman of Clan-na-Gael.

The Philadelphia Irish in the twentieth century were not segregated from other ethnic groups as much as Irish were elsewhere. Nor did the Pennsylvania Irish make their way into the middle class through politics, which were dominated from the Civil War through World War II by Republicans.

According to Charles R. Morris, "Philadelphia's construction trades were always controlled by the Irish, on both the labor and management sides of the table, with a healthy assist from the ceaseless building activities of the Catholic Church. . . . Construction families like the Kellys, the McCloskeys, and the McShains were, and to an extent still are, threefold pillars of the business community, the Democratic Party, and the Church. When Catholic Italians and Poles began arriving in large numbers in the

early twentieth century, Irish Catholics were already moving to the affluent suburbs in the north and west."

The three best-known Pennsylvanians of Irish descent in the mid-
1950s—Grace Kelly (of the Philadelphia contracting family); dream
dancer Gene Kelly, originally from Pittsburgh; and the class-obsessed
novelist John O'Hara, from Pottsville—attest to the mid-century ascen-
dance of an Irish middle class.

It's a great day—almost everywhere

The contrast between traditional Irish Boston and the conscripted culture of the New York St. Patrick's Day parade with Irishness in the rest of
America is, not surprisingly, most striking on and around March 17.

The main interest of those in charge of the New York St. Patrick's Day
parade, the late activist Paul O'Dwyer used to say, is to see whom they
could keep out. Organizers of the South Boston parade won a Supreme
Court ruling in 1994 that allowed them to keep a contingent of openly gay
marchers out of the pageant. Since then, community leaders perennially
tout the ruling as a victory for "family, Irish tradition, and Southie pride."
Battle cries during the busing era, those phrases are widely recognized as
code for "Keep out."

Boston's attracts more spectators; Chicago's boasts twice as many
marchers; and Philadelphia's lasts longer. But float for float, viewer for
viewer, and hoopla factor for hoopla factor, the St. Patrick's Day pageant
in Savannah, the Southern city better known for lavish gardens, good,
and evil than its Irish heritage, is rivaled only by the New York parade.

Half a million Georgians turn out to watch ten thousand paraders in
Savannah, where one in ten residents are of Irish ancestry, many of them
descendants of immigrants who came in the 1830s to build railroads and
canals. A city that prides itself on knowing how to party, Savannah has
put on a pageant in honor of Ireland's patron saint nearly every year since
1824; these days, the St. Patrick's Day celebrations start when the local
Irish arts and culture festival kicks off, around March 1.

St. Patrick's Day in the country's consummate party town, New Orleans, is a less-drawn-out affair—albeit an occasion with distinct local
flair. The day begins at Mass at St. Alphonsus Church, where congre-
gants pray for forgiveness for sins they intend to commit. Later in the

Irish Channel (which has long since ceased being Irish), horse-mounted men in masks tease paraders by throwing cabbages, potatoes, onions, and Moon Pies in a parody of Mardi Gras.

San Francisco's St. Patrick's Day parade, as might be expected in a multicultural mecca, is eclectic: longshoremen, a gaggle of gay organizations, Catholic religious, and the Irish-Mexican Association—an organization that gets together to celebrate Día de los Muertos (Day of the Dead) and St. Patrick's Day each year—participate. Two noncompeting parades are held in Chicago, where winters are long and a chance to make merry in mid-March is welcome; plenty of people go to both.

When Maureen Lennon, a San Francisco librarian and registered nurse, brought her daughters to step dancing competitions around the country, she was struck by the seriousness of kid competitors from the Northeast and their families. "It just seems to be more fun being Irish in San Francisco," she said, "than it is on the East Coast."

CHAPTER THREE

The Making and Remaking of the American CWASP

Catholic (or Celtic) White Anglo-Saxon Protestant

I wouldn't be true to my Irish roots if I thought this was an entirely good thing. . . . I can hear my grandmother saying, "Now don't get a swelled head." I will clutch onto my Irish humility with great vigor.
—Alice McDermott, accepting the National Book Award, 1998

Clever remarks made at the annual National Book Awards don't often grab mainstream media interest, and Alice McDermott's wry reaction to receiving the fiction honor might never have been noted outside publishing circles if *Charming Billy* hadn't beaten out Tom Wolfe's brash blockbuster novel *A Man in Full* for the literary prize that year. As it was, major newspapers reported what they cast as a David-versus-Goliath publishing industry upset and noted McDermott's Irish aperçu in the coverage.

The attention was fleeting. Yet for months after McDermott parsed the peculiar, quasi-comic Irish conviction that success is cause for trepidation and self-deprecation, versions of what she said to a crowd of writers, editors, and publishers in Manhattan cropped up in conversations among Irish Americans at a San Francisco courthouse, during a campus sherry hour in St. Louis, and in a Boston bar. Occasionally, her comments were recast as a joke (*Did you hear the one about the Irish writer and her grandmother?*). Clearly, one writer's remark resonated with any number of intelligent, accomplished postmodern men and women who harbor a similarly premodern sense of self-deprecation and free-floating anxiety

about success. For it is no accident that Murphy's Law—*Anything that can go wrong will go wrong*—is named for an Irishman or that Daniel Patrick Moynihan said famously, after John F. Kennedy was assassinated, "There's no point in being Irish unless you think the world is going to break your heart some day."

Celtic American traits are not often characterized as such. For one thing, the Irish way with words frequently loses its bearing when the subject is human feeling. For another, according to conventional wisdom, a distinct Irish identity has disappeared in the United States. America's oldest ethnic story ended with Kennedy's election, at which point the Irish had made it; they moved to the suburbs and were barely distinguishable from WASPs, save their Catholicism and perennial fondness for corned beef and cabbage, green beer, and sentimental songs around St. Patrick's Day.

As is often the case, conventional wisdom is wrong.

Ethnicity has not determined where the Irish live or work for at least two generations. A secular world of neighborhoods known by parish names, where the dads were union men, the moms stayed home, "Irish," "Catholic," and "Democrat" were interchangeable descriptives, and a "mixed marriage" meant Tommy Leary and Teresa Garofolo were tying the knot, has for the most part turned into the stuff of nostalgia. At least a generation of American media watchers would hardly know what to make of whistling police officers with brogues and cigar-chomping ward bosses. By last century's end, the best-known Irish American flashing a law enforcement badge on television was Agent Scully, and veteran Irish pol Moynihan was shortly to retire from one of the more cerebral careers in the United States Senate.

Traditional, institutional Irish Catholic subculture "collapsed when the bulk of Irish Americans became middle-class suburbanites and revolted against authoritarian Catholicism," according to the historian and author Lawrence J. McCaffrey. Intermarriage and prosperity diluted the strength of most ethnic traditions and traits. But as John Steinbeck, whose mother was Irish, once observed of his own heritage, "Irish blood doesn't water down very well; the strain must be very strong."

Alice McDermott's worries to the publishing world recall shibboleths that were recited over rough-hewn farmhouse tables on the Dingle peninsula in 1900 and are repeated over Waterford and imported linen in dining rooms in Winnetka, Illinois, and Garden City, Long Island, today. "Don't get a swelled head" is a quintessential Irish maxim; the fear that "this is not entirely a good thing" is an invocation of the Irish worldview that "this could all be gone tomorrow."

Middle-class Americans of Celtic ancestry today resemble WASPs in enough respects that they can puckishly be called CWASPs (Catholic— or Celtic—White Anglo-Saxon Protestants). But if Studs Lonigan's grandchildren are at least as likely to be found sipping and nibbling at American Ireland Fund cocktail parties held in majestic homes in Nantucket or Pacific Heights as at parish bingos at the local Knights of Columbus hall, they remain oddly oblivious to the fact that they have arrived.

As a group, Irish Catholics have been among the best-educated and wealthiest people in the country for at least a generation. Not many know it—and those who do evince a seemingly atavistic need to downplay it. In a 1995 *Irish America* magazine interview with media entrepreneur Tom

Murphy shortly after Disney bought his company Capital Cities/ABC for $19 billion, for example, Murphy answered questions about his career with a series of disclaimers: "The timing was right"; "I'm not an intellectual or anything like that, but I happened to be very good at the selling end of the business"; "It was the luck of the Irish, honest to God."

Prosperous, white-collar Irish America is several worlds removed from west-of-Ireland villages where children suspected of getting highfalutin ideas about themselves were duly warned, "Now, don't go getting above buttermilk." Yet self-effacement remains sine qua non in the subculture—and one of the traits that distinguishes it from others. Witness McDermott and Murphy; talkmeisters Phil Donahue and Rosie O'Donnell; avuncular adviser to Everyinvestor Peter Lynch, whose regular-guy signature style was the basis of a major print and TV campaign touting Fidelity Investments in the late 1990s.

Much in the way a Bronx accent becomes muted in Westchester or a South Side twang softens on Chicago's North Shore, American Irishness loses some of its sharper distinctions as second and third generations move out of tight-knit, mostly urban communities and suburbanize. But it hardly vanishes. Culture is a set of inherited and shared beliefs about body and soul, family, marriage, birth, death, food, sex, and friendship that may not be explicitly acknowledged—and in the case of the American Irish, seldom is.

What is more, the Irish may have assimilated *less* than some other American ethnics, because it was easier for them to blend in. "The Irish came here speaking English, so, unlike other groups, they didn't have to learn everything in a new language," pointed out Monica McGoldrick, coauthor of *Ethnicity and Family Therapy.* "If you can pass—and the Irish had been passing for centuries—there's no need to change much of what's really going on with you."

In addition, deeply rooted Irish values were preserved in realms beyond hearth and home. British colonialism and the brutality of the Great Famine essentially destroyed what was left of native culture in Ireland by the mid-nineteenth century. But immigrants to the United States brought with them their communalism, a tradition of popular education, and their church, which they replicated first in urban wards and parishes and then in a massive parallel culture of Catholic schools and colleges, social service networks, unions, clubs, and sports and professional organizations.

Many of those institutions did things in the good old Irish way through much of the twentieth century. Some of them still do.

"There's this unspoken sense among the Irish that we aren't like other people, and there's a moral fiber to that," said Seattle artist Matthew Lennon. "It doesn't matter if you're middle class. You had the same home schooling." When he was a child in Philadelphia, he went "with my grandmother to Gimbel's to see Santa Claus one year. There was a picket line, but I didn't care, I wanted to get the list in. And I remember my grandmother whacking me in the head and saying, 'You better learn this, and learn it now. *We* don't cross picket lines.'" To be Irish in America is to learn that "we do it this way—and you can be anything you want to be in America, as long as you remember who you are."

Generations removed from the raucous wakes of the old country, the American Irish still celebrate death—which confirms their fatalistic sense that life is long and hard and the end a release to something better—and they still enjoy drama. They keep track of friends, family, and everyone else who passes peacefully to their eternal rewards in the Irish sports pages (known to most others as the obituaries). But they maintain an awed reverence for the sadder, more unusual deaths: a demise that is un-expected (*She was gone in a month*); inevitable (*The drink finally got him*); or singularly tragic (*Three little ones under six with no mother— and, God love him, he can hardly change a diaper*).

The notion that disappointment and disaster are sure to follow life's fleeting fortunes is part and parcel of a distinct Irish American culture. So is an obsession with human tragedy. Culture explains the fact that the Irish put a premium on remembering where they came from and remain obdurately, sometimes irrationally, loyal to family and friends. It is why their get-togethers tend to be loud and lively even before the spirits start flowing—and are more likely than most to include a gaggle of glad-handers, at least one person no one else can stand, and a few people who've had a few too many—as well as a splendid speaker, a retiree who runs a soup kitchen, and a voracious reader.

Culture is the reason the Irish always get the joke.

So many shades of green

As far as Chicago public school teacher Mary Jo George is concerned, being Irish "means that I have always been true to my God. That I am more concerned about my children's souls than anything material. . . . And that I feel as if I've been volunteering for things since I was in pre-school." Veteran New York reporter Dennis Duggan calls himself a lapsed Catholic—"It is a label I cherish"—and carries in his pocket a symbol of his Irish heritage: a newspaper obituary of his father, an IRA captain sentenced to death by the British, then pardoned and exiled to the United States. Art Institute of Chicago conservator Timothy Lennon is a "cultural Catholic" and a member of the Georgian Society, which, to his mind, is "one expression of Irishness among many consumer choices, from wearing green pants to enjoying certain kinds of esoteric literature and art."

Jerome Frese, a superior court judge in Indiana, said "there was almost no oral history" in his mother's family when he was growing up in Baltimore during and after World War II. "We never knew much about their background, except that they had terrible lives. My grandmother's attitude if we asked was that we had no idea how bad things were, and pray God we would never find out." What he did learn was that "to be Irish was to be defensive, downtrodden, and meant you had to fight for yourself. It meant you would be firm and staunch and that disaster was a heartbeat away. The verities were that the world was harsh, and it was going to break your heart."

Former Massachusetts public safety secretary and strategic consultant Kathleen O'Toole, by contrast, developed an "incredibly romantic feeling, a sentimentality for my Irish roots because I used to sit and listen to my grandmother's stories. My other grandmother played the mandolin, and my family used to sit for hours and hours and sing old Irish songs. We always had a great appreciation for the art, for the music, and the success of Irish Americans—this whole romanticized version of Irish history."

When he got to Loyola Marymount University in the mid-1990s and met students who identified themselves as Irish, Jonathan Mooney realized there was much more to his heritage than "drinking, having a temper," and his orange-red hair. "There's this very nice mix of being intellectual without being pretentious, this love of literature and writing, . . . this commitment to thinking" that is every bit as Irish as a sense that "money's not important, it's a means to an end. It's never an end unto itself."

"The Irish are not just the people in South Boston," said Rosemary McGrath, bristling a bit, as many are wont to, that the white, working-class neighborhood that won worldwide notoriety for bigotry during Boston's busing crisis in the 1970s is so often assumed to represent the political ethos of the American Irish. Nor are the people of South Boston well represented as they are most often portrayed, as Michael Patrick MacDonald points out poignantly in *All Souls*, his memoir of growing up in Southie, a story that underscores the blatant class discrimination inherent in that failed experiment in forced integration and the way Boston political leaders manipulated communal resentment, pitting poor against poor.

"Everyone thinks the Irish are conservative—easy to label. Well, they're not; they're all over the map," said McGrath, offering herself as an example. Born in 1929, she is a single mother of two grown children, a former model and "beatnik," and a longtime Republican community activist in one of the country's more liberal enclaves, New York's Greenwich Village. None too typical by some standards, McGrath actually has a fair amount in common with the people who share her ethnic background. She is a college-educated woman, her politics are difficult to categorize—and she seems a study in contradictions.

Look both ways

The late historian Dennis Clark observed, "Almost anything you can say about [Irish Americans] is both true and false."

The Irish "have a tremendous flair for the bravado, but inwardly tend to assume that anything that goes wrong is the result of their sins. They are good-humored, charming, hospitable and gregarious, without being intimate. They love a good time . . . yet they revel in tragedy," writes Monica McGoldrick. The Irish are wits and optimists who struggle with loneliness and depression, fighters of fanatic heart who assume much of life is predestined. Known for their extraordinary loyalty to family, friends, and community, they can also be relied on to completely cut off relationships. The Irish value conformity and respectability but tend to have a high tolerance for eccentricity and subversion.

"Hail fellows well met without being met at all" is how Anna Quindlen described the American Irish. "The unknowable extroverts. It is no accident that some have taken to professions that give the illusion of being among the people while remaining essentially separate. Newspapermen, who are of events but outside them. Politicos, who always stand apart in the crowd. Priests."

Irish Americanism is a hybrid of contradictions all its own. Immigrants from Erin in the nineteenth and early twentieth centuries were a rural people who transformed themselves into city dwellers once they reached American shores. They have been simultaneously loyal to one of the world's most liberal states and more authoritarian religions. "We have a false modesty that comes from a tradition where the community is more important than the individual and, historically, people haven't had an opportunity to define themselves on their own terms," noted Timothy Phillips, cofounder of The Project on Justice in Times of Transition at Harvard. "But the U.S. cultural tradition is very individualistic."

Emotional reserve and humility are considered virtues in Ireland; it is in the Irish tradition to wait to take one's turn. In the United States, brashness and egotism are assets to the many for whom life is a series of competitions. The Irish are drawn to the spiritual, the dark side; Americans are materialistic and giddily optimistic. The Irish are ironic, black-humored; they write poetry and tragicomedy. Americans are innocent and exuberant; one of their key contributions to world culture is the musical.

"The Irish have managed to do these things no one else could do," observed the author Mary Gordon. "The English told them they couldn't learn to read, and they produced some of the best literature in the English language. Their church wasn't supposed to exist, and it became the strongest Catholic church in the world. A whole population is wiped out by famine, and they come here with no skills, no money, no family, and prosper beyond anyone's expectations."

But the children and grandchildren of Famine Irish immigrants put a premium on assimilation and American respectability, looking straight ahead, moving forward. "What will the neighbors think!" became "lace-curtain Irish-America's secular catechism," according to the historian Kerby Miller. John Gregory Dunne has written bitterly of a lace curtain mentality ruled by "the injunction 'Don't make waves.'" What that meant was "know your place, don't stand out so that the Yanks could see you, don't let your pretensions become a focus of Yank merriment and mockery. . . . It never seemed to occur to the diaspora Irish that playing the Yanks' game only encouraged a servant mentality, one laced with a sour envy, and worse, one that made lives of caution and contented mediocrity attractive."

By many measures, it is remarkable that Irish identity has survived in the United States at all. Sociologists, family therapists, and historians alike have noted that the Irish are unusual among American ethnic groups in failing to pass on family histories or cultural traditions to their children. Branches of family trees, burnished narratives, songs, and legends have been lost in part because so few saw any reason to talk about them or write them down.

"There seems to have been a strong element of humility and self-abnegation in the typical Irish-Catholic upbringing that discouraged individuals from feeling that they were important enough to record their own stories," writes the historian Thomas O'Connor, "or that any project in which they were engaged was of sufficient consequence to warrant being set down for future generations. Fear of the unpardonable sin of pride was still strong enough to preclude seeing one's small and insignificant self as an important element in the great scheme of things. As a result, most Irish people had an acute, often ironic, and usually comical sense of the present but seldom a personal sense of the past. They harbored the conviction that they were not good enough, important enough, deserving enough, influential enough to be part of real history."

Suffice it to say, then, that these are not people who encourage a sense of self-awareness and self-esteem in children. Not all that long ago, an Irish American woman leaned over her six-month-old grandson's crib and cooed: "H-a-n-d-s-o-m-e." She wanted to compliment the child but wouldn't want a young relative of hers getting highfalutin ideas about himself.

Generations of Irish American families have worried about keeping their young healthy, out of harm's way, and free from that pernicious, insidious syndrome: the swelled head.

———

Egoism, extravagance, even inquisitiveness were seen as symptoms of the syndrome, and therefore to be discouraged. Catholics were brought up to seek the rewards of the spiritual, not the material, world, and the parents of a young man who showed talent and promise were as likely to see a future priest as a doctor, lawyer, or scholar. The American Catholic subculture took pride in measuring its success by a different set of standards than the secular world. "We were thus a chosen people," writes Garry Wills, "though chosen, it seemed, to be second rate."

Irish Catholic "parallel culture" expanded after the Second World War, as Irish priests and nuns took charge at hundreds of the parishes and parochial schools built for Catholic suburbanites. Many of the "new neighborhoods" were as homogeneous as the old.

"The first black I ever met was Bryant Gumbel, who was my roommate at Bates!" said the actor and director John Shea, shaking his head, recalling his youth in Springfield, Massachusetts, during the Eisenhower and Kennedy years. "The first Jew I met was a girl I used to play tennis with at Forest Park in Springfield. One Friday, I said to her, 'Do you want to play tennis, Marsha?' and she said, 'I have to go to temple.' And I said, 'Temple? I thought you were going to Mount Holyoke.' She had to *explain* to me that temple was where Jews went to worship their God. It was a very sheltered way of living."

Suburban Irish American culture seemed "soulless" and "antiseptic" to Tom Hayden, founder of Students for a Democratic Society and anti–Vietnam War activist, who was brought up outside Detroit, in a Midwest, mid-century, middle-class America. He came of age feeling antipathy for the men he understood were Irish American ideological icons: Father Charles Coughlin, the infamous anti-Semitic radio priest; Senator Joe McCarthy; Chicago Mayor Richard Daley. "My Irish roots had been obliterated completely in my parents' generation, through assimilation," Hayden said. "I knew nothing about the diversity of the Irish heritage. I was totally unaware of the more romantic or liberal or radical Irish traditions—the poets or the progressives, the labor movement. As I understood it, the guys who were waving the Tricolour were the people who were blind to justice issues here. The Irish were the people who dragged us into the Vietnam War."

As a political progressive who has pursued a keen interest in his heritage for more than thirty years, Hayden marveled at the extent to which conservatives and reactionaries like McCarthy came to represent the American understanding of the Irish tradition. Mother Jones was Irish, he noted. So were radical labor organizer Elizabeth Gurley Flynn and birth control pioneer Margaret Higgins Sanger. Feminists Kate Murray Millett and Mary Daly are among contemporary women and men of fanatic heart. The list of notable liberal activists is even longer. To many minds in the latter half of the American Century, "Irish" and "conservative" became synonymous—and a number of Irish Americans born in the postwar years rejected both designations. It hardly seemed a loss.

"We didn't grow up with a sense of culture or of characteristics shared," said novelist and Lesley College professor Marjorie Farrell. "If it was Irish, it was 'Danny Boy' or James Joyce. It was never Eugene O'Neill or the literature of assimilation and loss."

Unlikely endurance

For much of the twentieth century, of course, the cultural identity that set most Irish Americans apart was their Catholicism. Through the 1960s, the Church absorbed many of the best and brightest into its religious orders, and many lay Catholics' intellectual and psychic lives were centered in their religion and religious institutions. All that has changed (see Chapter 7).

It is a truism that there is no such thing as an ex-Catholic: The burdens and blessings of growing up in the faith that holds itself out as the "one true church" have permeated the lives of most people raised within it. The tenacity of Irish Catholicism is readily evident among those who would appear to be most assimilated, the oxymoronic Catholic (or Celtic) White Anglo-Saxon Protestants.

CWASPs live side-by-side with well-to-do Protestants in the toniest suburbs and play golf at the most exclusive country clubs. Since at least the early 1970s, they have gone to the same universities and graduate schools, held the same professional and managerial jobs, and pulled down virtually the same salaries. Studies show that Americans of Irish and English descent drink comparable amounts of alcohol—that is, more than most others. They share a peculiar fondness for "well-made" casual clothing emblazoned with extraordinary designs—garish plaids, for example, and arrays of blue whales on green backgrounds.

But CWASPs are different. According to *Harvard Encyclopedia of American Ethnic Groups*, even three or four generations removed from the motherland, Irish Americans score consistently higher than most Americans on measures of sociability, localism, trust, and loyalty.

They tend to be gregarious. "Thirty-eight percent of all Americans socialize with friends at least several times a month, as opposed to 49 percent of Irish Catholics; 16 percent of Irish Catholics socialize in a bar several times a week (twice the national average) and 28 percent socialize in a bar at least several times a month (again twice the national average). Eighty-eight percent of Irish Catholics drink, 21 percent above the national average," according to data gathered at the National Opinion Research Center at the University of Chicago. "Thirty-five percent of Irish Catholics as opposed to 30 percent of other Catholics belong to a Church-related organization."

CWASPs like to laugh and are given to exclamations—"Hey, how are you!" "That's terrific!" They are loath to talk down to people or speak through their teeth. As their phenomenal success in organizing people and politicking suggests, many Irish possess an emotional intelligence about human interaction. They remember—and use—other people's first names; they know how to ask questions—and listen. At other people's weddings, their hostesses seat them strategically, assuming "they can talk to anyone."

One of the most flattering things that can be said of an Irish American woman (from her own point of view, at least) is "She is one of the most down-to-earth people you would ever want to meet." It is considered a supreme compliment to call someone "a regular guy." The more accomplished one is, the more admired he or she will be for "playing it down."

In the secular trinity of Irish American values, loyalty and humor are father and son. Self-deprecation is the spirit that works in mysterious ways.

———

As a description, "Irish Catholic" has taken on new meaning in the United States.

Consider a thirty-five-year-old, third-generation defense attorney—call him Kevin—and his fiancée, a thirty-two-year-old advertising account executive—Molly—whose maternal grandparents emigrated from Ireland but never spoke of the past and whose father's family is Scottish-German-English-Irish. The couple live together for three years before they get married. At the end of their first year together, they give each other Claddagh rings.

Just as stodgy Church officials might maintain the couple are not Catholic, natives of Ireland might sneer at their identification with things Irish. But Molly and Kevin call themselves Irish Catholic, and when they get married, it is in a Roman Catholic church they usually don't attend. Molly's brother reads a poem by Yeats at the wedding. At the reception, the best man's toast is an Irish blessing that brings tears to the guests' eyes. Molly and Kevin name their first son Rory and seriously consider spelling it Ruari. They have him baptized. Rory will most likely go to public or secular private schools. If Molly and Kevin take him to Mass, it won't be every week. They may well dispense with their parish's religious instruction for children—but not its volunteer efforts.

The Church's enduring social mission has withstood the cataclysm much of the institution has suffered, and its religious mission to the poor and disenfranchised inspires a sense of obligation—and guilt—in the laity. The CWASP capacity for guilt is copious—as might be expected of those who attended traditional parochial schools, where children are taught from the age of seven that they are personally responsible for the suffering and death of Jesus Christ. Just as critical to the ethos of Catholic schools—and to the Irish inheritance—is a sense of social obligation.

Most CWASPs have been imbued with the admirable Catholic belief that all souls are equal, and they harbor the visceral Irish sense that they are no more deserving of riches or success than anyone else. "Irish Catholic guilt," which is usually attributed to feelings about sex or other passionate behaviors, can also come from the anxiety, common to church-going, lapsed, and cultural Catholics alike, that they ought to be doing more for others.

CWASPs are Irish—their lives are filled with paradox. And so it seems perfectly normal to them to spend Saturday mornings serving food at a homeless shelter and Sunday afternoons golfing. The road that rises to meet them runs from the country club to the soup kitchen. (See Chapter 7.)

Lack of passion play

CWASP identity is by its very nature an imitation of WASPism, with some significant distinctions. There is the issue of money and status, for example.

As the home of the famed Fighting Irish, the University of Notre Dame is the sentimental alma mater of thousands of Irish American football fans. But it is Boston College, founded to educate the children of immigrants from Ireland's Famine, that in many ways epitomizes the Irish experience in the United States—and for that reason the Jesuit university provided a fitting backdrop for a widely watched, poorly reviewed morality play about Irish identity in the United States today.

In 1995, the Wall Street Council of Boston College, a flock of high-flying Eagles in the New York financial world, came up with the dubious notion of presenting former British Prime Minister Margaret Thatcher with the Ignatius Medal, a Jesuit humanitarian award and BC's highest honor. They planned to present it at their annual benefit dinner in Manhattan. As the council saw it, Thatcher's presence would be a fundraising coup; they hoped to make $1 million for a scholarship fund at the gathering.

Apparently, BC's administration and board of trustees did not subscribe to the conviction that Thatcher perpetuated the conflict in Northern Ireland with blatantly anti-Irish and anti-Catholic policies, nor did they anticipate that many others might. They gave the council the go-ahead, and a brouhaha broke out almost immediately.

The conflict unfolded like a passion play about Irish American identity. Positions were entrenched—pragmatists versus idealists—and political maneuvering was elaborate. Irish American activists promised "the biggest demonstration since the 1981 hunger strikes" outside the dinner (no idle threat, since the event—as if to add insult to injury—fell on the anniversary of the death of Bobby Sands). Influential Irish Americans such as Ethel Kennedy pressured the university to reconsider the award.

Reportedly to the surprise of university officials, numerous alumni from across the American political spectrum—including some significant donors—adamantly opposed the recognition. More than eighty Jesuits registered objections to the decision. In the end, Thatcher found an excuse to bow out of the dinner, saving face for those involved.

As is frequently the case in Irish conflicts, positions assumed in the dispute did not fit standard political constructs like liberal or conservative. There were prominent local multimillionaires on either side: computer software entrepreneur John Cullinane, who opposed giving the honor, and noted that "when you get into fundraising, you do funny things," and construction magnate and BC trustee Thomas Flatley, who favored it, saying that the college should "rise above the past." Alumni performed the role of deus ex machina, warning: "You cannot have it both ways." "It seems you are forgetting the past." The source of the furor, after all, was not just politics but a centuries-old blood feud—not to mention the perception that Boston College was selling out to the British.

Irish eyes rolled in amazement and amusement for some time after the BC -Thatcher episode, and not just because the Irish tend to take glee in the misfortunes of others. Boston College had gotten into trouble because it lost sight of where it came from—over money, no less.

If CWASPs are equivocal about success, they are utterly ill at ease when it comes to money, particularly a lot of money. As educated, middle-class Americans, they are encouraged to strive for success. As Irish Catholics, they have very likely been through what Wilfrid Sheed called "boot training in self-abnegation." Among "basics" taught in this life-shaping drill is the maxim "No matter how hard you come to believe in the secular world and what needs doing there, you will retain this reflex about yourself: 'I must not use it for my own glory—even if what it needs is my own glory.' "

Going along, getting along, all the way

"There is a definite distrust of wealth" among the Irish upper-middle class, observed Chicago hotel executive Nora Gainer, who grew up in Beverly, Illinois, an affluent Irish-dominated section of Chicago. "People make excuses for it. I don't think people are comfortable with it for a couple of generations. There's a fear that it will interfere with friendship and community. When fortunes are made, someone gets left behind."

The fortunes of the group are critically important to the Irish, observed *Boston Globe* editor Matthew V. Storin. In the Irish community in which he grew up in Springfield, Massachusetts, "there was a feeling that we were people of great sentiment and strength . . . who had to struggle, who had to overcome the Famine, had to come to this country, stick together, and help each other out. That we were a people who had talent. Now, I don't think we were told [as some were] that they were the greatest, or the smartest. It was not that. It was that by sticking together, by helping your own, everyone could move forward."

Much of the American Irish advance in the United States was made through politics, the Church, and the labor movement. Second- and third-generation Irish gravitated to the civil service and industries that were run by benign, paternalistic authorities who "took care of" people. To a number of Irish, entrepreneurship has meant starting a business that can bring others along.

Several American Irish have made fortunes in contracting, for example. Ambitious construction company managers took advantage of their network of connections to government, unions, and the Church to build lucrative enterprises that employed plenty of people with a range of skills. There was a job for the new CPA who was marrying into the family, the cousins from Ireland without green cards, and so on.

In the private sector, the Irish have long been a presence in law, journalism, television, and advertising—fields that made use of their skill for communicating through talking or writing. (As women have entered the workforce in large numbers, they have made their mark in many of the same fields as Irish American men did in the past, such as journalism— Pulitzer winners Anna Quindlen and Maureen Dowd of the *New York Times* and Eileen McNamara of the *Boston Globe*, to name three—and law—Supreme Court Justice Sandra Day O'Connor and Stanford Law School president Kathleen Sullivan come immediately to mind.)

The Irish have done well in industries like banking, "where there is stress on personal qualities and accommodation of conflicting interests, and not a little involvement in politics," Daniel Patrick Moynihan has noted. Many a corporate marketing department has been an Irish domain. Men and women of Hibernian ancestry are ubiquitous on Wall Street today. But it remains an Irish point of pride to know whom to call, who really runs things, how to trade favors. Those who lament the waning Irish influence in American politics should look beyond their nostalgia to corner offices of skyscrapers in New York, Chicago, and Boston, where networking is de rigueur and deals and decisions involving business and government are made.

And who would you be?

In a society that boasts a surfeit of cutthroats and self-satisfied egomaniacs, Irish self-effacing loyalty has considerable appeal.

But Irish ties can be constricting. "For years the Irish in this country hit what I've called the green ceiling," said veteran journalist and author Pete Hamill. Beneath that imaginary barrier, "to have an ambition beyond the cops and the firemen was to be guilty of the sin of pride. It meant you didn't accept your lot in life. You didn't pay enough attention when you were asked, over and over, *'Who the hell do you think you are?'*"

That searing, sneering demand—easily the most recognizable epigram of traditional Irish Catholicism—evokes shudders of recognition among the many of whom it was asked. A rhetorical question, it is a verbal slap, meant to shock nonconformists and shame upstarts. It was uttered repeatedly in homes, classrooms, and parishes for generations. It echoed in the "certainties, rhythms, and traditions of the Neighborhood," Hamill wrote in his memoir *A Drinking Life.* He asked it of himself as a teenager, when he was trying to assuage his own "arrogance" at thinking he might do something other than "what everybody else does; drop out of high school, go to work, join the army or navy, get married, settle down, have children. Don't make waves. Don't rock the boat."

Hamill said he suspects that "enough guys have made successes of themselves at this point that kids who are coming up today aren't discouraged in the same way." Unfortunately, the green ceiling is a state of mind that materializes all too easily to middle- and upper-middle-class communities, where limning one's ambitions is expected, screenwriter David McLaughlin observed. After living in Los Angeles for a while, McLaughlin found that he assumed a different persona when he went home to visit family and friends in West Roxbury, the middle-class section of Boston where he grew up during the 1980s.

"Out here, I'm working away, full of confidence and energy, my skills are sharp, and when people ask me how things are I say 'Great.' I'm not apologetic. When I come home and someone asks, I say 'Pretty good.' I feel almost obliged to say good things may happen, but if they do it will be some sort of luck," he explained.

McLaughlin recalled a night he was out with some friends in a West Roxbury pub and told them he'd decided to take time off from college to write a book. "And they just started laughing at me. It was the craziest thing they'd ever heard of. The idea that maybe you *could make a living as a writer?* That someone would want to hear your voice?" he said.

"Everyone got a laugh out of it. The joke didn't have to be explained to anyone in the bar. No one said 'Who do you think you are?' on that particular night. But it was sure said later."

In CWASP culture, departures from what are considered acceptable career and social norms are frequently thought to be arrogant, and anti-intellectualism masquerades as antielitism. It is a milieu in which "the worst thing anyone can say about you is that you're some sort of a snot," said Nora Gainer. "If you do anything different—if you wear different clothes or talk differently—you constantly want to play it down." After spending a year as a graduate student working her way through Europe, she realized when she returned to Chicago "that there [were] just things that [were] not worth bringing up" when she was with her old friends. "You wouldn't want to talk about going to the Sistine Chapel," for example, because people would either ask " 'Where's the Sistine Chapel?' " or mock the "pretense" of going there. "They'd say things like 'Oh, *the Sistine Chapel!*' " she said, imitating the sarcastic, put-upon tone Americans adopt to repeat clichés like "Well, *excuse me.*"

Ridiculing the traditional privileges and preserves of wealth—Ivy League educations, summer homes, positions on museum boards—has long been a feature of traditional Irish Catholic culture. It was one of the insidious ways in which Joe McCarthy made his appeal to Catholics.

In the United States, "the whole emphasis of Catholic education has been for respectability, not creativity," said historian Lawrence McCaffrey. "You were expected to read books, not write them. Listen to music, don't compose it. Study art history, but be a lawyer, be a doctor. Bright young men—and women, more recently—want to be lawyers, not poets." Even top-notch Catholic universities produce far too many graduates whose notion of a peak cultural experience is tailgating at a BC or Notre Dame football game—and who are quick to dismiss those who think otherwise.

Now that they own the homes their grandparents might have worked in and sit on the boards of institutions that were loath to let their parents in, Irish Catholics have come to terms with exclusive golf clubs, vacations in Irish castles, and calling the "help" who address them as "Mr." or "Mrs." by their given names. Yet many retain intolerance and skepticism of high culture and other intellectual pursuits. Hence the hubris among college-educated descendants of Ireland's fabled scribes and scholars, who laugh someone who wants to write a book out of a bar or somehow form the opinion that touring Michelangelo's mural in the Vatican is an exotic, if not supercilious, thing to do.

Because this is a culture of paradox, of course, the opposite is true. For all their failure to nurture creative or intellectual pursuits, Irish immigrants put a premium on education—since the early twentieth century, a higher proportion of Irish Americans have gone to college than WASPs. And Irish America has produced a plethora of autodidacts. Numerous children and grandchildren of immigrants recall fathers "who seemed to read all the time," as Rosemary McGrath's did. "He made us sit up and read Shakespeare so we would talk well. He always had a book in his hand," and she said the same is true of both her and her son today. Like many characteristics the Irish share, she added, "I think it's just one of those things we do—we don't talk about it."

Michael Lennon, a retired commander in the San Francisco police department, studies Gaelic so he can better recite Irish poetry; it is one of his hobbies. Chicago alderman Ed Burke, an acknowledged expert on local history, led the effort to clear the O'Leary family name—and cow—of culpability for the Chicago fire. Film and television actor Martin Hanley, a marathon runner, was plodding through *Finnegans Wake* one day in the early 1980s when he seized upon the idea for what became the annual James Joyce Ramble in Dedham, Massachusetts. Costumed actors read selections from *Ulysses, Dubliners,* and *Finnegans Wake* at the ten-kilometer race, which is dedicated to human rights and free speech (the first ramble was dedicated to Václav Havel, who was imprisoned at the time) and raises money for cancer treatment.

The self-motivated, self-directed, and self-taught are not exceptions. Indeed, there are enough of them to suggest there might be an underground autodidact organization operating somewhere in Irish America: a sub-rosa society for the firefighter with an encyclopedic knowledge of the Irish independence movement, the economist who studies Latin as a hobby, and the Yeats-scholar bank executive. A large number of them are men, so perhaps there is a secret initiation into the tradition at boys' Catholic high schools. Surely the priests and brothers would encourage this little-recognized if admirable proclivity.

Paradox lost, and found

"Somebody once said to me, 'Boy, you really know how to work a room,' and I was insulted," said Mary Pat O'Connor, a special events planner in Chicago, who saw the comment as a put-down, a suggestion she was behaving like an insincere politician. "But he was complimenting me! Knowing how to work a room is something the Irish take for granted, but it's a gift. And what about that incredible sense of humor and that awesome ability to laugh at yourself? It's magic. There's nothing like it. Also that sense of purpose—and loving people. Some of that has to be a gene thing. And we don't think it's anything special, because they're ours."

"The very things that the Irish were once vilified for—being boisterous, charmers, social animals, storytellers—are seen as wonderful attributes in American society today," observed political scientist Paul Green.

Americans admire characteristics that have long been associated with the Irish—gregariousness, wit, charm, and "the flavor of the underdog," according to Michael Hout, a sociologist at the University of California at Berkeley, who has studied how people of mixed ethnic backgrounds identify themselves on U.S. census forms and found that more claim to be Irish than immigration and natural selection statistics indicate should exist. Americans are least likely to choose British ancestry, noted Hout. "For all the Anglophiles at Harvard, there seems to be some antipathy west of there to be identified as British."

Having made the trajectory from rejection to acceptance to success in the United States by "passing," many Irish never developed a sense of ethnicity extant their religious identity that wasn't sentimental or superficial.

They have little appreciation of their heritage or of the values and nuances that distinguish them from others. They are more likely to recognize negative cultural characteristics—the tendency to drink too much—than attractive attributes like loyalty or humor. Not many see themselves as adding much in the way of texture and flavor to the American concoction. Even fewer realize that the very assumption that they don't contribute much is a trait of their tribe.

That may be changing—as well it should. "Irish Americans have been looking at the Jewish experience, the African American experience, and going through this business of looking across the ocean with this kind of deferential posture to the Irish," said Frank McCourt, author of the cele-brated *Angela's Ashes*. "But they're the ones who've been successful. They're the pioneers. They're the ones who came here and unleashed an explosion of energy, taking over every political machine in the country, building schools and churches all over, getting into the construction busi-ness. And they don't give themselves any credit!

"The Irish were ashamed of themselves when they got here. They dropped the O's and the Mc's from their names. They were so busy hanging on and then prospering and coming right up against the estab-lishment they lost sight of themselves."

CHAPTER FOUR

Bridget, Open the Door

idway through the first act of Frank McCourt's *The Irish . . . and how they got that way,* a theatrical mélange of music, history, and moments to muse on, a pair of players speak briefly of the Irish male in love: "An Englishman who wants to propose says 'Darling, I love you, will you marry me?'" observes one to another, who riposts: "An Irishman asks: 'Mary, how would you like to be buried with my people?'"

The punch line usually gets a laugh, layered as it is with allusion to the quirkiness of gender relations among the Irish, the preoccupation with death, and the recognition that romance renders many among this poetic people laconic. All such subtleties were lost on a woman who saw the Irish Repertory Theatre perform McCourt's play in Boston and complained in the lobby of the Wilbur Theatre during intermission that the joke was "just another example of how women are oppressed in Irish culture." Irish women are powerless in this retrograde realm, she explained to a clutch of earnest-looking men and women dressed in rumpled natural fibers and sensible shoes. They, in turn, nodded sagely at the stereotype of the only major ethnic group it remains safe to caricature in polite company in turn-of-the-millennium America.

Sexism, to be certain, flows as freely as fine talk and a sense of im-
pending doom among the Irish. But as those who've spent any time
around Erin's heirs are well aware, there is much more to Mary's story
than acceding to the wishes of her tongue-tied suitor.

Of the hackneyed stereotypes of things Irish in America, images of
rosary-clutching, rocking-chaired, long-suffering mothers and sweet

colleens may be the most misleading. They are, after all, synthetic. "Mother Machree" and "My Wild Irish Rose" are Tin Pan Alley creations—enduring elements of an imaginary Irishness conjured most vividly for the first time in song by the Buffalo-born composer and performer Chauncey Olcott, popularized by John McCormack, and revived and recorded for the ages by Bing Crosby. Olcott also sang the simple little ditty "Toora-Lural-Lura," "When Irish Eyes Are Smiling," and a slew of songs that generations of Americans have come to think of as traditional Irish music (to the consternation of traditional Irish musicians).

Olcott's pop culture paeans to wide-eyed feminine duty and devotion captivated the American imagination in the early twentieth century. By that point, Irish American womanhood had been honed by a generation of dauntless single women, immigrant widows, mother superiors and superior mothers—any number of whom had more in common with the fearsome labor leader Mary Harris ("Mother") Jones than Mother Machree.

Social scientists describe Irish culture as matriarchal, and mothers hold considerable if not singular sway in Irish American families. Unmarried women command far more respect than in other ethnic groups. Irish girls are raised to be respectable, responsible, resilient—and rarely with any expectation that they're going to be taken care of. For better or worse, there is no such thing as an Irish American princess.

Though "few people realize it, it was the women—the mothers and aunts, the teachers, the nuns—who brought the wild Irish into the modern world" and sustained the subsequent Irish rise into the middle class, observed the historian Thomas N. Brown. The Irish Catholic Church's phenomenal infrastructure of schools and social service organizations would never have existed were it not for the efforts of nuns, nurses, and laywomen.

Nevertheless, most religious, academic, and popular chronicles of the Irish in America have been written as if females were in purdah. "There is virtually no mention of women in the standard texts of American Catholic history," notes the historian Mary Jo Weaver. In James Hennessey's 1981 book *American Catholics,* "fewer than 50 of the nearly 1,300 index items refer to women in any way. . . . In 331 pages of text, the material about women [nuns included] adds up to approximately 10 pages."

Nonreligious texts are not much better. A handful of women warrant more than a paragraph in William Shannon's comprehensive *The American Irish: A Political and Social Portrait,* and most who do are present by virtue of their relationship to men. There is a paragraph-and-a-half panegyric to the selflessness and devotion of Al Smith's mother, Catherine Mulvihill Smith, for example.

Just as Irish American and Catholic historians have failed to pay attention to women because they are female, feminists and other "progressives" ignore them because they are Irish and Catholic. In academe in particular, those traits are synonyms for conservative, and therefore undeserving of high-minded liberals' attention.

Rediscovering Bridget

Any reclamation of the female heritage is cause for small celebration—particularly in Irish America, which often lags behind the "old country" in coming to terms with women's independence.

A group of 450 professionally and politically connected Chicago women turned out on an unseasonably warm February 1 in 1999 for the inaugural Brigid Award luncheon, which has become a yearly recognition that honors women whose lives and work reflect the sense of justice, generosity, and compassion associated with the fifth-century abbess and saint. Brigid of Ireland "was not just good, she was smart," Irish journalist and memoirist Nuala O'Faolain noted in her keynote speech that day. A wealthy woman who was converted to Christianity by St. Patrick and went on to spread his word, Brigid was "impassioned in her charity," sharing her bounty, her home, and the monastery she founded in Kildare with rich and poor, pagan and Christian alike.

Mary Pat O'Connor, the energetic organizer of the Brigid Awards, pointed out that American Irish Catholic laywomen have a history of giving abundantly of their time and talent. In the days before most women were in the workforce, it was not unusual for "stay-at-home" mothers to volunteer dozens of hours a week to organizations; that tradition dates to Brigid. Indeed it does.

Yet, as is often the case when Irish Americans get together to revel in their ancient roots, there was a palpable sense of overreaching at the luncheon. For while Brigid's spirit is worth celebrating, fifteen centuries and four thousand miles separate her era from present-day Chicago. Surely socially conscious, activist Irish women shouldn't have to return to the late days of the Druids for inspiration?

Any number of accomplished women of Irish heritage in the banquet room at the Four Seasons Hotel that day were, after all, immediate descendants of one of Brigid's namesakes—"Bridget," the immigrant maid, a formidable, unheralded, singular influence on Irish American family life and culture.

In late-nineteenth-century theater and popular culture, Bridget was portrayed as the stage Irishman's opposite: a bumbling but warmhearted girl who broke dishes in the kitchen and variously disrupted order in well-appointed dining rooms and parlors of the Gilded Age. In a sketch that dates to the time, a lady of the house points out that she can write her name in the dust the maid has let build up on the furniture. "It's a wonderful thing to have an education, isn't it, missus?" Bridget replies.

But the Irish servant girl was a sociocultural phenomenon. Tens of thousands of peasant farmers' daughters who had spent their lives in peat-heated cottages bid their families good-bye, sailed across the Atlantic in steerage, and months later were serving squab from Limoges china in Boston's Back Bay or polishing silver in Fifth Avenue homes.

Two features distinguished Irish immigration: It was largely female, and most Irish who came to the United States between 1850 and 1925 intended to stay. The typical European immigrant of the late nineteenth and early twentieth centuries was a single man or male head of household, often a transient—a sizable number of Italians, Swedes, and Greeks in particular returned to their native lands. Most women who migrated from European countries came as daughters and wives.

At the turn of the twentieth century, 60 percent or more of the Irish who immigrated to the United States were single women. In the decades before that, women made up about half the immigrant population. Irish women were usually young and unmarried; they migrated with sisters or female cousins or emerged from steerage alone.

Bridgets—and Noras and Kathleens—had no recourse but to find work. Their occupation of choice was domestic service, a field that was wide open. Household labor was difficult, poorly paid, and sometimes so degrading that most "native Americans" simply refused to do it, according to Hasia Diner, one of a handful of social historians who have written about Irish women. But it offered better benefits than factory work, because it gave girls a place to live and regular meals along with their wages. In 1850, three-quarters of Irish immigrant women in New York were employed as domestic servants. As late as 1900, some 60 percent of Irish-born women in the United States were "in service."

They earned their keep, and then some, according to the historian Lawrence J. McCaffrey. "In general, Irish women were more sober and responsible than Irish men. They saved their money, sending it home in the form of ship passages for siblings or in cash or bank drafts to help their parents. . . . And they contributed a significant amount of their income to the Catholic Church."

Taking leave

Agnes Morley left County Mayo by herself at age thirteen, because some cousins sent her an "American ticket"; they paid her passage and promised they would help her find a job. On the boat to New York, she met a young man, and the two of them had such a grand time they agreed to meet again once they settled into their respective lodgings in Manhattan. When they docked, Agnes assured him: "I'll see you at Mass on Sunday."

"Can you imagine the innocence?" marveled her granddaughter, Chicago public school teacher Mary Jo George. "She had no *idea*" what New York was like. Wide-eyed though she may have been, Agnes Morley made her way to Chicago, where she worked as a back-parlor maid in a home on Superior Street until she married Tom O'Reilly, a public transit worker. Like most Irish women of her era, she stopped working when she became a wife and mother and, like all too many of her peers, she was widowed; her husband was killed in a train accident when her children were young. She took the small settlement she got from the transit authority and bought a "two-flat" on Chicago's South Side, where she lived with her children in one apartment and rented the other for income. Eventually, she remarried. She never went back to Ireland.

Irish women immigrants left behind a motherland that offered them little in the way of love or work. Ireland was destitute and defeated in the years after the Great Famine. Marriages were arranged, and a system of inheritance in which fathers willed their farm to a single son and arranged a dowry for one daughter rather than dividing it among their children discouraged young men and women from marrying and kept them dependent on their parents. There were few opportunities to earn an independent living or start families. "Boys" could work the land. But often their unskilled sisters were faced with a prospect of spending their adult lives at home with their fathers and mothers, entering the convent, or emigrating—particularly if they wanted to get married.

Irish society paradoxically expected that women should be either "sweet good mothers" or "young women out in the world doing their duty," according to Catholic University historian Timothy Meagher. Female purity and passivity were so venerated in the decades after the Famine that the constitution adopted by the Irish Free State forbade most married women from working outside the home. Girls were schooled to model themselves on the Blessed Virgin Mary, to be handmaidens and helpmates, except when duty called—as it often did. In that case, unmarried daughters were urged, if not "forced," to take jobs to help support the family, even if it meant traveling thousands of miles to do so.

Contradictory demands that made some economic sense to struggling families in nineteenth-century Ireland persisted in the new world, even as the Irish made their way up the socioeconomic ladder. According to Meagher, census figures from 1880 and 1900 in Worcester, Massachusetts, home to a fairly typical Irish community, show that nearly 80 percent of first- and second-generation single women but fewer than 5 percent of married women worked outside the home.

———

In the house on Superior Street, Agnes Morley learned how to arrange a formal dining room. For the rest of her life, she always put damask cloths and napkin rings on her own table. Irish servant girls gleaned a sense of social currency along with the wages they earned in wealthy homes, learning what sort of books, music, and manners belonged in a respectable family's home—and, more significantly, just how much an American education could buy.

The Irish on both sides of the Atlantic put a premium on education—for daughters as well as sons. Few of Bridget's daughters worked in service; they were secretaries, teachers, and nurses, who entered the white-collar world a generation before their brothers did, according to the historian Janet Nolan. Most better-paying jobs open to women in the late nineteenth century required at least a four-year high school education, and girls often stayed in school longer than their brothers. By 1910, one-fifth of all public school teachers in Northern cities—and one-third of those in Chicago—were Irish American women. Miss Sweeneys, Miss Murphys, and Miss Sullivans would remain a prominent presence in urban school systems for decades.

Women's ambitions and earnings brought many Irish families "up." It was Finley Peter Dunne's mother, Ellen, who introduced the first chronicler of Irish American life to Dickens, Scott, and Thackeray, and it was his eldest sister, Amelia Dunne Hookaway, who convinced their father to send the seemingly unmotivated boy with an eye and ear for local color to high school. Dunne, the creator of "Mr. Dooley," credited Amelia with urging him not to abandon the famous newspaper series in which the fictional Roscommon-born Chicago barkeep and wit Martin Dooley watched the world through wary eyes ("Alcohol is nicissary f'r a man so that now an' thin he can have a good opinion iv himsilf, ondisturbed be th' facts"). Mr. Dooley held forth in the pages of Chicago newspapers and in syndication for nearly twenty years; his droll observances have several times been anthologized.

Finley Peter Dunne's brothers became carpenters. His sisters were teachers. When her mother died in 1884, Amelia became the family's "chief breadwinner," and the Dunnes' moves from a declining neighborhood in St. Patrick's Parish to more and more prosperous sections farther west in Chicago followed "in the wake of Amelia's steady rise" from classroom teacher to principal in the Chicago public school system, according to Nolan. When she died in 1914, Hookaway's obituaries lauded her as both a singular Catholic educator and a literary talent in her own right, who wrote and directed plays that were performed in the Chicago schools. She corresponded with Mark Twain. It was said that some of her Irish dialect rivaled Mr. Dooley's.

Rabble-rousing toward respectability

The history of Irish women in the United States in the late nineteenth and early twentieth centuries is a story of women breaking ground, said Sister Karen Kennelly, president of Mount St. Mary's College in Los Angeles. "The Irish are rightly thought to have a heightened political sense. They're organizers, adept at developing networks, making contacts, promoting people for office, or pursuing particular points of view. Politics is the art of the possible. The Irish are less inclined to cling to a theory, an ideological position."

Like Irish politicians and priests who have been credited—and criticized—for their organizational skills and pragmatic political maneuvering, Irish women made the inroads into communities, established an institutional presence, and in many instances had a lasting impact. Irish women were at the vanguard of the American labor movement in the nineteenth century. Today, said Kennelly, "a disproportionate number of seats in Congress held by women are held by graduates of Catholic women's colleges."

After her husband and four small children died in a yellow fever epidemic in 1867, Mother Jones supported herself as a dressmaker. "Sewing for the lords and barons who lived in magnificent houses on Lake Shore Drive" in Chicago while "poor, shivering wretches, jobless and hungry" walked along the frozen lakefront in sight of their plate-glass windows radicalized her, and she soon got involved in the labor movement. A woman who possessed both the Irish skill for organizing and a flair for the dramatic, she became one of the most formidable champions of the downtrodden of her day. She once led a band of children to the steps of the New York governor's summer home on Long Island to draw attention to child labor practices; on another occasion, she rallied miners' wives wielding mops and brooms to protest dire conditions in the mines.

A fabled figure who lived to be one hundred, Mother Jones is the best known of a cohort of Irish women who were at the forefront of the labor movement: teachers union organizers Kate Kennedy in San Francisco and Margaret Haley and Catharine Goggins in Chicago; Mary Kenney O'Sullivan, who was recruited by Samuel Gompers to be the first woman organizer of the American Federation of Labor; Leonora O'Reilly, who led the Women's Trade Union League's 1911 campaign for reform after the Triangle Shirtwaist Factory fire, and whose public speaking skills were considered so extraordinary that one journalist compared her to the evangelist Billy Sunday.

Congregations of Irish religious women cared for destitute Irish immigrants in need, sheltering the poor, nursing the sick, and doing what they could to help women and children keep bodies and souls together. As a rule, Irish nuns did less proselytizing than organizing. In Boston between 1850 and 1900, they put a veritable social service network in place. Franciscans set up a home for servant girls who were sick or out of work. The Sisters of Notre Dame de Namur ran a girls' industrial school. The Sisters of the Third Order of St. Francis established St. Elizabeth's Hospital to treat women's diseases. Sisters of St. Joseph taught typing, bookkeeping, and accounting, and the Sisters of St. Francis ran a nursing school that was sponsored by the Boston Lying-In Hospital and Infirmary for Women and Children.

The American Catholic Church's 1884 directive that every Catholic parish should build and operate its own school required the services of thousands of teaching nuns. And Catholic religious women, a number of them Irish, also established what Kennelly called the "most extensive and accessible system of higher education in the country." By 1918, fourteen congregations had opened Catholic women's colleges such as Trinity College in Washington, D.C.; Manhattanville College; and St. Mary's in South Bend, Indiana, which were "pioneers in educating women."

———

Women were also very active in the nationalist movement in the United States from the time of Ireland's 1916 Easter Rebellion to the signing of the treaty establishing the Irish Free State in 1921, according to labor historian Joe Doyle's fascinating account in *The New York Irish* of a little-known episode of the era. In April 1920, an ad hoc group of suffragists, socialites, professional women, mothers of soldiers, and performers called the American Women Pickets for the Enforcement of America's War Aims marched on the British embassy in Washington. The theatrical women involved in the demonstration directed the drama, as well-dressed Irish women "bombed" the embassy with leaflets denouncing Britain's military campaign in Ireland and chained themselves to the embassy gates, ensuring that they would be arrested—for protesting British rule in Ireland—and that their pictures and cause would appear on the following day's front pages.

In the summer of 1920, the Women Pickets and the Irish Progressive League organized a dramatic, unprecedented strike on the Chelsea Pier in Manhattan to protest the arrests of Irish Archbishop Daniel Mannix and Cork Lord Mayor Terence MacSwiney. Irish-born New York surgeon Dr. Gertrude Kelly, Leonora O'Reilly, Irish activist Hannah Sheehy-Skeffington, and Eileen Curran of the drama troupe the Celtic Players organized women who dressed in white with green capes, carrying "neatly lettered signs with grandiloquent slogans that were their trademark: 'There Can Be No Peace While British Militarism Rules the World.'"

Thousands joined the work stoppage on British ships docked in New York, including workers on a British passenger liner, Irish longshoremen, Italian coal passers, and African American longshoremen—who shared a contentious history of strikebreaking, violence, and discrimination with their Irish counterparts. The protest lasted three and a half weeks. According to one newspaper account at the time, it was "the first purely political strike of workingmen in the history of the United States," spreading to Brooklyn, New Jersey, and Boston.

The action didn't save MacSwiney, who died on the seventy-fourth day of a hunger strike in London's Brixton Prison. But it surely raised American awareness of British suppression of republicanism in Ireland. And it gives a glimpse of the will and skills and political leanings of a group of middle-class Irish American women, whose role in the fight for Irish independence is among the missing chapters in Irish American history.

Doyle points out that hundreds responded in 1914, when Kelly called on "women of Irish blood" to form an American chapter of Cumann na mBan (the Irish Women's Council) to raise money for Irish Volunteers and solicited "societies of Irish women," from industrial organizations to dramatic groups. Those organizations didn't simply spring into existence in 1914, and it may be that women had been working in groups for the Irish cause for the better part of the previous two decades—but that their activities weren't covered in the Irish press.

Patrick Ford, the editor of the *Irish World,* the influential Irish

American paper of record, was an ardent, articulate champion of the rights of downtrodden Irish peasants and industrial workers in America, and supported the Ladies' Land League. But he came to disapprove of women activists, writes Doyle. From the mid-1880s until early in the twentieth century, the only women featured in the *Irish World* were "saints, nuns, and, on rare occasions, women involved in labor disputes."

Women's work

Viewed through the prism of today, some of these Irish pioneers certainly seem like feminists. It appears, though, that only a handful of turn-of-the-twentieth-century Irish American activists rallied wholeheartedly to the cause of women's suffrage—activists like Lucy Burns, Alice Paul's deputy in the American Woman's Party (who claimed to have spent "more time in jail than any other American suffragist"), and Margaret Foley, known for chasing candidates opposed to voting rights around western Massachusetts while driving a car she called her big suffrage machine.

Mother Jones, by contrast, dismissed suffragists' concerns as trivial compared with those of industrial workers, and even supporters of the cause saw feminist issues as integral to broader social goals. O'Sullivan spoke out for suffrage, and the *New York Times* of June 11, 1911, reported that Miss O'Reilly, the leader of "several thousand wage earning women," was the "newest addition to the recruiting suffrage army." Irish American women often coupled the right to vote with trade unionism, making the case that workingwomen needed both to protect their rights.

The very notion of increased rights for women made male religious and community leaders sputter. John Boyle O'Reilly, an ardent advocate of rights for Indians, American blacks, and Irishmen and respected author and editor of the Catholic newspaper *The Pilot,* called suffrage "an unjust, unreasonable, unspiritual abnormality . . . a hard, undigested, tasteless, devitalized proposition . . . a half-fledged, unmusical promethean abomination . . . a quack bolus to reduce masculinity even by the obliteration of femininity." Suffrage, O'Reilly added, is "the antithesis of that highest and sweetest mystery—conviction by submission and conquest by sacrifice."

Many women "turned a cold shoulder" to feminism's first wave, according to Diner. Social class, religion, and cultural background separated Bridget and her daughters from many of feminism's most visible organizers and supporters—well-educated, often well-to-do women whose families employed Irish "girls" as maids. Suffragism grew out of abolitionism, a movement that had demonstrated a strong anti-immigrant, anti-Catholic streak. It was "an upper-middle-class, Protestant, Anglo-Saxon, self-conscious movement that didn't make a whole lot of sense to those women," Janet Nolan explained. "This was an alien group of do-gooders seeking to advance their elite agenda."

Some of feminism's founding mothers, including Susan B. Anthony and Lucretia Mott, were active in the temperance movement, a reform effort disdained by many and particularly noxious to the Irish, who were so frequently the targets of nineteenth-century nativist Protestant social reform. The vote notwithstanding, goals like property law reform meant little to women who had no tangible assets. And liberalizing divorce laws and easing access to contraception flew in the face of their religious beliefs.

Erin's daughters in America braved new worlds for their families, not for ideology but because, by temperament and tradition, Irish women do what they think has to get done. Feminism's righteous rebellion against the Victorian cult of womanhood and its fetishization of female frailty belonged to a world they knew only as handmaidens. The right to work wasn't an abstract ideal and feigned helplessness was not an option open to most. Nor was it part of their inheritance.

The Celts are said to have viewed women as morally superior to men, and under Brehon law women could pick their partners, divorce them, head families, and own property. The warrior queen of Connacht, Medb (or Maeve), dominates the ancient Irish prose poem the *Tain* "as does no other woman in any epic," Thomas Cahill has written. Medb was a warrior, ruler, and demanding lover. There has never been a cult of romantic love in Ireland; waiting women, damsels in distress, and spurned, suicidal lovers do not figure in the stories. When King Ailil suggests to Medb that she became better off the day she married him, her rejoinder is "I was well enough off without you."

Irish nationalists and Catholic pedants rewrote elements of history in the late nineteenth century, to propagandize religious, rural, republican ideals. According to Luke Gibbons, "Standish O'Grady, one of the main architects of the Literary Revival, was so flummoxed by the 'very loose morality' of Queen Medb and her companions" when he was writing popular accounts of early Irish history that he changed her personality, endowing her with traditional female traits that better conformed to the conceits of Victorian narrative.

The story of Brigid of Ireland went through similar rewrites over the centuries by Catholic chroniclers distressed by evidence that Brigid had presided over a religious community at a time when high abbesses were thought to possess "hands that had the power to heal . . . almost certainly heard confessions, probably ordained clergy, and may even have celebrated Mass." According to Cahill, conservative scribes consistently downplayed evidence of female power in the Irish Church, and one account went so far as to claim Brigid was ordained "by mistake."

Poverty and humility were valorized, and that remained true for many women well into the twentieth century. The female icon and inspiration for Ireland's devotional revolution during the late nineteenth century was the Blessed Virgin Mary, handmaiden, intercessionary. Devotions to Our Lady of Knock, the most popular shrine in Eire, "focus on the hardships of Irish mothers in their family kitchens," writes Marina Warner. "One fast-selling picture at the shrine shows a wan young mother in an apron stirring a bowl by a steaming stove. It is inscribed with the 'Kitchen Prayer' ":

> *Lord of all the pots and pans and things*
> *Since I've got no time to be a saint*
> *By doing lovely things*
> *Or watching late with Thee*
> *Or dreaming till the dawn light*
> *Or storming heaven's gates*
> *Make me a saint by getting*
> *Meals and washing up the plates.*

As Warner points out, the feminine virtues "degenerate easily: obedience becomes docility; gentleness, irresolution; humility, cringing; forbearance, long-suffering."

The ascent of the sainted mother

> *There's a spot in my heart, which no colleen may own,*
> *There's a depth in my soul never sounded or known;*
> *There's a place in my mem'ry, my life that you fill,*
> *No one can take it, no one ever will. . . .*
> *I kiss the dear fingers, so toil-worn for me . . .*
> *Oh, God bless you and keep you, Mother Machree.*

The mother of Irish American sentimental mother songs, a secular hymn to self-sacrifice, underscores a verity of the subculture: that in the realm of human relationships, none is so precious as the bond between a boy and his mother.

The relationship between mothers and sons in post-Famine Ireland was "proverbially close, at times smotheringly so," according to the historian Kerby Miller. Women "trapped in loveless marriages to men much older than themselves" doted on their male children, who often returned the favor, sometimes throughout their lives. Anthropologists who have done fieldwork in Ireland have observed that mothers spoiled their sons—waiting on them at mealtimes, ironing their clothes—and expected their daughters to do the same.

The devotional revolution's emphasis on the Blessed Virgin Mary encouraged a tendency toward mother worship, a pattern that repeated itself in America, where widowhood and abandonment left many women practically as well as psychologically dependent on their sons. Historic accounts and criminal records show that domestic violence, alcohol abuse, and abandonment were commonplace in Irish immigrant communities.

The biographies of well-known Irish Americans such as Al Smith and the Kennedy family often begin with stories of struggling widows in the latter half of the nineteenth century, when Irish male life expectancy was less than ten years in America and it was often said that "you never see a gray-haired Irishman." The father of James Tyrone in Eugene O'Neill's autobiographical *Long Day's Journey into Night* may be the most famous example of a man who walked away from his small children and their mother, leaving her "a stranger in a strange land"—a pattern of abandonment that came to be known as "Irish divorce."

The idealized Irish mother assumed a place in sentimental Irish American iconography as those struggles receded to the past for many in the second and third generations. Her pop persona loomed large in the dramatic disconnect between things Irish and Americans' imaginings of them. In 1916, the year of the Easter Rebellion in Dublin, for example, one of the most popular songs Stateside was "Ireland Must Be Heaven for My Mother Came from There" (see Chapter 1).

Like the Virgin at Knock, Mother Machree is silent, distant, and adored. So is the mother who used to sing "Toora-Lural-Lura" to Barry Fitzgerald in *Going My Way*. Ditto two of the three or four marginally significant female characters in Edwin O'Connor's classic Irish American novel of politics, *The Last Hurrah*—the women are not only reticent, removed, and selfless, but dead: Skeffington's late, lamented wife and his dear mother, his inspiration, he tells his nephew, for evening scores and tormenting the Yankee establishment during his years as mayor of a red-brick city.

———

A professional tenor who performs in many of the world's capitals, Robert White includes in his repertoire a moving rendition of "Mother Machree." A son of an Irish woman with ambitions for her family, he winks knowingly at the song's saccharine assumptions. White was a child star. Among his eclectic collection of milestones is a recording of his 1948 appearance with Bing Crosby on the Fred Allen radio show. The walls of his New York apartment are covered with photos of meetings, greetings, and peak moments with Alice Tully, Tip O'Neill, Bishop Fulton J. Sheen, and—the singer points out proudly—the family of the legendary McCormack.

As far as his Irish-born mother, Maureen, was concerned, the acme of her son's career occurred in April 1963, when Robert sang at a dinner for the duchess of Luxembourg at the Kennedy White House. Three pictures of him taken that grand evening were among the many published in a 1967 coffee table tome, *The Kennedy White House Parties*. The book hadn't been out very long at the time Maureen White was dying. Robert recalled sitting quietly by his mother's hospital bedside, certain she had fallen into a coma, when his sister-in-law mentioned the book and asked him if he was in it.

His mother, who hadn't spoken for hours, opened her eyes immediately and demanded: " 'In it? Why, he's all over it!' " White paused for effect before adding: "Now *that* is an Irish mother."

It is an article of Irish American faith that "herself" should have the last word. As she might put it, "Why would anyone think otherwise?" Bing Crosby once made the mistake of attributing his success to luck, and his mother duly informed him: "Your luck has been my prayers and the prayers I've asked the Poor Clare nuns to offer up for you." The crooner's biographers describe Catherine Harrigan Crosby as a woman who ran her household as if she "had a direct hot line to God."

———

In monumental works of Irish drama and literature, it is often a woman's voice that speaks the denouement: Synge's Pegeen Mike ("I've lost the only playboy of the Western World") and the keening women in *Riders to the Sea;* Joyce's Molly Bloom; Juno in Sean O'Casey's *Juno and the Paycock;* Josie Hogan in Eugene O'Neill's *A Moon for the Misbegotten.*

In Irish American fiction, the unequivocal feminine voice is on many occasions throttled by the stifling forces of piety and propriety—key elements of middle-class, or lace curtain, life.

The term "lace curtain" came into common usage in the late nineteenth century, when upwardly mobile Celtic Americans flaunted panels of Galway and Limerick lace in living room windows to symbolize the relative prosperity and sense of refinement that distinguished them from poor, "shanty Irish." The adjective has always signified a mind-set more than a window treatment—a hybrid of Victorian primness, Catholic Puritanism, and social insecurity that would characterize much in Irish American life long after many families packed away the diaphanous fabric that hung in the windows of brownstones, triple-deckers, and two-flats, and moved to the suburbs.

The "lifestyle" was a family enterprise. But women were in charge, and they were the ones who fussed over the windows, stretched the family budget to pay for white gloves and starched white shirts, and made sure everyone made it to Mass in clean, well-pressed outfits on Sunday.

Women, as historian Thomas Brown pointed out, deserve credit they have yet to receive for turning the wild Irish into upstanding members of the middle class. At the same time, because women are the caretakers of customs and culture, they have been blamed for most of what went wrong behind the lace curtains: the "chilling and repressive" elements of bourgeois Irish Catholic life, in Shannon's words, "a mania for the respectable and pious, the sober and genteel . . . epitomized in the cliché that hushed many a family quarrel: 'Ssh. What will the neighbors think?' "

American writers of ranging talent and insight have portrayed the lace curtain Irish mother of early- to mid-twentieth century as an iron-fisted, velvet-gloved matriarch, firmly in charge of a family unit in which an emotionally absent Dad sits at the head of the dinner table, where he and everyone else nod in agreement with what Mom has to say.

Mary Lonigan, mother of the eponymous antihero of James T. Farrell's Studs Lonigan trilogy, alternates between cursing her son's pregnant fiancée, Catherine, and saying the rosary as Studs lays dying. She is duly enraged, the critic Charles Fanning has observed, at losing the beloved son she had hoped would be a priest and the scandal Catherine's pregnancy will cause at his funeral.

But Farrell has created a near caricature. "Momma" Towne in Alice McDermott's *At Weddings and Wakes*, who regales her daughters and grandchildren relentlessly with stories of her toil and suffering, demanding they pay homage to her self-sacrifice, is a far more astute portrayal of the martyred, manipulative Irish mother.

Elizabeth Cullinan's *House of Gold* presents a searing portrait of such a woman in Julia Devlin, a self-righteous, steel-willed matriarch who sees herself as a "saintly paragon," Fanning observes. Julia has so skillfully dominated her grown children—two priests, two nuns, a military man, and a son and daughter who have never left her home—that they have "thoroughly internalized their mother's vision of herself."

The tragicomic centerpiece of Cullinan's novel is Julia's nineteen-page, handwritten autobiography, "The Story of a Mother," a document that could be a primer of lace curtain delusions and obsessions, religious rigidity, and self-absorption masquerading as self-sacrifice. In it, Julia recalls in detail the events that supposedly led to each of her children's religious vocations—portraying each "calling" as a sacrifice *she* made to God. Characters and episodes that might tarnish her sentimental trajectory are edited for consistency: Her feckless bartender son is a successful businessman; her husband is wholly peripheral to "The Story," as is her daughter and unheralded handmaiden Elizabeth, who adds little luster to her mother's glory, being neither a member of a religious order nor a son.

The controlling American Irish mother's prerogative is endemic to a milieu in which children are raised not to question authority, particularly religious authority, which she represents. Suffering is thought to make one a better person in Catholic culture. In his one-man show *Colin Quinn: An Irish Wake,* one of Quinn's characters recalls a woman named Margaret, who assures another mourner who steps on her foot not to worry: "I'll offer it up." Margaret, as Quinn explains, "would do anything for you—as long as you never did anything for her."

Offering it up has won many women admiration and the blind affection, loyalty, and obedience of their children, particularly their sons, who may be utterly devoted to assuaging their distress, whatever its source. As one man who grew up in a dysfunctional Irish alcoholic family, in which the mother stoically endured her husband's abusive behavior, said, "My father was in the gutter, my mother on a pedestal—just a step below the Blessed Virgin Mary. I would do anything to keep her from crying."

But within the traditional Church, Irish women's responsibility is frequently without authority, their power without glory. Designated domestic purveyors of the faith, they are barred from sharing equally with men in the Mass and bestowing the spiritual glories of the sacraments.

For all the restrictions it places on female roles, its prohibitions about marriage, sex, and birth control, the Church has offered women relatively few earthly protections. Not only have all Catholics been forbidden to seek divorce, many women have been counseled by priests that it was their duty to stay married to negligent, abusive, and alcoholic husbands. In his memoir *All Souls,* Michael Patrick MacDonald recalls that his mother sought help from a priest when she was married to a womanizing drunk who beat her regularly and at least once tried to strangle her. Divorce was out of the question, the prelate told her, adding helpfully: "You're a Catholic, make the best of it."

In her way, Helen MacDonald did. Her kids shared her pride in her favorite line: "I was always a fighter."

Indeed, it is an assumption of both Catholic and Irish culture that women can—and will—make the best of it, no matter how trying the circumstances. "There's an expectation that women are the strong ones.

They're the practical, responsible ones," said Joan O'Donnell, a New York psychologist with an interest in ethnicity. It is their duty to be that way—which leaves ample room for the men in their lives to be dreamers and ne'er-do-wells. "Men can be little boys—in fact, they're expected to be absent and irresponsible," she added. Look at Brian Friel's *Dancing at Lughnasa.* "The three men in the play are a little boy, a crazy priest, and an unreliable man!"

In families under duress in particular, "Irish women tend to think they have to do it all themselves," said family therapist and author Monica McGoldrick. Women with children take on the responsibilities of mother and father, a near-impossible task; human beings—even Irish mothers—are neither superheroes nor saints, and all too many lives have become exercises in "trying to keep a lid on things." O'Donnell concurred. Too often, they become stern and demanding, resentful, self-righteous. "They feel they have to tolerate men and keep them under control, and that means blocking off feelings. There's a fear of intimacy . . . and these women lose touch with their tenderness at times."

In *That Most Distressful Nation,* his sociological and impressionistic consideration of American Irish Catholics, Andrew Greeley maintains that many Irish women "have far more power in the family life than do women in some other ethnic cultures; and in some instances this produces a situation in which a strong and domineering mother rules either by sheer force of will or by the much more subtle manipulation of constantly appealing to the sympathies and guilt of her husband and children."

Greeley pulls no punches in criticizing this kind of control. Most male alcoholics he knows "are sons of mothers who rule the roost who have married women just like their mothers," he writes. So are underachievers: "The Jewish mother encourages her children to overachievement so that she may be proud of them," the priest, social scientist, and novelist opines. "The Irish mother encourages underachievement in order that she may continue to dominate them."

———

Caveats are in order here: Women like Momma Towne and Julia Devlin are readily recognizable to many American Irish Catholics, but they are not *representative* of the tens of thousands of warm, supportive mothers who have raised reasonably happy and adjusted Irish American children. Similarly, while alcoholism and underachievement are prevalent and problematic in the subculture (see Chapter 5), Irish families are no more or less dysfunctional than those of any other American ethnic group. Storytellers do not tell tales of the quotidian, nor do social scientists focus on the sanguine.

Fiction writers and social scientists who have written about them sometimes give short shrift to the fairly obvious fact that Irish matriarchs, like most people on the planet, are part of a cultural dynamic. What is more, as the Irish critic Declan Kiberd observes, "Women could not have achieved such dominance if many husbands had not also abdicated the role of father."

Kiberd points to O'Casey's tragedy *Juno and the Paycock* as an example. In the penultimate scene, Juno braces herself to see the bullet-ridden body of her son, who has been killed in revolutionary cross fire, and then to seek shelter for herself and her unmarried pregnant daughter, Mary, who's been disowned by her father, abandoned already by both her feckless lover and her boyfriend. When Mary moans to Juno, "My poor little child that'll have no father!" swiftly her mother assures her: "It'll have what's far better. It'll have two mothers."

As if to prove her point, "Captain" Jack Boyle then staggers drunkenly onstage with "Joxer" Daly, slurring platitudes: "Irelan sober . . . is Ireland . . . free . . ." and ". . . th'whole worl's . . . in a terr . . . ible state o' . . . chassis" in the final scene.

O'Casey, Kiberd observes, is pointing to a grim fact of early-twentieth-century Irish life: that troubled times bolstered female resolve and encouraged male retreat. Irish fathers had "lost face," writes Kiberd, "because they had compromised with the occupying English in return for safe positions as policemen or petty clerks, or because they had retreated into a demeaning pattern of alcoholism and unemployment. The Irish father was often a defeated man, whose wife frequently won the bread and usurped his domestic power, while the priests usurped his spiritual authority."

The move from countryside to city (be it New York, Boston, or Dublin) threw the Irish family into flux, undermining time-honored truths about what it meant to be a father, mother, son, or daughter. The rural father's traditional sphere of authority was the land; the mother's was the household, which included matters of faith as well as domestic finances, and the family's spiritual life. Once the family left the farm, the male role was diminished—a phenomenon that some observers, Hasia Diner among them, say contributed to tension and fractious, sometimes abusive, relationships between men and women.

There is "no question" that as the Irish assimilated, there were many middle-class families in which "women called the shots," said Danny Cassidy, a filmmaker who teaches Irish studies at San Francisco's New College. "People used to go to Rockaway Beach to see my grandfather fight—they'd watch the bodies come flying out of the doors of the bars. But like most of these big, tough, classic Irish guys, the tough stuff stopped when he walked through the door. When the men got paid at the construction site, the women were there to take the pay envelope. They'd give them something to go to the pub. Then they paid the bills, took care of the money, took care of the family. Women ran the whole thing."

The lace curtain rises

"The Irish American women I know today are more like their grandmothers than mothers," said Seattle artist Matthew Lennon. "I think a lot of women suffered from that sweet colleen generation of sentimentality . . . the middle-class standard that put the mother on a pedestal and said they were pure. I remember at family parties [in the 1950s and 1960s], my mother and the American women were in the kitchen, talking about children and losing weight, and my grandmother, who worked in a factory, was in the living room, smoking Luckys and talking about baseball with the guys. Nobody would have dared suggest that she go into the kitchen."

Generations of women born since World War II "have learned to be nice and polite and get through the system in a gentler fashion," he continued, "but they know that if you want the job, you have to fight for it. And I always find Irish women are more ready to intellectually grapple with a guy."

At a time when many American men and women have struggled with changing assumptions about gender roles, Irish women enjoy some signal advantages. Few are raised with any expectation that a man will take care of them, and many have witnessed female resourcefulness and independence from an early age. The very concept of "Daddy's little girl" boggles the mind of Chicago hotel executive Nora Gainer. Growing up in Beverly, Illinois, in the 1980s, she and her sisters "cleaned the gutters. We cut the grass. We did everything. There was never this idea that girls didn't do that!"

And while unmarried females are woefully undervalued in a male-centered society that casts a wary eye on women who seem not to need men, the "maiden lady"—call her "Aunt Mary"—has long been a respected, pivotal figure, sometimes even the matriarch, in Irish American families.

"In Italian culture, or Greek culture, or many others, single women have very little status," said Monica McGoldrick. "We have this Auntie Mame character—this strong and admirable person who has status and power and guts and charm. She has clothes, she has a good time, she has a good sense of humor. She tells the nieces and nephews where they ought to go to school," a decision of enormous importance in Irish families. "There is much about her to be admired and taken."

The Irish pattern of delaying marriage persisted for two, sometimes three, generations in the United States, and in many families it was simply assumed that at least one unmarried daughter would stay at home and care for aging parents. Until her parents died, her wants or needs were of secondary concern—at most.

The syndrome sometimes encouraged unhappy, indeed harrowing, family lives. William Kennedy's Albany trilogy provides a chilling portrayal of a single woman strangled by family ties that bind in Sarah Phelan, whose father announces on his deathbed when she is twelve: "I don't care who gets married as long as Sarah stays home with her mother." Sarah does, assuming the role of that smothering, sex-obsessed matriarch when she passes on, devoting her life's energy to the hopeless task of trying to maintain pious respectability among a family of iconoclasts and half-mad eccentrics.

Isabelle Moore in Mary Gordon's *Final Payments* and Mary Agnes Keely in Maureen Howard's *Bridgeport Bus* put their lives on hold as long as they are needed—in Isabelle's case, until her widowed father dies. After Mary Agnes's father died unexpectedly when she was sixteen, Mary

Agnes explains, there was no question in her family's mind that she shouldn't quit school and take a job to help support her mother: "I had to pay for [my brother] Francis to study sixteenth-century logic and rhetoric with the Jesuits."

Throughout the twentieth century, Irish women outnumbered men in their own families and communities; even at the time of the 1990 census, there were 30 percent more females than males of Irish ancestry in the United States. The so-called man shortage was more acute in Irish America than it was in other substrata: Few Catholics separated or divorced; marrying outside the faith was frowned upon; many of the best and brightest boys went into the priesthood; and the appeal of a sizable number of "available" males—"the gelded, balding boys that my mother finds in limitless supply," as Mary Agnes Keely describes them—was limited.

In the days before most women worked, Aunt Mary was a nurse, a teacher, or an executive secretary who seemed to embody some of the more admirable Irish American traits—humor, resourcefulness, respect for learning—while enjoying the benefit of her exposure to the world outside the Irish Catholic milieu.

Agnes Towne, the eldest of the Towne sisters in *Weddings and Wakes,* is an Aunt Mary—an executive secretary who owns every book, newspaper, and record album in her family home and whose stock-in-trade, as far as her nieces and nephew can tell, is knowing things: "how to keep cut flowers fresh, how to clean brocade or velvet or silver . . . which cocktails called for bitters or onions or round red cherries and what kind of glass should be served with each . . . good china, fine cheese, and the best seats in every Broadway theater."

Peter Quinn's Aunt Mary was "Aunt Marion, actually. My mother's older sister. She was an executive secretary at Saint Vincent's Hospital, went to Fordham at night—the first woman to graduate from college in Edgewood, New Jersey. When my grandfather died in '36, she stayed home with my grandmother. All the others left. It was never spoken, but that was her role, she was social security for my grandmother. But she lived a very fulfilling life—she never seemed unhappy.

"Her constant companion was Father Daniel Ryan, a Jesuit, after whom my son is named, who taught Marion psychology at Fordham. Looking back on it, the great irony is that they were the perfect couple. If they were alive today, he'd probably leave the Jesuits. They were the only two people I ever met who took children seriously. Listened to them. They would take us out to dinner all the time. To Broadway plays. Anything I ever saw in New York was because of them. And of course they had no children. They were the only two people who weren't dysfunctional."

Aunt Mary is admired by her nieces and nephews for many reasons, not the least being that she is often matter-of-fact about family matters that other adults refuse to discuss. *Why does Grandma purse her lips and stare fixedly out the window when certain names come up?* Some in the younger generation might want to know. (Your grandmother thinks those people betrayed Grandpa's loyalty, Aunt Mary explains.) *What happened to Uncle Billy, who appears in every family picture taken before some unnamed, unacknowledged incident occurred, then seems to have disappeared?* (Billy left his wife because he is gay, explains his sister—who may well be the only family member in touch with him.) As for *her* sexuality, the assumption is that she is celibate. Then again, that is one of those things Irish families don't bring up, so no one has ever asked about it.

Generations of Irish American teachers, many of them single, took girls' and women's education seriously, as did many nuns and young Irish Catholic women who had the advantage of being exposed to educated, working women long before most women had careers. Memoirs of Catholic girlhoods look back with what is often well-reasoned skepticism on the rigorous training in ladylike conformity the daughters of wealth and privilege received in Sacred Heart convents. Still, the Madames of the Sacred Heart and other orders of teaching sisters gave up the secular world for lives of faith, learning, and teaching, and the better Catholic women's colleges had highly accomplished female faculty members who encouraged high standards; Catholic girls came into contact with more educated role models than many others did.

As the American Church expanded during the 1940s and 1950s, certain avenues that were largely off-limits to women in the secular world opened to Catholics. Nuns were "two or three times as likely to be administrators or bosses" as their lay peers, according to the Catholic cultural historian James T. Fisher. Women were also members and leaders of many of the lay apostolates that formed after the war. Feminism was not the inspiration for this ascendant female leadership; the Church had new needs and, as always, counted on women to fulfill them.

Recording a legacy

Thomas Brown and Hasia Diner both speculate that, if women's economic, social, and educational achievements had been taken into account, the history and sociological profile of the American Irish might well have been significantly different.

In *The Fitzgeralds and the Kennedys,* Doris Kearns Goodwin describes John F. Kennedy's great-grandmother Rosanna Cox Fitzgerald as a woman who was "indispensable in life, but only vaguely remembered in death." She was pregnant with her thirteenth when she died at forty-eight. A two-line obituary for her ran in the *Boston Herald.*

JFK's paternal great-grandmother Bridget Murphy Kennedy, who arrived in Boston on a boat from County Wexford in 1849, was left a widow with four children when her husband, Patrick, died of cholera. Working in a notions shop, which she eventually bought, she scraped together enough money to put her son P.J. through private school and helped him buy a tavern. A mover and shmoozer, he went into politics, where his world intersected with that of Mayor John "Honey" Fitzgerald, father of Rose. Against her father's wishes, she married P.J.'s son, Harvard-educated Joe Kennedy.

The rest, as the cliché goes, is history.

The Kennedy legacy is sometimes described as a larger-than-life example of the Irish experience in the United States, which, in the case of the Kennedy men, it most certainly is not. Yes, many Irish American men did make their way from rags to respectability through the bar business and politics. But only a very few were raised to be so ruthless, such sexual predators.

The lives of the Kennedy women, however, reflect those of many in the diaspora. Rose was a young woman with a "vibrant mind and an active temperament" who very much wanted to go to college at Wellesley. One of her great disappointments in life was that her father wouldn't let her, because Boston's archbishop told him that sending his daughter to a secular school might lose him Catholic voters. It was one of many times she would be forced or force herself to sublimate her wants and desires to a man's ambitions and appetites.

"Rose wanted sons who looked like gentlemen, but who still had the brashness and bravado of the Irish streets," Laurence Leamer writes in *The Kennedy Women: The Saga of an American Family.* "She wanted daughters devoted to the church and faith, dedicated to their brothers and their husbands."

She got both, and everyone involved paid a price.

In an op-ed piece celebrating Irish women that appeared in the *Boston Globe,* Jean Kennedy Smith wrote that her mother once asked her what she wanted to be when she grew up. "I answered, 'I want to get married.' She asked my brother the same question, and he said, 'I want to be president.' We both achieved our goals. Many years later, when I asked my young daughter that question, she replied, 'I want to be president.'"

This upbeat anecdote of generational evolution belies certain essentials of the Kennedy saga, of course. For example, when Rose was in the hospital delivering Jean, she got a bouquet from Joe Kennedy's mistress, Gloria Swanson. She ignored that taunt—and countless others—teaching her daughters by her example to put up, shut up, and put a good face on all of it. Joe Kennedy invited showgirls and secretaries to the family homes, where Rose entertained cardinals.

Rose Kennedy did not encourage her daughters to pursue the intellectual life she was denied. Like their mother, they went to convent schools and Catholic women's colleges. The Kennedy "girls" didn't particularly interest their mother, who said to a young relative, "My daughters are nice women. However, I tire of them."

One can only wonder if she found more stimulation in her granddaughters, an impressive lot both personally and professionally. Kathleen Kennedy Townsend is Maryland lieutenant governor; Courtney Kennedy Hill is a human rights activist; Kerry Kennedy Cuomo is an activist attorney; Rory Kennedy an accomplished filmmaker whose documentaries have focused on female addicts and impoverished families in Appalachia. Their cousin Caroline Kennedy Schlossberg is an attorney whose books on privacy law have been respectfully received; and cousin Maria Shriver is a successful television journalist and writer.

Jean Kennedy Smith has not had an easy life. Four of her siblings died tragically. She married a man who was apparently a womanizer, but she stayed with him until he died of cancer in 1990. The following year, her son was acquitted in a rape trial that made public some of the raunchiness that was de rigueur male behavior for decades at Kennedy family retreats.

When she was in her late sixties, Kennedy Smith became a "most improbable, controversial, and ultimately successful" U.S. ambassador to Ireland, Kevin Cullen wrote in the *Boston Globe* as she departed the post. Her role in pushing forward the peace negotiations in Northern Ireland and encouraging Washington to abandon its "hands-off policy" earned her "a mention in the history books for her own actions, not those of her brothers. Someone who lived most of her life in the shadow of powerful men, she has stepped out into the light and, critics be damned, got the job done."

Her obituary will recognize that.

Mary, Mary, quite contrary

In 1990, when Mary Robinson was elected president and wowed the world with her vision of a new Ireland, many in the media described her as an anomaly: an independent, clear-sighted woman in a tradition-bound, Church-cowed country. In fact, Robinson was a woman of both her time and her inheritance. She assumed her post in an Ireland that was emerging from a chrysalis of postcolonialism and latter-day devotional Catholicism—a culture that had tried and failed to keep a formidable female heritage dating to Brigid of Ireland under wraps.

The history of Irish America that is written most often—as a political allegory—and the anodyne renderings of popular culture from Tin Pan Alley through *The Quiet Man* and *The Last Hurrah* have diminished the significance and muffled the voices of Irish American women. Even a cursory look at *Notable American Women* turns up an impressive number who have made their mark since early activists like Mother Jones, Margaret Sanger, and Lucy Burns. Dorothy Day, cofounder of the Catholic Worker movement; painter Georgia O'Keeffe; entrepreneur and philanthropist Margaret Fogarty Rudkin, who turned her talent for baking into Pepperidge Farm Bakeries, which she sold to Campbell's Soup for $28 million in 1960; Jane Hoey, the first director of what became the U.S. Department of Welfare; and marine biologist and poet of environmentalism Rachel Carson, author of *Silent Spring*.

Throughout the twentieth century, as sentimentalists sang about reticent colleens and silent mothers, Irish American women were making their mark as pioneers. A few examples: Margaret Bourke-White, the first female photographer allowed in the Soviet Union when Germany invaded; Maureen "Little Mo" Connolly, the first woman and youngest tennis player ever to win the Australian Open, French Open, and Wimbledon; Doris Kearns Goodwin, first female journalist allowed in the Red Sox locker room; Sandra Day O'Connor, the first woman on the Supreme Court; Kathleen Sullivan, the first woman dean of Stanford Law School; Eileen Collins, the first female to command a space shuttle, and so on.

As for the Irish voice in America, three female commentators on the *New York Times* op-ed page in the last decade of the last century were Anna Quindlen, Maureen Dowd, and Gail Collins. Quindlen, Dowd, and Eileen McNamara of the *Boston Globe* all won Pulitzers for commentary in the 1990s. Peggy Noonan, who wrote the more memorable speeches delivered by Ronald Reagan, the "Great Communicator," opines for the *Wall Street Journal* and on television. It seems that Irish American women are reclaiming the clear voice of feminine authority that resonates in their collective past.

The popularity of the music troupe Cherish the Ladies, all Irish American women, stimulated the Irish traditional music revival that started in the 1970s and that seems to have eclipsed the Tin Pan Alley tunes that fans of "trad" music refer to derisively as "Bing Crosby Irish."

Meanwhile, American writers for big and small screen have been creating female characters whose names underscore their independence, tough-mindedness, and humor: Cagney and Lacy; Murphy Brown; Lieutenant Colleen McMurphy in *China Beach*; Maggie O'Connell in *Northern Exposure*.

For sheer contrast with the sentimental mother of Irish American song and movie myth, though, few characters come close to matching Geraldine Page's last screen performance. An Irish matriarch no one would want to mess with in the 1984 film *The Pope of Greenwich Village*, she faces off with a pair of duplicitous police officers who come looking for incriminating evidence against her son, who has been killed in the line of corrupt police duty. "My Walter was tough as a bar of iron [eye-yun]," she tells them, "and he didn't get that from his fathah."

God bless her and keep her—and the many like her.

CHAPTER FIVE

The Creature and Related Demons

"Here's how."
—Edmund Tyrone, raising his glass
in Eugene O'Neill's *Long Day's Journey into Night*

It should go without saying that the overwhelming majority of men and women of Irish descent are no more alcoholic than Italians are members of the Mafia.

The fact that it doesn't underscores what many people who have spent much time in their presence might suspect: The Irish drink when they are happy and when they are sad. They drink on special occasions and at the end of the day; to dull the pain of living and to make the good things in life grand; to loosen the tongue and to stifle words of love and affection. "It is remarkable," a group of researchers who studied ethnicity once remarked, "that the Irish can find an outlet for so many forms of psychic conflict in this single form of escape."

Studies of ethnic drinking in America have shown that, among regular drinkers, Irish, WASP, Slavic, and Native Americans tend to drink more heavily than most others in U.S. society. The Irish are somewhat less likely than people of Slavic or English heritage to suffer serious alcohol problems. But because the Irish are far less likely to abstain from alcohol than many others—88 percent of Irish Catholics in the United States drink beer, wine, or spirits as compared with 67 percent of the overall population—they are more problem-prone.

"Alcoholism has been a major public health problem among Irish Catholics for centuries," observes the Irish-born Los Angeles psychiatrist Garrett O'Connor, a specialist in the psychology of addictions. Alcoholism researchers and clinicians for the most part agree that the very fact of being of Irish ancestry puts a person at risk for developing drinking problems. Some of the reasons appear to be genetic. Others are cultural, as evidenced by the fact that American Irish drink more—and more problematically—than their cousins in Eire.

In Irish America, drinking is more than retreat, more than recreation, more than release. Since the late nineteenth century, it has been an ethnic identity, a substitute for culture. It isn't Irish music, literature, or accomplishment that are celebrated most often on American St. Patrick's Day. It isn't even Irish conviviality emblematized by a glass. It is weakness for drink and what drunkenness engenders: the fightin' Irish; the tears near beer; the lachrymose renditions of "Danny Boy" sung in Irish theme bars.

The journalist and author Pete Hamill has said that "a lot of Irish American men have their first real conversations with their fathers while they're standing at a bar."

"At a bar or at the cocktail table," agreed a recovering alcoholic raised in a wealthy Midwestern suburb. "That was like an altar in our house. You went there right from Mass. Mixing martinis was a holy ritual" after late-afternoon Mass on Saturdays. The "Irishness" of the act made it all the more spiritual. To second- and third-generation Irish Americans, increasingly removed from Ireland and their immigrant past, drinking stood for everything attractive about their heritage. "It was romance," he said, "it was rebellion, it was the Irish writers and all the songs."

"You grow up thinking the fact that you're Irish meant you had to drink" is how Kathleen Corrigan (a pseudonym) put it. "Somewhere it is embedded in your genes that drinking and fun are synonymous. A sip of Daddy's beer was fun, a sip of Southern Comfort under the sink; drinking your way through Europe after college was a great time—that's just what you did. The fact that you hold your liquor better than anyone else does isn't a warning sign—it's admirable."

In many Irish American eyes, a little bit of booze makes one friendlier, funnier, and more loquacious more Irish, in other words. It undercuts the straight and serious. The historian William Shannon once observed an Irish predilection for "satire and self burlesque"—a tendency to play the court jester who "poked fun at king, commoner, and himself" at every opportunity. Sodden self-effacement that devolves into self-loathing is everywhere.

The stage Irish drunk of the turn of the twentieth century, consummate jester, was supposedly booed off the American boards in the early 1900s. But he still struts his stuff on St. Patrick's Day and when men and women get together to celebrate the "Irish pride" of getting drunk. As Daniel Patrick Moynihan writes in *Beyond the Melting Pot*, "The Irish are commonly thought to be a friendly, witty, generous people, physically courageous and fond of drink. There is a distinct tendency among many to live up to this tradition."

Traits and traditions

George Vaillant, a professor of psychiatry at Harvard Medical School who studied the drinking behavior of hundreds of inner-city men over four decades, found that Irish Americans were seven times as likely to develop alcohol dependence as Italian Americans—even though the Irish had a substantially higher abstinence rate. Vaillant concluded that of all traits that influence alcohol addiction, the most salient are a family history of alcoholism and growing up in a culture that promotes or condones adult drinking.

Sons of alcoholic fathers, including those who are adopted and raised by foster parents, "have a four to five times greater rate of alcoholism than the general population," Vaillant concluded. Having an alcoholic relative outstrips family mental health and stability, depression, anxiety, and environment in predisposing a person to alcoholism. Vaillant's subjects who had one alcoholic parent but grew up in an otherwise stable environment were five times as likely to develop alcoholism as those who came from troubled families without an alcoholic mother or father. At the same time, being a child of an alcoholic parent does not a problem drinker make; almost half the *nondrinkers* in Vaillant's studies were sons of alcoholics.

Cultures that incorporate drinking into religious rituals and family occasions and encourage drinking in moderation and with food, such as Jews and Italians, have very low rates of alcoholism. Italians start introducing children to small amounts of alcohol and give them "a long education in moderate alcohol use." Their beverage of choice is wine, which they drink with food, diminishing the alcoholic high of beer or whiskey. Drunkenness is frowned upon. French children, by contrast, are taught to drink, but not necessarily in moderation, and "in France, unlike Italy, public drunkenness is condoned." France for many years had "the highest alcoholism rate in the world."

Vaillant and other alcohol researchers have found that drinking disorders are prevalent among groups like the Irish and American Indians, who don't imbibe at table or with their families, but "tolerate—and covertly praise—the capacity of men to drink large amounts of alcohol."

Contrary to much of the Western world's perception, the people of Ireland drink less and have lower rates of alcohol-associated illnesses than many other Europeans. In 1998, Ireland ranked eighth among seventeen European Union nations in "adult alcohol intake per year." France was first (though alcohol consumption has dropped dramatically in France in recent years). The French have the highest number of deaths from cirrhosis of the liver in western Europe; cirrhosis deaths among the Irish are comparatively low.

Notably, the French are rarely typecast as alcoholic, and the stereotype of the Gallic imbiber is benign: the cosmopolite ordering a bottle in a bistro or the farmer settling down to a lunch of bread, cheese, and a bottle of good Bordeaux. The stereotype of the Irish drinker, by contrast, is much more demeaning, owing largely to its origins; the Wild Irishman, the apelike Irishman, and the stage Irishman are among the colonial legacies the British bestowed upon the world.

"The assumption, mainly promulgated by visitors and observers who've gone to weddings and funerals, that this country [Ireland] has a large alcohol problem is not true and has not been true historically," said Irish psychiatrist and epidemiologist Dermot Walsh. Data show that alcohol consumption and related medical and social problems in the nineteenth and early twentieth centuries were hardly different in Ireland than in Great Britain as a whole, said Walsh. Studies done in the 1980s showed "proportionately fewer drinkers in Ireland than in England and Wales." Indeed, it appears that the British have historically been every bit as fond of the glass as the Irish.

"The Irish abroad are in a different category," said Walsh. "In Britain and the U.S., they have been greater drinkers. It is part of a cultural identity." Many Irish emigrants, he added, have been "poorly educated people" living in impoverished circumstances that can exacerbate a tendency to alcohol addiction.

That is not to say Ireland has no alcohol problems. The Irish spend a higher proportion of their per capita income on alcoholic beverages (13 percent) than many other Europeans. And alcohol consumption has burgeoned dramatically in recent decades, noted Walsh. In 1960, the country consumed 4.88 liters of alcohol per capita. Forty years later, that has risen to nearly 11 liters.

According to the National Health & Lifestyle Surveys conducted by Ireland's Department of Health and Children, "overall, 27% of males and 21% of females consumed more than the recommended weekly limits for alcohol." Recommended limits were twenty-one "units" of alcohol for men and fourteen units for women, a "unit" being the equivalent of a half pint or glass of beer, lager, or cider; a shot of whiskey; or a glass of wine, sherry, or port.

"One would have thought that with affluence" in Ireland, "there would be a much more civilized approach to drinking—less binge drinking, and so on," said Walsh. His sense is that there is not, and one health study in Ireland showed that more than one-third of regular drinkers binge—or consume more than the weekly recommended limit in one day—on a weekly basis.

Walsh also "worries about young people, who do seem to drink an awful lot," he said. "More of them are doing it, and there are consequences in relation to aggression and accidents." Among children under eighteen who responded to the National Health & Lifestyle Surveys, 35 percent of boys and 24 percent of girls reported having been drunk; 8 percent of boys and 3 percent of girls reported being drunk more than ten times.

For all the Irish associations of drink with geniality, families don't teach their children to drink beer or wine at meals, or even at weddings and wakes. In Ireland, a boy's first pint has traditionally been a rite of passage—part of a long tradition of convivial male imbibing that became institutionalized in the late nineteenth century, when drinking was a symbol of masculine identity in a defeated society, according to sociologist Richard Stivers, who has studied Irish American drinking patterns in *A Hair of the Dog: Irish Drinking and American Stereotype.*

In the years after the Irish Famine, men began drinking heavily and routinely in what Stivers and other social scientists call "bachelor groups," though the cliques included married and unmarried men. The groups fulfilled important economic and religious functions in Irish society, the fundamental one being that they kept young men and women apart. Overpopulation had exacerbated the disasters of the Famine, and Irish families anxiously tried to keep the birthrate under control by discouraging young marriages. The Catholic Church, obsessed with preventing sins of the flesh, eagerly abetted social customs that confined one sex to a place that was largely off-limits to the other, such as the pub.

Bachelor groups diverted attention from traditional symbols of male adulthood such as marriage, family, and farm ownership, which were unrealizable goals for many young males, according to Stivers. The focus instead was on sports, storytelling, and the pleasures of all-male drinking company—a substitute for sex for some. The "hard-drinker," writes Stivers, "was a stalwart of Irish social structure and culture."

(Intriguingly, in this milieu the teetotaler was eyed with suspicion. Not only was he beholden to the world of women and priests—recall the sniveling Shawn Keogh, scorned fiancé of Pegeen Mike in *Playboy of the Western World*—but he "posed a threat to sexual standards." Who was to know where that one was when he went missing from the male realm of the pub?)

While hard drinking was greatly admired in Ireland, drunkenness—"a good man's weakness"—was something to be tolerated though not encouraged. Not so Stateside.

Prodigious Irish imbibing on both sides of the Atlantic has been attributed to everything from gray and soggy weather in the west of Eire, to sexual repression, to the stereotype of the Irish drinker itself.

Stivers makes a compelling case that the latter was quintessential in the development of Irish American ethnic identity. The Irish bonded around booze in nineteenth-century America, when their propensity for hard drinking was initially viewed much as it was in Britain—as one among the more deplorable of Irish traits. Famine Irish immigrants settled in shanties surrounded by many sorts of human misery. Employers who *didn't* hang out signs bearing the infamous admonition "No Irish Need Apply" often paid laborers part of their wages in rotgut and encouraged them to drink so they would work harder.

The police were more likely to arrest "deviants" than upstanding citizens. And the Irish were lampooned mercilessly in the media and made fun of themselves on the stage. Diseased, depressed, downtrodden, the Irish in America behaved as they were expected to behave. They drank because they were homesick. Lonely. They also drank to show their group identity, Irish nationalism, their Catholicism, and what made them different from other ethnics.

"As a sacrament in the religion of Irish-American nationalism, it differentiated the Irish from other ethnic groups," writes Stivers. "It became a spiritual value symbolizing Irish group identity. It implied that the more one drank, the more Irish one became. Drink in Ireland did not fundamentally symbolize one's Irishness or one's Catholicism."

"Catholic Ireland," Stivers observes, "had little desire to be assimilated by the English. But in America, the great desire of the Irish to be accepted by native Americans, coupled with the impossibility of remaining authentically Irish, meant that they were doomed to become a caricature—the only terms on which native Americans would accept them."

Drunkenness, humor, and haplessness, stocks-in-trade of the stage Irishman, became sacralized. To some extent, as the Irish acculturated, as newer groups of non-English-speaking immigrants—who struck Anglo-Americans as even stranger than the Celts—started arriving and those characteristics became interchangeable, drinking made the Irish happy, bighearted, harmless people to be around. Toward the end of the nineteenth century, traits identified with Irishness were increasingly seen as benign. The persona of the stage Irishman evolved into the happy Irish inebriate—the price paid for assimilation into American society, Stivers maintains. "The happy drunk was a bastard born out of an unholy union of Irish culture and American stereotype."

Silences and shame

Psychiatrist Garrett O'Connor's Irish Catholic patients who seek help for alcoholism today are "frequently crippled by shame, guilt, and a mortal fear of being exposed as inherently bad or perpetually wrong," he writes. The singular behavior has earned them a moniker in some chapters of Alcoholics Anonymous, where they're known as "CIA" (Catholic Irish Alcoholic). O'Connor is among those who attribute the prevalence of Irish alcoholism and psychological problems to the legacy of colonialism and the Irish Church's espousal of a "grim theology of fear that led Irish Catholics to believe they had been born bad, were inclined toward evil, and deserved to suffer for their sins."

"CIA is a kind of shorthand," explained Kathleen Corrigan, a self-described sufferer of the complex. "It means that you probably have a lot of shame and guilt in your story," the individual narrative of drinking, "hitting bottom," and achieving sobriety that AA members tell at meetings. "And chances are that you grew up with [alcoholism]. Your first conscious memory probably has a bottle of beer or something to do with drink."

The lure exists despite the fact that many homes in which heavy drinking is norm and ritual are veritable advertisements for its disastrous effects. "Both my parents were seriously affected by alcohol, and there was chaos in the home," said Corrigan. "It never occurred to me that other people's homes weren't like that. That the fighting wasn't there, you didn't live in fear of anger and the temper and the belt hung over the table. I just didn't know this wasn't the way it was for everybody."

In many families, "the creature" turns sinister in part because problem drinking dominates the very crowded category of things the Irish don't like to discuss. A recovering alcoholic once tried to apologize to her mother-in-law for her past behavior, and the older woman cut her off, saying, "Drink is the curse of the Irish, and we needn't talk about it."

Any number of Irish families would rather have a freewheeling discussion about sex or money than broach the subject of Dad's near-intolerable grouchiness or talk about why and when it was that Mom started nodding off every night during dinner.

Frank Malley (a pseudonym) recalled trying to approach the subject of what he jokingly calls "Irish sickle cell anemia" with his father's brother, a successful lawyer and "the smartest" member of his family. He asked his uncle whether he thought a "strain" of very heavy drinking among the Malleys might be alcoholism.

" 'There's no alcoholism in our family; people drink a lot,' " his uncle told him. "It was as if we were unsullied by this," Malley recalled. "And I said, 'What about Pete—he was the town drunk!' One of my earliest memories is of Uncle Pete coming up the street with a bucket of suds. And he said, 'Well, Pete was very sensitive, and people treated him badly.' " Drinking is " 'a good man's weakness,' " said Malley, reiterating one of the most frequently uttered Irish aphorisms—a mantra of denial.

"In the old country, people drank because of lonesomeness or poverty, or the two mixed together, and the Irish grow up thinking that's what you do at reunions and family get-togethers and gathering places. You drink when you're lonely or moody, which means you drink a lot of the time," Malley, a recovering alcoholic, continued. "We do think dark, the Irish. My wife always tells me, 'Don't worry—nothing's gonna be all right.' "

For a long time, repeated drunkenness "wasn't considered a danger, or improper, or embarrassing. The priests et al. might get someone to join a group" if his or her alcohol consumption seemed out of control, "but it's hard to tell someone not to drink when everyone else does. Everyone can give you examples of an Uncle Harold or Uncle Pete, but there's bafflement as to what it's all about. And a way of excusing it is to say 'I'm Irish.' It's easier that way."

Some of the refusal to confront alcohol problems is generational—"there's more awareness of it now," said Malley. But not enough, in the opinion of Jonathan Mooney, who is young enough to be Malley's grandson and who also grew up thinking that getting drunk was as much a part of being Irish as his own freckles and red hair. "There's this idea drinking is natural, it's inevitable and out of one's control. It's a way of dealing with intangible emotion. And you joke about it. It's funny that there's no such thing as one beer—there are twelve beers. Using a little humor to express pathological behavior makes it bearable, I guess."

Suffering and swallowed words

"She's had a hard row to hoe," Kate said [of a family friend], directing her sister toward it. "Her girl with the drugs and Jim with Alzheimer's. And those babies she lost."

"And Tim Schmidt," Rosemary said, "in the war."

"She's a marvel," Maeve said, and Kate touched her shoulder and told her, "You too, my girl."

Maeve laughed a little. "A marvel of what?" she said. Her shoulders seemed boneless.

"Of endurance," Kate said.

"Of patience," Rosemary added. "And loyalty."

Maeve smiled, dipping her head. It was clear that it pleased her, to have this much recognized and acknowledged. Her endurance, her patience, her long suffering.

It is the night of the day of Billy Lynch's funeral in this passage from Alice McDermott's novel *Charming Billy*. The life of an endearing drunk, the kind of guy who was loved by everyone who knew him, has come to a premature, if predictable, end. His sisters, Kate and Rosemary, and his widow, Maeve, are engaged in a middle-class American version of keening—the wailing, weeping lamentation for the dead that their great-grandmothers and their mothers took part in as they sat by the bodies in farmhouses in Ireland. They are reciting a secular litany of "holding up."

There is a rhythm and internal rhetoric to this incantation: First, the premise that life is hard is established (the daughter with the drugs; the husband with Alzheimer's). Next, it is bolstered with examples of loss that make living all the harder (lost babies; Tim Schmidt in the war). Finally, it is agreed that one woman's tragedy has been gracefully, stoically endured—though not quite so impressively as Maeve's.

Young widowhood doesn't garner someone like Maeve Lynch automatic empathy—an Irish woman, she's expected to carry on in the face of life's difficulties. Her years of long-suffering, however, win her accolades. Maeve is a "marvel" because she has spent so many years dutifully propping up her alcoholic husband while he drank himself to death. She did the same for her own father, who, unlike Billy, was *not* a great guy when he didn't have the drink in him.

There is deep admiration for stoicism, coping with compounded psychological pain and tragedy, in this subculture. It is for living through so much of it without breaking or losing her faith that Rose Kennedy was much admired among her own. "God gives us no more than we can bear," the matriarch told Bobby Kennedy's fatherless children, whose lives have proven both the truth and the folly of their grandmother's brave claim.

"It's a great life if you don't weaken," substance abuse counselor Bill Regan's mother used to tell him. "This is a culture," he said, "where people think the light at the end of the tunnel is a train. Life is a painful experience, and catastrophe is to be expected. If I'm Irish and I lose my arm, someone is going to tell me 'It's a good thing you didn't lose them both.'"

"Alcohol is the strongest thing you can get without a prescription in [a larger] culture that says 'If you're feeling something, for God's sake take something,'" he continued. In Irish culture, "which is hubbed around pain, alcohol is a great way of self-medicating. It gives you relief, and it allows you to express yourself—it allows you to dance." The Irish "are great at storytelling and great at being tough. A lot of people have been taught, basically, to keep their feelings to themselves."

In the 1960s, a Brandeis University sociologist studied carefully controlled groups of Irish and Italian patients who were being treated for eye, ear, nose, and throat ailments at the Massachusetts General Hospital and the Massachusetts Eye and Ear Infirmary. He found that while their physical symptoms were much the same, their responses were markedly different. "Not only did the Irish more often than the Italians deny that pain was a feature of the illness but . . . when the Irish were asked directly about the presence of pain, some hedged their replies with qualifications. ('It was more a throbbing than a pain . . . not really pain, it feels more like sand in my eye.')

"The Italians presented significantly more symptoms, had symptoms in significantly more bodily locations, and noted significantly more types of bodily dysfunction." Dramatization, the researcher concluded, was an Italian defense mechanism for coping with problems. Its Irish counterpart was denial. Disapprovingly, he noted that the Irish patients made their diagnosis and treatment more difficult. He suspected that their behavior assured "some degree of continual suffering and thus further proof that life is painful and hard."

At John Kennedy Jr.'s funeral, his uncle Ted, delivering yet another eulogy for a family member taken long before his time, rallied his Irish humor, recalling jokes John had made about the presidency at Ted's expense; he quoted from Yeats. The family prayed together and would go on to play together. Humor and poetry have helped them get on with life. But stoicism has also tightened tragedy's grip on the lives of Irish America's first family and all too many others who have sought release in "alcoholism, addiction, risk-taking, and self-destruction," as Joan Walsh, reflecting on "the Irish way of grief," writes in *Salon* magazine.

"I have always heard a strange double meaning in the phrase 'bottled up,' as though it was inextricably, etymologically linked to alcoholism. It's the bottling up of feeling that leads to the unbottling of alcohol, and to the morbid excesses of families like the Kennedys, and so many of the Irish," she ruminates.

When Walsh lost her mother as a child, she was taught the importance of bearing up—and that drinking brought relief. Her father had difficulty talking about her mother; her uncles would "keep a friendly distance at family events when sober; collapse in tears, unable to talk about my mother, when drunk. (My aunts were a little better, though all of them were undone by crying, so I learned not to.)"

Years later, the woman who had been that brave little girl read *Angela's Ashes* "reluctantly, in pieces, because I couldn't stand it, it felt so close and real: the loss, the sorrow, the anger, and the drunken, broken men. Clearly, there are millions of Irish Americans who escape these patterns." But all too many have succumbed to the Irish way of grief.

The Irish, to paraphrase James Joyce, wrote in a language that was not their own, stamped it with their genius, and produced what would be called English literature. A people with enormous regard for the word, they express themselves splendidly in literature, drama, oratory, and a lot of everyday blather. Yet a remarkable number never acquire an active vocabulary of human emotion. Among the most voluble families and the closest of friends, there may be a great deal said, much of it about little that matters.

Brian Friel's play *Philadelphia, Here I Come!* provides one of the more poignant contemporary portrayals of an Irish emotional silence that Van Morrison has called "inarticulate speech of heart." The play takes place in Ballybeg, the fictional County Donegal setting of many of Friel's dramas, on the eve and morning of Gareth O'Donnell's reluctant departure for America. There are two Gareths—"Public Gar" and his alter ego "Private Gar." Public bids hale, hollow farewells to an unrequited love, a pathetic teacher, and his lug-headed friends. He keeps up appearances with a teasing, affectionate banter with Madge, the woman who raised him, and a guise of gruff indifference that has long been his unhappy way with his elderly, widowed father. Private speaks of the resonant loneliness in his casual good-byes.

On what may well be the last evening they spend together, Public and his father laconically go over the inventory in the family store, say the rosary, talk about the next day's weather, each groping for a few words of affectionate recollection he cannot bring himself to say.

Irish families go to great lengths to avoid emotional scenes, said New York psychologist Joan O'Donnell. Leave-takings like the one in *Philadelphia, Here I Come!*, which marked the beginnings of what might be lifelong separations, were a constant of Irish family life from the time of the Famine until emigration leveled off in the 1990s. The breaks were made all the grimmer by the fact that Mother Ireland simply couldn't sustain its young. Early generations of immigrants were sent off at "American wakes," where they were celebrated and mourned as if they had died.

That custom waned, then disappeared. But what is at times a mawing muteness took its place.

Such reticence is partly an adaptive response to the trauma of repeated family ruptures. "I have a friend who's a private-duty nurse from Ireland, and during the '80s, she was in demand all around the world," said O'Donnell by way of example. She and her mother were close. Yet "every time she left, her mother would go over to a neighbor's house just before it was time for her to go. There was no good-bye; she just couldn't cope" with the sadness of her daughter's departure. At a certain level, she denied it was taking place.

Some of that denial is understandable. "But at some level, you're also left wondering: 'Well, does she really care?' Yes, it's awful to go through one of these tearful separations, but at least when you do, you know there's a connection. Those feelings are there, whether you acknowledge them or not—and they're better off expressed," O'Donnell contended.

Couch and Confessional

"This is one race of people for whom psychoanalysis is of no use whatsoever," Sigmund Freud is said to have observed about the Irish. Though it may well be apocryphal, the remark is repeated often: For one thing, it seems plausible; for another, the Irish have traditionally evinced little interest in psychotherapy.

"You don't get people coming in and saying, 'I want to explore myself' or 'I want to understand my unconscious,'" confirmed O'Donnell. "What has usually gotten them to come in [if they come at all] is that something has become so traumatic that they have to deal with it." Once in therapy, many "have a remarkable inability to express feelings—an inability to say what's going on."

The attitude toward "talking cures" is surely influenced by the Catholic ritual of going to confession. Until the sacrament of Penance was updated and renamed the sacrament of Reconciliation in the early 1970s, Catholics in the darkness of the confessional revealed not the intellect, strength, and splendor of their spirits, but the *sins* of their souls. To reveal oneself in confession is to seek judgment and ask forgiveness, to acknowledge guilt or weakness.

Self-revelation outside the confessional, then, is a tacit admission of unworthiness and vulnerability. It puts one at peril, particularly in Irish families who stifle emotions and prefer to leave painful problems undiscussed. Self-disclosure is all the riskier when drink introduces candor to the conversation. Alcohol eases—but ultimately corrodes—emotional expression.

"Let's not kid each other, Papa. Not tonight. We know what we're trying to forget," Edmund Tyrone says to his father, James, in *Long Day's Journey into Night.* In the final act of O'Neill's autobiographical drama, Edmund and James, then Edmund and his brother, Jamie, and finally the three of them drink, declaim, and tear one another apart. Drunk to begin with, they consume quantities of whiskey that would render many men speechless. Boozing turns the Tyrone men poetic—at first.

"Here's how," Edmund says more than once, raising his glass. But no amount of lavish language or liquor can allow them to forget that Mary Tyrone has regressed again to morphine addiction; that Edmund is gravely ill; that Jamie's alcoholism has turned him into an abject failure; and that James feels utterly defeated at the end of the day.

When James Tyrone can bring himself to talk about it, he refers disgustedly to Mary's drug of choice as "the damned poison." Whiskey, though, is the palliative that turns truly toxic in this play, seething beneath the surface of the Tyrones' recitations of Shakespeare and Baudelaire, agitating their arguments over relatively benign matters of dispute, such as James's insistence that Shakespeare was an Irish Catholic ("The proof is in his plays"). Booze releases venomous emotion and eases its flow, bloating every confession, bitter accusation, and recrimination made.

The Tyrones refuse to confront the demons of the past and will continue to live with them. The tragedy of this play, which has been called the quintessential Irish American text, is made bleaker by the fact that no one can trust anything that has been said: Drink undercuts, it contradicts, it excuses. For all the wounds inflicted and merciless reopening of scars during this long night of angry accusation and bitter revelations, little understanding is achieved; no reconciliations are reached. Jamie claims that one of his confessions to Edmund is "not drunken bull, but 'in vino veritas' stuff." Yet moments before, he'd apologized for a particularly insulting crack he made about their mother, saying it was the "booze talking."

Irish men may drink so they can talk to one another, but they don't expect to be held accountable for anything "the booze" has had to say.

Speaking no praise

Recall that it was the Irish who invented the boycott.

"Himself," the formidable Irish father figure and stereotype, is almost by definition remote and taciturn. The mother is his buffer; the one who expresses parental love and affection, the emotional nexus of the family. "Just because he doesn't say much doesn't mean he hasn't feelings like the rest of us," the surrogate mother, Madge, tells Gar O'Donnell in *Philadelphia, Here I Come!* "Say much? He's said nothing!" Gar responds. "He said nothing either when your mother died," Madge assures him.

Ostracization and silence are acceptable ways of showing disapproval in many Irish families, a social unit oft noted for both its extraordinary loyalty and willingness to cut off relationships abruptly and completely. "If someone does something wrong in an Irish family, the rest of the family just stops talking to them," said Regan. "They may put up with it. But they don't talk to you. If they did, they would have to tell you" what was bothering them, which would mean letting down their defenses. Alcoholics in particular often "become totally isolated from their families."

It is not unusual for Irish family members to live within miles but never see or communicate with one another, until a relative dies. The close, indifferent, and estranged are expected at wakes and funerals— the Irish will show up to bury someone they haven't spoken to in years. Reconciliations do occur among the living at these gatherings—if for no other reason than that there is truth to the wry observation that Irish grudges go on for so long that people forget what they were about to begin with.

In contrast to emotional silence, which is defensive, refusing to speak to someone else is hostile and punitive. Irish Catholics are raised in a tradition that teaches absolute truths and a moral cycle of sin, guilt, and redemption, and punitive silence is judgmental and self-righteous. It brooks no questions or compromises; the offended expects nothing less of the offender than repentance.

Punitive silence is a hallmark of the "sainted Irish mother" (see Chapter 4), who may "offer up" anything that upsets her—a drinking problem, a divorce, a gay child—in a muted martyrdom of silent, sometimes seething, suffering. Deflecting difficult subjects is a way of pretending they do not exist.

While Irish women have always been less likely to drink than Irish men, biology and culture put Irish of both sexes at higher-than-normal risk for developing drinking problems, and Irish women "do drink more than women from other ethnic groups." Middle-class American women in general tend to tipple in secret, and female alcoholics may get sick more quickly and more often than their male counterparts, but denial—their own and clinicians'—increases the likelihood that they will be treated for "secondary depression or anxiety rather than primary alcoholism," according to Harvard professor Vaillant.

The respectable Irish mother who does stealth drinking in her domicile is unlikely to be confronted. Mom has excuses: She is the bearer of the family's problems; she may well suffer anxiety and depression. She needs the sherry or martini or white wine to calm her anxieties or get a little lift from her depression. And why would anyone want to raise an emotional ruckus?

Today, working and professional women have more occasions to drink publicly, socially, and in more copious quantities than their mothers did. Anecdotal evidence suggests that, for all its welcome social advances, feminism may have engendered a new type of problem drinker: the high-functioning female alcoholic.

Irish women are particularly well suited to that role. They are raised to be independent, self-sufficient, to forge forward in the face of obstacles—and those can include being drunk or hung over. Corrigan recalled that while she was drinking very heavily, she went to graduate school, held down a job, and raised children. "The kids did great at school, they were well dressed and taking violin lessons, I was on the PTA. There was insane stuff going on inside, and when you drink like that, you're there but you're not there. But I was looking pretty good." At least for a time.

Heavy drinking among women is taboo in most societies, and an Irish woman who drinks violates her church's teaching that alcohol abuse is sinful and the expectations of her family and self that she be competent, reliable. The pain and sense of failure are profound. According to Regan, "any time a woman starts drinking there's a lot of shame involved," and that is "reinforced by priests, who tend to be very judgmental in a culture where there's lots of harsh judgment anyway." A female veteran of Alcoholics Anonymous agrees: "When they come in to AA, most women's self-esteem is at about zero. With Irish women, it's in the negative. There's so much more tolerance for men drinking—hey, he's earned a few beers, ya know? For women, it's all shame."

Stiletto smirks, emotional clubs

Psychotherapists attribute the "need to keep people at bay" to a fear of love and loss that makes one vulnerable—to pain, dependence, disappointment. The collective Irish experience has left many individuals with "a deep fear of negative judgment and a constant need for approval by others," according to Garrett O'Connor.

And there is plenty of negative judgment to go around.

Awkward though many may be at expressing love and tenderness, the Irish are altogether too adroit at wielding words as weapons. Ridicule is as much a part of Irish discourse as humor, and it is used to convey a remarkable range of emotions, from affection to disapproval to disgust.

When Edward Burns's first film, *The Brothers McMullen,* was released in 1995, moviegoers uninitiated to the Irish ways of filial affection were puzzled as to why these brothers, who appeared to be close, spend so much time and energy insulting one another.

"Being sarcastic is a way of showing you *like* someone," said Regan. As Andrew Greeley explains: "Ridicule is the matrix for many presumably intimate relationships in Irish-American families. Husband and wife, parents and children, brothers and sisters, use it constantly" to keep a distance from one another.

In *The Brothers McMullen,* Barry McMullen's caustic tone of voice when he talks about his late father—"our favorite wife-beating, child-abusing alcoholic"—is barely distinguishable from the sarcasm with which he advises his younger brother, Patrick, about love interests. "How the hell did a fruitcake like you end up as my brother?"; "I could give two shits about you and your true love"; "Don't flatter yourself, Patrick, all right? Nobody is killing themselves over you." But the McMullen brothers are touchy-feely compared with the Fitzpatricks in Burns's second movie, *She's the One,* in which Dad Fitzpatrick, played by John Mahoney, speaks to his sons with all the tenderness a prison guard might use talking to inmates.

Burns's points of reference were Hollywood ethnic movies, American coming-of-age tales, and his own experience growing up in Queens, New York. Yet some of his dialogue bears an at times astonishing resemblance to exchanges in Synge, specifically those that invoke the absolute that we're all a sorry lot, but the ridiculer is better off than the ridiculed for knowing and saying so. ("It's a wonder, Shaneen, the Holy Father'd be taking notice of the likes of you," Pegeen Mike says to Shawn Keogh in *The Playboy of the Western World.* "For if I was him I wouldn't bother with this place where you'll meet none but Red Linahan, has a squint in his eye, and Patcheen is lame in his heel, or the mad Mulrannies were driven from California and they lost in their wits.")

Evidently, not all that much emotional distance has been traversed between either end of the twentieth century in County Mayo and County Queens.

Greeley compares Irish ridicule to African American mockery—the high-spirited and, by some lights, outrageous gibing that goes on in all-black company. Unlike its Irish counterpart, black ridicule is essentially good-humored—a competition in verbal virtuosity, with symbolic honors going to the wisest crack, the first taunt to go over the top.

At a chic Martha's Vineyard restaurant and nightspot in the late 1990s, for example, a group of black women dressed for dinner and dancing were waiting in a cocktail lounge for their husbands when Jesse Jackson appeared on the evening news on a TV set over the bar. Jackson was shaking hands, grinning with delight as he was cheered and applauded and, for whatever reason, looking extraordinarily pleased with himself. When it caught their attention, the women erupted. Lines flew, fast and funny—"That Jesse. Thinks he's somethin'—ooo-eee!"; "Just because you run for president doesn't mean you *won* for president!" There was laughter all around.

At first glance, the women's ragging on Jackson because he thinks he's somethin' seems like Irish mockery—"Just who does he think he is?" But African American teasing is more like Irish *craic* (which translates, roughly, into having a riotously good time) than Irish ridicule. The put-downs are more playful; more intent on riling up than dragging down. A group of Irish Americans in another bar making fun of Ted Kennedy wouldn't be content to take a few stabs at his self-importance or failed presidential ambitions. That would merely deflate the man. Irish ridicule demands an all-out assault on dignity—in this instance, deriding Kennedy's politics, his past, his future, his manhood, his weight, his family. Targets of Irish ridicule are to be "brought down to size," which means they must be reduced to something less than their ridiculer—a pathetic stature.

Irish ridicule—which the native Irish, who have turned it into an art form, call "slagging"—is deliberately hurtful. It is also meant to tame ambition and render the grand mundane. Not that the bar for either is all that lofty. Setting one's sights high is seen as a sign of elitism or egoism—an open invitation to derision, as Pete Hamill learned when he was hanging out with friends in the neighborhood in Brooklyn.

Getting drunk was proof that while he might have his eye on a bigger prize than some, he was still "one of the guys," Hamill writes in his memoir, *A Drinking Life.* It was "a way of saying I would never act uppity, never forget where I came from. No drunk, after all, could look down on others. Being drunk was the great leveler."

Drinking makes Irish ridicule easier, louder, nastier. In his one-man show *Colin Quinn: An Irish Wake,* set in a rapidly changing Brooklyn neighborhood in the mid-1970s, the comedian enacts the roles of several friends and family of Jackie Ryan who are gathered for his untimely wake and funeral.

Unlike some middle-class scribes who evoke the hoary days of the neighborhood parish, pub, and precinct with nostalgia, Quinn recalls "a group of people who had spent their whole lives doing what they were told, kept their mouths shut, beaten by the nuns and told that sex was bad. Then twenty years later, when our marriages were filled with silence, violence, and bad sex, we blamed each other." It was a circumscribed world in which, as one character puts it, "We didn't go after what we wanted. We went after what was left."

The characters in *An Irish Wake* are shrunken souls, though none so withered—or withering—as the heavy drinkers among them. "There was the sober Jackie, who played stickball with the neighborhood kids, and there was the Jackie three beers later who chased an Econoline van with a broken-off car antenna, because he thought he saw a peace sign in the window," one character ruminates of the deceased.

Among those who come to pay their respects to Jackie at his wake is Aidan, a vicious, erudite, inveterate boozer, who hisses "Whore!" at a little boy who brings him the wrong drink. "The little pimple-faced Judas has sold me out for thirty pieces of silver," he says scornfully, in a fit of whiskey-imbued verbal acuity that is all too common among Irish alcoholics.

God, but he was funny . . .

As the fact they've acquired a nickname in Alcoholics Anonymous groups suggests, Catholic Irish Alcoholics are a prominent presence in AA.

Irish abstinence mirrors Irish drinking in many ways. "It is consistent with Irish culture to see the use of alcohol in terms of black or white, good or evil, drunkenness or complete abstinence," according to Vaillant, "while in Italian culture it is the distinction between moderate drinking and drunkenness that is most important." Among alcohol abusers in Vaillant's study, the Irish were more likely than Italians to confront the problem by giving up drinking altogether.

The main influences that put Irish at high risk for developing alcoholism—that it runs in so many of their families and that heavy drinking is tolerated if not outright condoned in Irish social settings—also make it harder to give up. It may be that in Irish American milieus where drinking is ever-present, moderation is more difficult than sobriety for some. It's one thing to limit the number of glasses of wine one drinks with a five-course Italian family dinner where the focus is on food; it's another to stay sober at a bar or a cocktail party where everyone else is getting happy and someone is almost sure to demand: "You're not drinking? What kind of Irishman are you?"

Perhaps not surprisingly given the paradoxical tendencies in Irish culture, the social response to the shibboleth of drink has tended to extremes. On the one hand, in Ireland there is the Pioneer Total Abstinence Movement, founded in the nineteenth century and still influential, which encourages young people in particular to "take the pledge" never to imbibe. On the other, in a very small country, where few are without a family member or friend who has "died of the drink" or been "in hospital" because of it, "the drinker, even the drunk, is treated more with amused forbearance than social disapprobation," as one group of researchers noted.

Regan, for one, is convinced that AA works for a lot of Irish Americans—so long as they can convince themselves to ask for help. "There are no last names, and you don't talk about it" outside meetings, he explained. "There's a lot of storytelling, a lot of black humor. There's an emphasis on personal responsibility." Lapsing into an imitation of a brogue, he added, "And we are a people who've long been drawn to underground movements."

To a remarkable extent, drunks are considered harmless buffoons and out of control drinking a trait to be laughed at if not outright admired in Irish America.

In the late 1990s, the Irish actor Shay Duffin toured the country in a one-man show about the life and times of the Irish writer Brendan Behan, *Confessions of an Irish Rebel.* During a Boston run of the show billed as "Last Call," Duffin/Behan opened the performance by approaching an onstage bar, genuflecting, and making a sign of the cross. Irish abject reverence for alcohol is usually sure to get laughs, and in this case it did.

Behan, as the show made clear, drank himself to death. Evidently, there was a time when he was a great raconteur with a store of tales of a life of outrage and rebellion, a wit who could hold his liquor and his own in any setting. A friend of Behan's wrote that "when he took a few drinks to break the ice, he was the most wonderful company in the world. When he took one over the eight he became violent and unpleasant." Inevitably, alcoholics come to a point where eight is never enough.

Behan's addiction to the stuff that destroyed him is supposed to be amusing, though surrender to the bottle is anything but; nor is it typically portrayed comically unless the alcoholic is Irish. Think of Ray Milland in *The Lost Weekend* or Nicolas Cage in *Leaving Las Vegas.* Fans of the Behan show might argue that the fact he was a man of words distinguishes him from others who die drunk. If so, where are the stage portrayals of Dylan Thomas's last call? Or William Faulkner's?

Anyone who has known an alcoholic—and, truth be told, most Irish

Americans probably have—is all too aware that the creature is hardly a harmless, cuddly presence. It has turned many men and women monstrous, chewed up and swallowed all too many lives. Episodes in some of the best of contemporary Irish American performance, memoir, film, and fiction make that clear: Pete Hamill repeatedly trying and failing to talk to his alcoholic father; little Frankie McCourt watching his Da rest a pint on his son's small coffin in a pub in *Angela's Ashes;* the abusive off-screen father in *The Brothers McMullen;* the eponymous drunk in Alice McDermott's *Charming Billy,* so bloated and discolored from the drink that his best friend doesn't recognize him when he goes to claim his body.

Redolent with the real gifts of the Irish inheritance—humor, talk, irony—each of those works underscores a truth about Irish American culture that should go without saying but warrants repeating: The Irish voice in America, surly and sloppy when drunk, is most exquisitely expressed when the words aren't slurred.

CHAPTER SIX

The Urge to Serve

I got my roots off in the Catholic Church as an altar boy.

That's why I think there are so many good Irish actors—because from the time you are five years old, you're in costume, and you're learning lines, and you're onstage in front of a paying audience, and you're performing a ceremony, and you're taking it very seriously.

There's a backstage, the sacristy, where the priest and the altar boys get into costume, and there's this ritual transformation. The altar boys come in wild and rowdy from the farm or the streets or from wherever. And suddenly you put on that red and black cassock and slick your hair back and wash your hands and there's a kind of ritual cleansing of yourself and that rowdy tongue. And you ring bells and you recite and you sing and there's incense.

But it's not you, it's a role you're performing. Now you're a servant of God and you're about to serve this priest and go into this mystical transformation; a transubstantiation of wine into blood and bread into flesh. To be in military uniforms, onstage speaking poetry in front of audiences, is not that different. And the important thing is that it's like a religious calling. There's a spiritual responsibility. So it's not a superfluous occupation. . . .

What I got from being around priests and nuns was this concept of a calling: You have God-given gifts. What do you do with those gifts? And then: How do you serve humanity? That there is a higher purpose. Life shouldn't just be something selfish.

—Actor and director John Shea

Surely not all would make the connection between sacristy and stage that John Shea does. But his sense that life's bounties are meant to be shared is as elemental to the Irish American identity as loyalty, wit, or the gift of gab. If drink casts a shadow on this subculture, generosity gives it its radiance and warmth.

Most Catholics are taught that all souls are equal in the eyes of God and that of the gifts of faith, hope, and charity, the greatest is the third. A sense of duty to the less fortunate imbues secular Ireland and Irish America as well. The native Irish contribute heavily to organizations such as Concern and Oxfam; in 1985, when the country's economy was in the doldrums, they led the world in per capita giving to Live Aid, donating £8 million. Since the Irish Aid program was established in 1974, "virtually every Irish family has had involvement with Ireland's overall aid effort, either by way of having a family member working in the developing world or by contributing to the work of one of the many Irish humanitarian organizations," according to an Irish government white paper on foreign policy.

The social and humanitarian missionary work in the underdeveloped world begun by Irish nuns and priests continues among Irish religious, laypeople, and secular organizations today. When international relief efforts are launched around the world, "the Irish are always the first ones there and the last to leave," said Dr. Tom Durant, assistant director of Massachusetts General Hospital and a veteran of such undertakings.

"I don't think we should be complacent about it or flatter ourselves, but it is one of the nicer dimensions of the Irish character," said Sean O'Huiginn, Ireland's ambassador to the United States. "There's an egalitarian side to our society which is attractive and it's positive. It can be negative in the form of cutting people down to size. But its positive form is a very strong sense of being as good as the next person and an ability to empathize. I think one of the explanations is the memory of the Famine; that we're a first world country but still third world in memory."

"The Irish in Ireland had to support their church, and they did it out of a pittance," said Sister Mary Oates, CSJ, an economist who has written extensively on the Catholic philanthropic tradition. "In Italy or Germany or France, the state kicked in to support the church. In Ireland, you had the British," who were hardly supporters of the Catholic Church.

"Hands-on" giving became part of American Irish Catholic culture. Until recently, few Irish in the United States had "deep pockets, and if you don't have a lot of money, you have to give something of yourself besides your money," Oates said. From the outset, burgeoning Catholic parishes, schools, and charitable organizations "required voluntary services, not just of sisters, but of the laity. People give in kind."

As for Irish America, a 1996 National Opinion Research Center General Social Survey (GSS) showed that as a group, Irish Catholics in the United States volunteer more time and are more likely to give money—large or small amounts—to charitable organizations than many other Americans. Firmly established among the ranks of the country's well-educated, well-off, and white-collar elite, they continue to be overrepresented in health and human services and teaching, much as they once were in the protective service occupations like police and firefighting.

The most deeply rooted cultural traditions are those that people don't think to discuss. Growing up in an Irish family, "taking care of other people is just part of what we always did," Illinois Appellate Court Judge Anne McGlone Burke observed. "The families have a lot of kids, where the oldest helps the next one. And it's a logical extension to do it at church or at a community center. It seemed natural, to me, to go into the social service area. My kids grew up volunteering, and now all four are in some kind of public service."

"The Irish are givers," said Charles Daly, retired head of the John F. Kennedy Library Foundation and a founder of the American Ireland Fund. "The Irish in Ireland are very generous, even though the tax laws aren't nearly as conducive as they are here, and they're generous here. The Irish started their [rise to the top] in the corporate world without the philanthropic habits of the Jews. But there's been a rapid change from not having much to give, and they're increasingly generous."

Irish American philanthropy at this point is too new a phenomenon to characterize, much less quantify—and that may be so for some time. Giving away significant sums of money seems to be one of those things the Irish just *do* and don't like to talk about.

Multibillionaire Charles Feeney, who made a fortune in Duty Free Shops, managed to donate $610 million to charities without drawing attention to himself until a lawsuit involved in the sale of his business drew him briefly into the public eye in 1997. Feeney's wealth and contributions are extraordinary, but his low-key, self-effacing generosity is not, according to Joe Leary of the Irish American Partnership, a nonprofit charitable organization with eighteen thousand members, whose ledgers show that "there are a lot like him."

Tim McCarthy, an institutional bond salesman who took a leave from Bear-Sterns in 2000 to start CharityAmerica, a virtual volunteering and e-philanthropy organization, concurred. "A lot of Irish give to give, not to take a bow," he said. "In other cultures, it's more important to put your name on the front door." The reason, as he sees it, is that "Irish people have always just kind of helped each other out. My grandfather used to say, 'You just throw a little more water in the soup.' If you can do something, you do it. It's not a big deal."

A communitarian tradition of giving, sharing, and serving is an essence and impulse of Irish American liberalism, which has inspired American politics, policy, and social activism—though many liberals are unaware of, or loath to acknowledge, that contribution.

Liberals tend to equate Irish Catholicism with "Joe McCarthy, William F. Buckley, Francis Cardinal Spellman. There's this idea that the Irish are intolerant, if not racist, that the church is anti-Semitic," said Alan Wolfe, author of *One Nation after All* and the director of the Center for Religion and American Public Life Society at Boston College. "And there's a history there. That's real. But so is a lot else."

When Wolfe left a job at Boston University to go to Boston College, some of his Jewish and African American friends were shocked. The feeling among the latter seemed to come down to the belief that Irish Catholics were "on the wrong side in the busing wars," the infamous conflict over forced public school integration in the 1970s.

The Irish have been on the "wrong side" of some of the most visible fights in the country's ongoing battles over race, from the Draft Riots of the 1860s to the battle over forced public school desegregation in the 1960s and 1970s. But busing in particular was much more than a black-white, liberal-conservative struggle, Wolfe pointed out. And elements and episodes of the conflict point to the ways in which the Irish have served as scapegoats and symbols of the white American establishment's intolerance and racism.

"A lot of New Yorkers who think of themselves as people of unshakable tolerance take a sort of easement when it comes to the Irish," Calvin Trillin wrote in *The New Yorker*. Sneering at the supposed conservatism, bigotry, and backwardness of Irish Catholics is perfectly acceptable in some media and social circles in which prejudice and generalizations based on race, religion, or ethnicity are supposedly anathema. It is said often—though not often enough—that anti-Catholicism is the anti-Semitism of the American intellectual classes, and much of that religious bias is rooted in historic Anglo-American fear and loathing of the Irish Catholics.

Scoundrels, stereotypes, scapegoats

E. L. Doctorow's novel *Ragtime* was made into a 1981 movie and turned into a hit Broadway musical that won four Tony Awards in 1998 and toured North America to nearly unanimous critical acclaim. It is an epic American story of three families—WASP, black, and immigrant Jewish—set at the start of the last century, as peak numbers of immigrants were arriving at Ellis Island, labor strikes were erupting, and the NAACP was formed. It is as elegiac a tribute to American diversity and democracy as a Walt Whitman poem.

Doctorow has described ragtime music as a perfect metaphor for the age: "a paradox of a very formal, controlled music, almost European in its classicism, but with the striding bass and syncopated right hand that was the clear sound of the New World." The Irish provide the notes of discord in the humming multiethnic mix. *Ragtime*'s uplifting theme song is "Wheels of a Dream," a reference to progress in general and the motorcar driven by Coalhouse Walker Jr., the musician turned revolutionary who is ultimately destroyed by a complex of forces, racism being the ugliest and strongest.

What sets those dynamics in motion is a loutish group of dumb Irish firemen who are outraged because Walker, a well-dressed black man, is driving a Model T. They try to destroy his car. In a musical filled with complex, compelling characters, Willie Conklin, head of the firefighters at the Emerald Fire House (he's a drinker who speaks with a brogue, in case audiences don't catch the ethnic reference), is monodimensional: unrepentantly obdurate and ugly. Even the WASP father in *Ragtime*, burdened with a role that represents the rigid mind and mores of the establishment, has moments of valor.

In the touring production of *Ragtime* that showed in Boston in 1999, the actor playing Conklin slouched, simian-like, through some scenes. His knuckles nearly scraped the floor. At one point, as his silhouette appeared on a stage scrim, it bore an incredible resemblance to a Thomas Nast drawing of a simian Irishman (see page 142).

The unintended irony might not be so noticeable if the Irish were not conspicuous by their absence from episodes that are celebrated in *Ragtime* in which, in reality, they played a significant part. The Irish, for example, figure prominently in the American labor movement, yet the movement is represented here by the estimable Emma Goldman, who is just the sort of innovative, energetic American influence the firefighters are not.

Incidents like the one at the firehouse, of course, occurred.

African American–Irish American conflict dates to the time Irish Catholic immigrants started arriving in the United States in the 1830s and 1840s and found work building railroads and canals. A steady source of cheap, easily exploitable labor, they displaced the unskilled at the lowest levels of the socioeconomic ladder, including free blacks. Rootless, leading hand-to-mouth existences in work sites along the nascent byways to the west, they formed work gangs and trade associations, often on the basis of the region of Ireland they came from, and fought one another, other immigrants, and blacks for whatever work there was. Irish immigrants in the mid-to-late nineteenth century formed voluntary firefighting organizations that often did the legwork—and arm-twisting—for political machines.

To many Irish, abolitionism was a nativist and anti-Catholic movement that represented a profound threat to their livelihoods: the freeing of four million enslaved Americans who would compete with them as hod carriers, bricklayers, and stevedores. Even so, when the Civil War broke out in 1861, between 150,000 and 200,000 joined the Union Army—some to help preserve the union, others because they were in need of a meal ticket.

When the federal government, short of soldiers, passed a conscription law in 1863, protest rallies were held around the Northeast. Poor immigrants were furious at the economic unfairness of the measure, which allowed inductees to send men to fight for them or buy their way out of the draft for three hundred dollars (about what a laborer made in one year).

Ten days after the Battle of Gettysburg, in which Irish soldiers fought and died on both sides, an anticonscription rally in New York City turned into the Civil War Draft Riots, the largest and bloodiest insurrection that has ever taken place in the United States. Blacks had been used as strikebreakers in New York and were exempt from the draft, and Irish laborers turned on African Americans. Burning, looting, and destruction went on for four days. Rioters attacked draft boards, the office of the *New York Tribune,* and the Negro Orphan Asylum, according to Charles R. Morris. Residents of the orphanage fortunately had been moved to a safe haven by the time rioters screaming "Burn the niggers' nests!" set fire to the building at Fifth Avenue and Forty-third Street.

The riots, Morris writes, confirmed the prevailing opinion of American Protestants that the Irish were racist. Citizen leader George Templeton Strong, for example, excoriated "Celtic brutes" for the riots, failing to note that "the police and firemen and a good number of the militia who quelled the disturbance were also Irish Catholics." Morris maintains that "the Irish and their Church [whose Holy See had yet to condemn slavery] were racist, even by the standards of the time. . . . But racism of all kinds was endemic in America, and the charge of Catholic racism loses much of its force when it comes from Protestants who delighted in Thomas Nast's cartoons portraying the Irish as a race of gorillas."

Religion as race, religious racism

Religion and class were the "race" of the nineteenth century, and endure today.

Civic worthies took a rather hands-off approach to the Orange Riot of July 12, 1871, which is said to be the bloodiest day in American peacetime history. To celebrate their ancestral victory at the Battle of the Boyne (the event that is commemorated during the inflammatory "marching season" in Northern Ireland today), the Protestant Orange Order of New York planned a march from what is now the border of Chelsea and Hell's Kitchen to the Lower East Side of Manhattan. "Green" Irish Catholics planned to protest the march, and the press reported rumors that 10,000 of them would be armed. Orange leaders said the marchers would be carrying weapons. The mayor of New York sent 800 police and 2,300 militia to protect the 160 Orange marchers who turned up.

Protesters threw bricks and stones, a shot was heard, and the militia fired indiscriminately into the crowd of Irish Catholics, wounding women and children and setting off a deadly fracas in which 76 were killed, more than 150 injured, many of them wounded by guns, and some 90 people were arrested.

The *New York Times* heralded the incident primarily because it showed that Boss Tweed's grip on Tammany Hall was weakening. The "ignorant, unthinking, bigoted hordes which Tammany brought up to its support year after year are hopelessly scattered" and New York City would "no longer be tyrannized over by our esteemed friends from the Emerald Isle," as the *Times* told it.

Forced busing in Boston was a liberal social program. That does not mean it was necessarily "progressive"—or that it achieved the aims of those who initiated it.

An Irish American, Judge Arthur Garrity, ordered mandatory public school desegregation through busing when he found that Boston's elected officials had "willfully and systematically maintained separate but equal school systems for black and white children."

Twenty-five years after the fact, many Bostonians tended to agree with *Boston Globe* columnist Brian Mooney's assessment that Garrity's was "the correct finding but the wrong remedy." Tens of thousands of white residents fled to the suburbs. The Boston public schools, which had a 60–40 white–minority balance in the mid-1970s, are not racially integrated today; 15 percent of the school population is white. Many in South Boston still seethe with anger over the era.

Busing was perceived as an African American–Irish American conflict. But it was as much a class struggle as a racial battle, as J. Anthony Lukas illustrated in his brilliant book *Common Ground*. It was also "an Irish family feud" between those who had made it, like the judge and the politicians, and those who had not—the families whose children were being bused.

The people of South Boston, home to some of the poorest neighborhoods of the city, had been left behind in the middle-class exodus to the suburbs in the 1950s and 1960s, and they deeply resented the college-educated, suburban "social engineers" who forced integration upon them. They reserved a special loathing for the upper-middle-class liberal Irishmen who engineered the busing plan, like Boston Mayor Kevin White and Judge Garrity.

Because class conflict is almost never acknowledged in the United States and because dramatic black-white battles were taking place in Boston, the so-called cradle of liberty and a supposed liberal bastion, images of violent race hatred defined the busing crisis: a black lawyer in a three-piece suit pummeled with an American flag in City Hall Plaza; South Boston mothers clutching rosaries in one hand and giving the finger to a bus filled with black children with the other; political leaders—future Boston Mayor Ray Flynn among them—proudly marching in Southie's St. Patrick's Day parade at the head of the antibusing forces.

Antibusing leaders like Louise Day Hicks maintained that liberals and the media scorned them, and they were right. The *Globe*, wrote Lukas, ridiculed Hicks in particular. "She was once depicted by a cartoonist as a bloody bitch of Buchenwald bestriding the city."

But for astonishing liberal arrogance, "nothing quite matched the lofty condescension of *Newsweek*'s 1967 cover story," Lukas wrote: "'They looked like characters out of Moon Mullins, and she was their homegrown Mamie made good. Sloshing beer at the long tables in the unadorned room of the South Boston Social and Athletic Club sat a comic-strip gallery of tipplers and brawlers and their tinseled over-dressed dolls. . . . The men queued up to give Louise their best, un-screwing cigar butts from their chins to buss her noisily on the cheek.'"

Dissonances among like voices

Racism is presumed to be the overriding reason for urban white ethnics' resistance to integration. But Catholics' attachment to their neighbor-hoods—which were often known by parish names—was deeper and more complex than is often assumed, historian John T. McGreevy observes in *Parish Boundaries: The Catholic Encounter with Race in the Twentieth-Century Urban North*. Until recently, Catholics didn't choose their churches; they went to Mass, baptized their babies, went to confession, buried their dead, and sent their children to school in *their* parish—the Catholic church six blocks away belonged to other people, sometimes a group of different ethnic origin; there were German parishes, Polish parishes, Italian parishes, and so on.

Unlike Protestant and Jewish places of worship, Catholic parishes were "immovable." When Jews and Protestants left urban areas, their syn-agogues and churches moved as well. Catholics invested heavily in their communities. "Working-class immigrants were often more likely than middle-class native Americans to own their homes," McGreevy writes. Attachment to those parishes kept many Catholics in Northern cities as Protestants and Jews moved to the suburbs in large numbers after World War II. Catholics had much more at stake in maintaining the urban status quo than those who had gone elsewhere.

The history of bitter urban conflict between African Americans and Irish Americans is striking in light of the parallels between the two cultures. Both are matriarchies, both church-centered, both transplanted abruptly from agrarian to urban settings.

Peter Quinn has written that the Irish in the nineteenth century and blacks in the twentieth were the "epitome of the urban underclass—tough, violent, jail-prone miscreants who changed the nature of city life, making it more threatening and volatile, a place widely perceived to be as intrinsically hostile to the real American family values of work, thrift and sobriety."

Irish and blacks, he points out, "organized gangs so powerful they not only ruled the street but formed the nucleus of political organizations. They drove the soi-disant respectable classes from the cities. Their lack of entrepreneurial skills and attachments to the public purse provoked a political reaction intent on ending the 'culture of dependency.' "

For black dependency, read "welfare"; for Irish, "Tammany Hall."

Weaving the safety net

"One of the reasons that American society developed its inclusiveness was because of the Irish," Sean O'Huiginn, a student of Irish American history, observed, "because they came at a very crucial time. They had been to school with a genius of modern democratic politics, Daniel O'Connell—three-quarters of the population had been organizing: party dues, newsletters, membership, mass rallies. They got here, and they set up this form of politics that got a lot of deserved criticism for its cronyism and so on. But if you look at it in a broader sense, it was a very important decompression mechanism, whereby immigrant groups could actually come to terms not just with American politics, but with the potentially harsh realities of American life."

Daniel Patrick Moynihan describes the Irish village as "a place of stable, predictable social relations in which almost everyone had a role to play, under the surveillance of a stern oligarchy of elders, and in which, on the whole, a person's position was likely to improve with time. Transferred to Manhattan, these were the essentials of Tammany Hall."

The communal life of villages in the west of Ireland was also replicated among extended families whose members were separated by an ocean—in parishes, in unions, and in communities where the Irish settled.

For generations, the Irish who "came out" to America were expected to send money home to support their families. They routinely paid for the passage of siblings and other relatives and provided for them to the extent that was necessary when they arrived. (Public payrolls were padded with relatives who needed more providing than others.)

The prevailing wisdom among the Anglo-American establishment in the second half of the nineteenth century was that good government governs least, that "the primary task of politics was to make government a tidy, efficient housekeeper," in William Shannon's description. "The business community developed the comfortable and useful mythology that social conflict was unreal, that the interests of employers and workers and of captains of capitalism and consumers were one and the same."

At a time when sweatshops, daybreak-to-sunset work hours, child labor, and horrific living conditions were the norm, the "men of means, education, and civic virtue" who ran good government had little interest in addressing the needs of immigrant hod carriers and domestics, impoverished widows and injured laborers, who needed representative government more than good government.

Having been persecuted by their governors in Ireland and then come up against the disdain and indifference of the ruling Anglo-American class when they arrived as the country's first unwelcome immigrants, the Irish in America hardly questioned the need for an alternative system. They had what it took to set up a shadow government: the advantage of speaking English—and speaking it well; familiarity with representational government; and a phenomenal talent for political organizing.

"Charity became a primary emblem of Catholic identity in American culture and the chief means by which the church established a public voice," write Dorothy M. Brown and Elizabeth McKeown in *The Poor Belong to Us: Catholic Charities and American Welfare.* Catholics in the United States began providing social security and salvation for "their own," in part to protect them from the attentions and intentions of Protestant do-gooders and " 'child-savers,' who labored diligently in the nineteenth century to rescue poor children from what they considered the baneful and antidemocratic control of the Catholic church and from the poverty and degeneracy of their parents."

In 1852, for example, the Protestant New York Association for Improving the Condition of the Poor reported that three-quarters of its assistance went to Catholics. Ten years later, in the wake of the Civil War draft riots, the AICP underscored the Irish Catholic character of New York's "dangerous classes," insisting that 70 percent of inmates of public almshouses and 50 percent of the city's criminals were born in Ireland. "AICP leadership . . . referred to the children of Irish Catholic immigrants as 'accumulated refuse.'"

Catholic charitable institutions offered an alternative to Protestant solutions to the "refuse" problem and showed a sense of civic responsibility that undercut nativist anti-Catholic claims that they were dangerous, impoverished, and hell-bent on remaining that way.

The success and staying power of Catholic networks won providers a voice in local, state, and national policymaking and "access to the public purse." Catholic social reformers influenced public policy at every level.

In the late nineteenth and early twentieth centuries, the Irish-led American Catholic Church built a virtual parallel society of parishes, parochial schools, hospitals, social service networks, and private charitable organizations. By 1920, Catholic Charities in New York was a $1-million-a-year operation. In the 1990s, Catholic Charities USA was the umbrella organization for the largest private social service network in the country.

One of the largely unheralded legacies of Irish Catholicism in this country is its continual dedication and service to the downtrodden, regardless of their religious beliefs. (See Chapter 7.) In Manhattan at St. Charles Borromeo in Harlem and Transfiguration in Chinatown; in Boston at St. Augustine in Southie and St. Brendan in Dorchester; in Chicago at Old St. Patrick's and Leo High, the faces of at least half the children wearing plaid uniforms or blue blazers are black and brown; about a third of them belong to children who are non-Catholics. According to the Catholic Schools Foundation/Inner City Scholarship Fund in Boston, parochial schools offer "secure, disciplined and culturally diverse" settings; the dropout rates are negligible, and the vast majority of students (85 to 90 percent) go on to postsecondary education. To struggling families seeking alternatives to public education for their children, the schools—no pun intended—are a godsend.

Though they are less expensive than private institutions, Catholic schools still cost more than many families can afford. The dioceses support the schools, to varying degrees. And wealthy Irish Americans have spearheaded efforts to raise scholarship funds for some of the systems. The sociologist and novelist Andrew Greeley put $1 million of the royalties from his best-selling novels toward a foundation for Chicago parochial schools. Former Los Angeles mayor and business executive Richard Riordan has contributed large amounts himself and led fundraising campaigns for Catholic schools in Los Angeles. Ditto Peter Lynch in Massachusetts, who was elected president of Boston's Catholic Schools Foundation in 1992 and, through a combination of investing and fundraising, increased the yearly amount it awarded in partial scholarships from $1 million to $5.3 million in 1999.

———

"The idea that 'Catholic' is clergy working in the inner city with kids for no wages or that at a place like Boston College the most left-wing department is the theology department hasn't caught up with a lot of people," said Alan Wolfe.

Facts don't fit with the widely accepted wisdom that Irish Catholics are conservatives.

Similarly, Irish American politics are typically characterized with c-words: *crony, corrupt, criminal, conservative;* and they have been each and all these things. But they have also been high-minded, earnest, and liberal. The best way to measure most things in Irish America, including politics and social activism, is to look at the paradoxes in each.

In 1886, heyday of Tammany Hall, for example, a coalition of union members, socialists, and proponents of land reform in Ireland backed reformer and labor champion Henry George, advocate of a single tax, as a candidate for mayor of New York City. George ran *against* the Tammany candidate, Abram Hewitt, who was also supported by the New York archdiocese. Hewitt won, but even ballot fixing couldn't give him a large margin: 90,000 votes, as compared with George's 68,000.

The Rev. Edward McGlynn formed the Anti-Poverty Society to spread George's benevolent word, ignoring the admonitions of New York Archbishop Michael Corrigan, who first took away McGlynn's parish and then had him excommunicated for his political activities.

Irish labor activism has been characterized by contradictory instincts and ideologies: a protective, sometimes pugilistic insularity in some quarters, like San Francisco, where Denis Kearney organized against both Chinese immigrants and railroad owners, and a liberal, sometimes radical egalitarianism in others.

Irish labor leaders in the building trades in New York and men like Terence Powderly, leader of the first national union, the Knights of Labor, prided themselves on forging alliances with workers of other ethnic backgrounds and races. Unlike German and Jewish union leaders, who tended to embrace socialist ideology, the Irish focused on pragmatic, bread-and-butter issues. In the twentieth century, many were opposed to communism and socialism. But then there were ex-Catholic Communists, like Harry Bridges and Elizabeth Gurley Flynn, and at least one prominent Catholic ex-Communist, "Red Mike" Quill, head of the Transit Workers Union, in the labor movement.

The priest played by Karl Malden in *On the Waterfront* ("Christ is in the shape-up. . . . Christ works on a pier") is modeled on the "labor priest," John Corridan, who ran a Jesuit labor school at St. Francis Xavier church hall in Manhattan, a few blocks from the waterfront.

According to Charles Morris, the school was set up partly to fight communism in the union movement. But Corridan spent less time doing that than combating "Joe Ryan, boss of the corrupt International Longshoreman's Association, and a 'Holy Namer,' as he put it, while the waterfront's 'Mr. Big,' Big Bill McCormack, who controlled much of New York's shipping, trucking, and cement industries and who was the power behind Ryan, filled the ear of his friend Cardinal Spellman with stories of the damage Corridan was inflicting on the Church's reputation," Morris recounts.

Spellman, of course, is among the conservative figures who loom large when the Irish come to the American mind. But his Church is also the Church of Dorothy Day and the Berrigan Brothers.

Irish pagan babies, pious apostates, and presidents

As noted in Chapter 2, the late socialist visionary Michael Harrington and the devoutly Catholic, anti-Communist "jungle doctor" Thomas A. Dooley were classmates at St. Louis University High School. Dooley arranged Harrington's first date—a double date to the movies in the Dooley family's chauffeur-driven limousine.

In his autobiography, Harrington describes his and Dooley's adolescent acquaintance as a "preposterous coincidence." Both men exerted singular influence on American government and social policy of the 1960s: Dooley as the instigator of celebrated medical missions to refugees in Indochina and as an adamant anti-Communist propagandist who greased the ideological skids that led to American military involvement in Southeast Asia, Harrington as the author of *The Other America: Poverty in the United States,* the book that "supplied the organizing concept, the target, the word, and thus was the idea for the War on Poverty."

Each in his way was driven by a sense of purpose and an extraordinary skill for articulating the needs of some of the world's downtrodden. By young adulthood, "we had developed profound political differences," Harrington writes. Yet some of what led him as a young man to the Catholic Workers, whose ideal was " 'to see Christ in every man,' including the pathetic, shambling, shivering creature who would wander in off the streets," inspired Dooley as well. "I suspect each of us was motivated, at least in part, by the Jesuit inspiration of our adolescence that insisted so strenuously that a man must live his own philosophy."

Dooley was a closeted homosexual, an opportunist, and a profound egoist who, according to his biographer James T. Fisher, simultaneously used and was used by what came to be known as the "Vietnam lobby." Nonetheless, he did care for and serve the greater good of the destitute of Laos and Vietnam and was an inspiration to lay activists who embraced "his cause as a special opportunity to immerse themselves in service to others."

Catholic schoolchildren prayed for the handsome, charming missionary doctor, who lent cachet and appeal to middle-of-the-road, mid-century American Irish Catholicism at a time when, as Daniel Patrick Moynihan famously observed, "to be an Irish Catholic became prima facie evidence of loyalty. Harvard men were to be checked; Fordham men would do the checking."

Sixth graders who collected money for MEDICO, Dooley's relief organization, adopted a "pagan baby" through a Catholic overseas mission and named him Thomas Anthony. In a thank-you note that captures the tenor of the times, Dooley wrote: "I hope he grows up to be an Irish pagan baby that will be able to say he's living in a world of peace because the Sixth Graders of Our Lady of Victory School put their shoulders to the wheel and helped launch a program called MEDICO." After Dooley's untimely death from cancer in 1961, children prayed *to* him.

A socialist who described himself as a "pious apostate," Harrington was named on Richard Nixon's enemies list, and was surely less conventional an Irishman than Dooley. But his lifelong effort to create a "left wing of the possible," which won him admirers and detractors on all points of the American political spectrum, echoes the difficult-to-pigeonhole pragmatism of other Irish American political activists and thinkers.

Those familiar with the history of the American left know that Harrington, a lead figure in what came to be known as the "Old Left" of the 1950s, first enjoyed an ideological alliance and then a major falling-out with New Left leader Tom Hayden, another Irish Catholic.

American Irish Catholics were deeply divided, as was the rest of society, over civil rights and the war in Vietnam. Spellman and Chicago Mayor Richard Daley represented the "establishment" Irish point of view in 1968, the year Hayden led the protests outside the Democratic National Convention in Chicago. Robert F. Kennedy's brief presidential campaign embraced the civil rights movement, and Eugene McCarthy ran for the presidency as an antiwar candidate. Radical activist priests Daniel and Philip Berrigan symbolized the depth of Americans' moral objections to the American military presence in Vietnam. By the late 1960s, Irish Catholic FBI men were arresting Irish Catholic priests and nuns for antiwar activities.

Tip O'Neill, one of the first congressional leaders to register his opposition to the Vietnam War, reflected in his autobiography on his relationship with Ronald Reagan and how it was that he and Reagan (whose grandfather was Irish Catholic, while the Great Communicator himself was raised Protestant) could be so different.

On the surface, President Reagan and I have a lot in common. We're both of Irish ancestry . . . sports buffs . . . sociable and outgoing. We both came from modest backgrounds and had FDR as our hero as we came of age in the 1930s.

We also both had a parent who was especially benevolent to our less fortunate neighbors and friends: my father was a one-man service institution in North Cambridge, and Reagan's mother used to visit hospital patients and prisoners in Dixon, Illinois. I've often wondered how we came to have such different visions of America.

Maybe it all boils down to the fact that one of us lost track of his roots while the other guy didn't. . . . As a man of wealth, he really didn't understand the past thirty years. God gave him a handsome face and a beautiful voice, but he wasn't that generous to everyone. With Ronald Reagan in the White House, somebody had to look out for those who were not so fortunate.

That's where I came in.

Leaving the best unspoken

Charles Feeney wowed Maureen Dowd of the *New York Times* during a brief foray into the public arena to accept an award from *Irish America* magazine, when he explained that he gave away much of what he made because "you can only wear one pair of shoes at a time." Dowd found Feeney's generosity "startling in an age when people stamp their names on every available surface."

Feeney was articulating a very Irish American point of view. So was John F. Kennedy when he said of politics: "It beats chasing a dollar."

Kennedy's attitude toward the business of America was archetypically Irish, in the opinion of William Shannon. The American Irish had been "outside of the business system" and never entirely reconciled themselves to its values, Shannon writes in *The American Irish*. "At the lower levels, they have been obsessed with the security of civil service jobs . . . more impressed with the failures and vicissitudes of capitalism than by its opportunities and rewards. At the higher levels, this same alienation reappears as an aristocratic disdain for mere moneymaking." The late president's father, Joe Kennedy, was a multimillionaire who aspired to nothing so much as the ambassadorship to Great Britain.

Shannon was writing in the mid-1960s, when a number of Irish Americans who have since reckoned well enough with American capitalism to become multimillionaires were launching their careers. But a lack of enthusiasm for "mere moneymaking" is still palpable in many provinces of Irish America. The glossy magazines *Irish America* and *World of Hiber-*

nia are rife in every issue with profiles of men and women who have made it big and made it a point to give back in a big way.

Few of Joe Kennedy's grandchildren followed his footsteps into the private-sector enterprises in which he made the family's first fortune. In choosing careers and avocations, several seem to have followed Robert Frost's advice to President Kennedy: "Be more Irish than Harvard."

Throughout the heartrending, hand-wringing media coverage of John Kennedy Jr.'s death and burial in the summer of 1999, commentators from all quarters dwelled on the so-called Kennedy curse, lamenting what was generally deemed to be recklessness among Kennedy men, their unfulfilled promise. Routinely overlooked was that many Kennedys, who could easily spend their time at leisure or set up philanthropic foundations that write checks to what they consider worthy causes, are actively involved in politics and social and human services. Even those tagged as "troubled" can lay greater claim to doing good than many other scions of wealth.

Robert Kennedy Jr., it is often noted, is a recovering substance abuser, but he is also an activist environmental lawyer. His older brother Joe served less than spectacularly in Congress (unlike his uncle Ted, who is one of the Senate's most liberal, effective, and underrated legislators) and went through a messy divorce, but he founded and now runs Citizens Energy Corporation, which buys and distributes fuel for the poor and low-income elderly. John Kennedy Jr. established a program to train caregivers for the mentally disabled and supported foundations for the needy. Cousin Timothy Shriver runs Special Olympics; his brother Anthony heads a program for the mentally disabled called Best Buddies. The Kennedy women are an even more impressive lot (see Chapter 4).

Catholic philanthropy in general tends to be community-oriented, and Irish generosity is often socially conscious, even altruistic, according to Frank Butler, executive director of FADICA (Foundations and Donors Interested in Catholic Activities). Those donors to urban parochial schools reap no personal rewards or status from their gifts; nor do their own communities benefit. Frequently, their generosity receives little recognition. They do it because they think it's the right thing to do, he said.

Lawrence J. McCaffrey maintains that Irish American philanthropists have been "stingy" in their support of Irish Studies programs and culture. "Irish Americans with money prefer law, medicine, and business schools," he said. "Unlike Jewish Americans, they have little interest in promoting their own culture." Indications are that may be changing. Donald Keough endowed the Irish Studies department at the University of Notre Dame, and Loretta Brennan Glucksman is a benefactor of Irish Studies at New York University and universities in Eire. The American Ireland Fund concentrates on peace, culture, and charity.

"There's very little flash about [Irish American philanthropy] as compared with other kinds," said Butler. Not much of it is "organized" or distributed by foundations at this point.

But the organized Irish philanthropy that does exist differs from other kinds of American charitable ventures; it tends to be less hierarchical, less formal, less self-important than some. There is little sense of noblesse oblige among the donors and less concern about taking credit for contributions made and deeds done.

Irish foundations, said Butler, "keep their perspective. They have a sense of humor about themselves and what they're doing. No one gets too full of himself or herself without getting cut down to size. They're self-deprecating. Irish foundations are run a lot like Irish families."

———

Jonathan Mooney grew up in suburban Los Angeles and Denver in the 1980s and 1990s. His uncle is a priest and he was baptized a Catholic, but his parents didn't practice their religion and he never went to Catholic school. When he encountered the Jesuits in his freshman year at Loyola Marymount, he was immediately drawn to their "liberalism and social service," he said. "And later I came to realize that *that* was an Irish tradition.

"There's a sense of social justice. My dad's a labor lawyer. My parents are activists. I started a federally funded tutoring program and went and worked for the labor movement—for justice for janitors."

Admonishments like "Don't get a swelled head" resonate in his, but "it didn't come from Catholic schools. In my family, it comes from a sense that there's a disaster around the corner. The road is never clear and you need to stay humble. You have to be on your guard. You can only hold your head up so high when there's so much injustice in the world."

Not that that was ever articulated, he added. "But it was always implied."

CHAPTER SEVEN

The Changing Church

If a religious stock analyst were to rate the American Catholic Church, he might say: "Dynamite product, great market, but you need to shoot some upper and middle managers."

—Charles R. Morris, *American Catholic*

The impression from the outside is that a splendid and sanguine American Catholic Church started hemorrhaging in the 1960s and has yet to stanch its bleeding.

Attendance at Mass has fallen off dramatically among all practicing Catholics, including some nuns who are dissatisfied enough with the pastorate that they conduct their own eucharistic services. Catholics live together before marriage and receive the Eucharist—a mortal sin compounded by a sacrilege, according to Baltimore Catechism standards. Nine out of ten reject the Church's position on artificial birth control; Catholics' attitudes on abortion are indistinguishable from those of Protestants. A majority disagree with Vatican teachings on divorce, clerical celibacy, the ordination of women, homosexuality, and the role of the laity—and 80 percent of those see no conflict between ignoring Church teaching and being good Catholics.

Religious orders are in crisis: There are nowhere near enough priests, nuns, and brothers to staff the Catholic parishes, schools, and social service networks. Thousands of religious left their congregations in the 1960s and early 1970s, according to one count; there are nearly as many

former nuns as there are active nuns in the United States today. In the last two decades of the last century, approximately one-fifth of priests gave up their ministries. "The priest-to-parishioner ratio was 1 to 1,110 in 1970, it was 1 to 2,200 in 1990, and it will be 1 to 3,100 in 2005," according to Charles R. Morris.

Rome dismisses even reasoned discussion of matters of concern to American Catholics, such as women in the priesthood, and the U.S. Conference of Catholic Bishops passes a resolution that, if enforced, would require theologians at Catholic colleges and universities to pass muster with local bishops. In an era of ecumenism, in which Pope John Paul II makes a point of improving the Church's relations with other faiths, the Vatican beatifies and canonizes demonstrably anti-Semitic Catholics and issues a proclamation reasserting the triumphalist claim that Catholicism is the one true religion. Members of the Catholic League for Religious and Civil Rights mouth off about books they haven't read and movies they haven't seen, garnering headlines and airtime that suggest a cranky conservatism is at the core—and is much of what's left—of American Catholicism.

Irish Catholics, once "the most docile and faithful" in the flock, now "tend to be the most critical and rebellious," according to historian Lawrence J. McCaffrey.

Hypocrisy has become institutional Catholicism's calling card.

Divorce is forbidden, but sixty thousand annulments are given in the United States each year—90 percent of people who apply for a "Catholic divorce" receive it.

Priests are expected to be celibate and homosexuality is "against natural law," but a book by the Rev. Donald B. Cozzens, rector of a Catholic seminary, argues that the priesthood is becoming a gay profession. In his best-selling *Papal Sin,* Garry Wills maintains that "the admission of married men and women to the priesthood—which is bound to come anyway—may well come for the wrong reason, not because women and the community deserve this, but because of panic at the perception that the priesthood is becoming predominantly gay."

At the same time, practice of the faith appears to be thriving. "There is no place on earth that Catholicism is more alive than on Catholic university campuses," said Timothy O'Meara, retired provost at the University of Notre Dame. Theology courses at Notre Dame and Boston College are more popular than ever. The majority of BC undergraduates are involved in some sort of Catholic social action, according to the Rev. Joseph Appleyard, vice president for University Mission and Ministry.

The church's long-standing and often unheralded commitment to those who are poor and struggling continues in parochial schools and community centers that were established for Irish in need in the nineteenth century and remain open for children of immigrants and impoverished families today.

Some fifteen to twenty million Americans, many of them suburban baby boomers with families, consider themselves "highly committed" Catholics and are very much engaged in liturgy, parish work like mentoring and family counseling, and social service.

"A lot of Catholics have taken the A train," said Monsignor Frank Kelley, pastor of Sacred Heart Parish in Roslindale, a middle-class section of Boston. "Twenty-five percent of our parishioners have left. But we still have two thousand families in the parish. We have twenty Hispanic families; eight to ten from African countries; four to five from Caribbean nations. Yuppies who grew up in the suburbs and were smart enough to buy in this neighborhood when the prices were low. Single people. They represent an extraordinary mix of what it means to be Catholic today."

A devotion built on desperation

The Irish Catholicism of "flickering candles in dim churches; the quick lash from the yardstick in a nun's billowing sleeve; a grimly dour view of sexuality; the cult of the mother, from the white haired 'Mother Machree' to the celebration of the Blessed Virgin; a world that is separate, strictly ordered, and submissively obedient" is now an anachronism.

Those who recall it wonder how so profound and powerful an institution has become as remote as the misty-isle mysticism of St. Patrick, whence it came.

In fact, Catholicism as it was practiced in Ireland and the United States for most of the twentieth century does not date to the days of Patrick but to the middle of the 1800s. It is the outgrowth of a "devotional revolution" that arose in the wake of cultural upheaval that followed Ireland's Great Famine.

Catholicism in Ireland before the Famine was as pagan as it was Christian—a "witches' brew of half-remembered pagan rites and fractured Catholic ritual—a jumble of hexes, fairies, banshees, saints, and Latin prayers," as Morris describes it. For centuries, it accommodated Celtic customs, some of which survive today. The festival that inspires Brian Friel's *Dancing at Lughnasa,* for example, honors the ancient god

Lugh; even now, Irish people living in rural areas worship at holy wells that were built as shrines to water spirits.

In rural Ireland in 1840, only one in three people went to Mass regularly, partly because there were so few priests: one for every three thousand people, according to the Irish Church historian Emmet Larkin. Irish priests complained that the peasants were a "raunchy lot," given to much drinking, fighting, "sexually charged" dancing at the crossroads, and procreation. A British Catholic cleric lamented to the Vatican in 1843 that Irish priests "not only did not keep to the rubric and practice of Rome in the Mass, but their sermons were of poor quality, and 'the ignorance of the people in matters of Religion is frightful.' "

Yet the Irish peasantry were ripe and ready for a "devotional revolution" even before the Famine, in Larkin's view. A multitude had joined Father Theobald Mathew's Total Abstinence movement, which saw the production of Irish whiskey fall from 12,296,000 gallons in 1839 to 5,546,283 gallons in 1844; and tens of thousands took part in Daniel O'Connell's massive campaign for Catholic emancipation. In addition, the population was exploding as the people's source of subsistence was failing. There were potato blights in 1822, 1831, 1835, and 1837 and a cholera epidemic in 1830. Emigration was mounting. Between 1845 and 1851, at least one million people died of starvation, disease, and neglect, and another one and a half million were forced to emigrate.

Paul Cullen, the architect of Ireland's devotional revolution, "derived very great advantage from the psychological impact the famine had on those who remained in Ireland," many of whom were convinced that "God's wrath was made manifest in a great natural disaster that destroyed and scattered his people," writes Larkin. Educated in Rome, a protégé of Pius IX, Cullen is described by historians as puritanical, premodern, and much given to pomp. He was appointed archbishop of Armagh in 1849 and became Ireland's first cardinal in 1866. Within a generation, he had Romanized and remade the Irish Church, building churches, schools, seminaries, and convents and raising thousands of pounds from the impoverished of Ireland for the Holy See.

Social and economic decimation in Ireland at the time of Cullen's rule worked to the advantage of the devotional revolution. Terrified of overpopulation, farm families discouraged their grown children from marrying by assigning family property, usually land, to a single son and providing a dowry for one daughter. Hundreds of thousands emigrated because there were so few opportunities to earn a living or to marry in Ireland. Those who stayed were often faced with extended or lifelong bachelorhood or spinsterhood; the religious life appealed to many of them.

By 1870, the number of priests in Ireland had risen 25 percent from 1850, while the Catholic population had dropped from five to four million. The ranks of nuns had more than doubled. In 1850, there were 1,500 nuns in Ireland; in 1870, more than 3,700. Weekly Mass attendance had risen to 90 percent by 1890 and remained that high through the 1990s.

Jansenism, which the Church considers a religious heresy because it holds that human beings have no free will, is often cited as the source of Irish puritanism. But historian Lawrence J. McCaffrey maintains that the mid-nineteenth-century mind-set drew its inspiration from conservative reformism encouraged by both Rome and Victorian England, a rule-bound society preoccupied with respectability and sins of the flesh. Celibacy and sexual abstinence were the order of the day. The devotional revolution "fostered a dour religious atmosphere in rural Ireland. . . . Segregating men and women in Catholic chapels and in many aspects of social life, priests frequently broke up crossroads dancing and harassed courting couples."

The devotional revolution, which fostered a wholesale embrace of an elaborate and rigid form of faith, succeeded spectacularly because it served as a substitute for native Irish culture, Larkin argues.

The English had been Anglicizing or "West Britonizing" Ireland for nearly a hundred years before the Famine. Education, business, politics, and communication were conducted in English. British and European history were taught in schools. Irish ways of life that weren't outlawed were discouraged. The devotional revolution gave the Irish a "substitute symbolic language" and offered them a new cultural heritage with which they could identify.

What distinguished the Irish from their British overlords now was a Catholic culture of "austere beliefs and elaborate devotions: the rosary, forty hours, novenas, benediction, . . . catechisms and holy pictures blessed by priests, . . . music, singing, candles, vestments."

"Irish" and "Catholic" became interchangeable terms.

Mission to the new world

Devotional Catholicism became the cultural link between Ireland and the new world. Irish seminaries and convents dispatched thousands of religious to minister to the millions who had made the journey across the Atlantic.

Erin's clergy struggled for control with the Church that existed in the United States, but not for long. By dint of their numbers, the fact they spoke English, and an uncommon skill for political organization and bureaucracy, they made the American Church theirs in no time. In the second half of the nineteenth century, almost nine out of ten men enrolled at major American seminaries had Irish names.

By 1900, three-quarters of the Catholic hierarchy were Irish—immigrants and sons of immigrants, officers in the devotional revolution. The Irish Catholic Church in the United States started as a survivors' Church. As the Irish population became more stable than it had been in the aftermath of the Famine immigration, its mission increasingly was one of "immigrant uplift," the tenets of which were as simple as those Cullen's Church had prescribed for the peasantry of Ireland: "Go to Mass, receive the sacraments, send your children to Catholic schools, do as the nuns and priests say, give money, avoid drunkenness and impurity," as Morris observes.

There were strong disagreements within the Irish American hierarchy over how much the American Church should assimilate—or compromise with—secular society. A trustee movement, whose members felt that laypeople should have more authority, including the right to name priests, was beaten back by opposition articulated by John Hughes, the Ireland-born New York bishop from 1842 to 1864.

Hughes and his successors John Cardinal McCloskey and Archbishop Michael Corrigan rejected a nascent Americanization movement that was led by men with more worldly outlooks such as John Ireland of St. Paul, Minnesota, who wanted to modify Church attitudes to draw converts. Ireland thought that parochial schools wrongly perpetuated the "foreignness" of Catholic schoolchildren and that building the number of schools required to accommodate the Catholic immigrant families streaming into America from Ireland, Germany, and later Italy and eastern Europe would put too big a burden on families.

Corrigan disliked even talk of dissent in the separatist, well-disciplined, Vatican-oriented American Church that was emerging in the 1870s and 1880s. According to the Rev. Thomas Shelley, a historian of the New York archdiocese, a core group of liberal-minded intellectual priests who met at St. Joseph's Church in Greenwich Village "raised questions about evolution versus the Bible's account of creation, priestly celibacy, and the infallibility of the pope. Archbishop Corrigan put a stop to this by scattering the liberal priests to upstate churches."

––––––––

At the Third Plenary Council of Baltimore in 1884—the gathering that gave the Catholic world the Baltimore Catechism—the American bishops decided that every Catholic child should have a Catholic education. The mandate required a massive infrastructure, not just of schools but of convents for nuns who would staff the schools. There was work to be done.

Bishops became businessmen and builders—CEOs in the multimillion-dollar enterprise of bricks-and-mortar Catholicism. Neo-Gothic churches flanked by parochial schools, convents, rectories, and sometimes high schools went up in working-class neighborhoods in Northern cities. In Rochester, Bishop Bernard McQuaid opened 26 parishes, 17 missions, and 30 parochial schools. Corrigan built more than 250 new Catholic institutions—churches, schools, convents, rectories, orphanages—in the archdiocese of New York in the 1890s, at a rate of about one every two weeks. Chicago Bishop Patrick Feehan boasted a record: 140 new parishes went up in the Windy City between 1880 and 1902.

By the mid-twentieth century, the demands of constructing the nation's "church-school complex formed a body of priests who advanced toward their monsignorate, their bishopric, by virtue of business skill," Garry Wills writes in *Bare Ruined Choirs*. "The most successful bishop was the one who had opened more schools than any other—Spellman [of New York] was the champion on the East Coast, McIntyre [of Los Angeles] on the West Coast.

"The priest had little time for theology, or for study of any sort. He adopted the businessman's 'no-nonsense' ways and practicality. He praised simple faith; he delivered a standard five-minute 'feverino' after the standard ten minutes of announcements and financial reporting on Sunday morning. His anti-intellectualism, defensive at first, and self-justifying—became in time self-gratulatory. 'If you want theological niceties,' he would say in effect, 'go to the Jesuits. . . .' The pastor was obnoxious, not for his theology or his transnational ties but for his lack of theology and parochialism. He was a Babbitt in a biretta."

The village center

To an extent that is now difficult to imagine, many Catholics in the first half of the American Century lived in a largely Catholic world. They were born in Catholic hospitals and went to Catholic schools where the nuns taught reading from Catholicized versions of the Dick and Jane reader (in which the children passed statues of the Blessed Virgin on their way to school). They played on Catholic sports teams and had Catholic neighbors. They went to Catholic colleges. They joined Catholic associations and professional organizations and read Catholic newspapers and magazines.

"Looking back, I'm amazed at how protected we were," said retired Chicago insurance executive John Scanlon, who grew up on Chicago's South Side. "We were sheltered, secure, and clannish—for better and for worse. We just weren't exposed to that much. I thought Catholic University was a citadel of learning! On the other hand, you have to give the Irish Catholics credit. We were encouraged to succeed—but to succeed at certain things. We learned a strong ethical code. Businesswise, if you came into contract with a Catholic layman, you knew his word was his bond."

The urban Catholic parish was a singular institution: a re-creation of life in a west-of-Ireland village; a place of refuge and shelter from the hostility immigrants faced in the new world; a center of faith and family and a way of life for children and grandchildren.

"It had all the functions of a castle," recalled Chicago Art Institute conservator Timothy Lennon, who grew up in Visitation Parish on Chicago's South Side during the postwar years. "It was the center of community, spirituality, even theater—because no one went to the theater. There were women's and men's organizations, sodalities, fraternities, acolytes, and the choir. The families were large—we were nine and by no means the largest. The church calendar was our calendar."

Lennon was bemused to return to Visitation for a friend's funeral in the late 1990s and find only glimmers of its onetime splendor. "I talked to the pastor, who was a Dominican, who told me that the neighborhood was now a mission. Here was a place that at one time was arguably the largest predominantly Irish parish in the Midwest, and a generation later, it doesn't exist. How did that happen? How did this place become a mission?"

Founded in 1886 by Irish who moved south from hardscrabble areas like Bridgeport or Canaryville in Back of the Yards, Visitation circa 1950 comprised four thousand families. There were twelve Masses every Sunday; nearly two thousand children attended the elementary school and another thousand went to the parish's girls' high school. Five priests resided in the rectory, and sixty Dominican nuns lived in the convent.

One and all turned out for Visitation's annual Mother's Day May Crowning of the Blessed Virgin Mary. Patriotic, devotional, and provincial, the pageant was a microcosm of the triumphal era of American Irish Catholicism. A throng of three thousand—nuns in habits, priests in clerical garb, students wearing Catholic school uniforms, first communion outfits, and white caps and gowns—made their way up Garfield Boulevard to the imposing statue of Mary that faced the thoroughfare. There they said prayers, sang the national anthem, and saluted the flag.

"Vis" in the heyday of its Maydays was parish, neighborhood, and way of life," said Chicago police officer Eddie Burke Jr., off duty and driving his own car past the church at dusk on a December afternoon in 1998. He was born in Visitation in 1971 and, like some others of his generation, expresses certain nostalgia for a past he never had. "My dad grew up here when everybody knew their neighbors, people used to sit out on their steps and would walk up and down the streets saying hello to each other.

"People who were raised in the neighborhood and left still say 'Visitation' when someone asks 'What parish are you from?'" The Burkes moved out of the neighborhood when Ed Jr. was a toddler, he said, turning down a side street, slowing to point out what had been the family's house. A teenage boy and a woman who looked to be in her twenties, holding out her hand and swaggering, approached the car. "They think we want to buy drugs," he said calmly, shook his head, and shifted gears.

"There are four murders a day in Chicago," he noted grimly, heading out of the old neighborhood. "And two of them are here."

The Irish Catholic life that flourished in the traditional parish "was not always pleasant," noted Lawrence McCaffrey. "It was very defensive, puritanical, often alcoholic. There was a great deal of gender segregation, a lot of late marriage, spinsters, and bachelors. All of it was great material for great American novels, but less so for life."

There has been a counter-backlash in recent years against a culture of complaint that developed among products of parochial school education. Self-absorbed whiners wearing T-shirts that brag about "surviving" or recovering from Catholic schools have prompted people like Peter Quinn to say, "Enough already! First, priests and nuns were all saints. Now they're all perverts."

Most religious men and women charged with the education of Catholic children were decent human beings. For every hysterical nun or sadistic priest a Catholic school kid might encounter, there was often another who was extraordinarily kind and inspirational. Nevertheless, well into the 1970s, many of them were part of an austere, puritanical, and punitive institutional Catholicism that condoned outright child abuse.

Those who have in fact survived traditional Catholic education can laugh at the overemphasis on sin and personal responsibility that was expressed in consummate Catholic epithets such as "You are personally responsible for the suffering and death of Jesus Christ." But a lot of what went on was not at all funny. Shaming children verbally—*Just who do you think you are?*—and physically was routine in all too many parochial school classrooms well into the 1960s. Children were beaten and a small but significant number were sexually abused.

As damaging to human dignity as any harm Catholic children suffered or feared was the apparent complicity of adults in others' brutal behavior. Pastors and principals rarely interfered with "discipline," regardless of how bizarre or extreme. Irish Catholic parents were loath to protest if a child came home bruised or in tears because Sister got mad—that was her prerogative. Some parents punished their child again for getting into trouble.

————

Though postwar suburbia is typically perceived as a place where the lingering flavors of ethnicity are stirred into the great American stew,

Catholic suburbia witnessed what historian James T. Fisher describes as "the final triumph of 'Irishization' in the American Catholic Church." Catholics to a great extent re-created the old neighborhoods in former cow pastures outside cities like New York, Boston, Chicago, and Philadelphia. "The hundreds of new parishes and schools created in the 1950s and 1960s were bound to be led primarily by Irish priests."

The entire country went through a growth period in the 1950s, but Catholic parallel culture had its own boom. Catholics had lagged behind much of the American middle class before the war. By the mid-1960s, they caught up and in some cases surpassed national income and education averages. They went to college in greater numbers than most Americans.

All of the new suburbanites needed churches and schools, and parishes were opening at a remarkable rate of four per week in the early 1950s. In 1964, some 5.6 million children were enrolled in parochial schools.

Those were heady days for the first-generation middle-class suburban Irish, Fisher recalls, "when all the world seemed to revolve around their loud, boozy cookouts; their paneled rec rooms . . . their Notre Dame football on the radio in the 'era of Ara' Parseghian."

Then, of course, "it all went sour. . . . The Catholic moment succumbed to an accretion of blows in the wake of a Vatican Council that had generated too many grandiose expectations. . . . For every guitar-slinging ponchoed priest celebrating at a folk Mass, there was an old timer who lost his vocation. Several of the nuns who taught in my junior high school took flight without even returning our homework."

The laity emerge

While the seismic changes in the Church are typically attributed to the Second Vatican Council, demographics played as significant a role as dogma in reshaping the institution.

"We went into World War II as a poor, lower-class church. There were a few upper-class Catholics, but the clergy were often more educated than the laity," explained Monsignor Kelley. "The GI Bill made the church mainstream." Men got back from the war, they went to college, and "by the sixties and seventies, priests and nuns who'd once had a free hand were now preaching to people who were as educated as they were if not more so."

The changes the Vatican Council enacted were profound: Altars were turned around, and priests shared the celebration of the Mass facing the people of God. Mass was said in English instead of Latin. Guitars replaced organs. Transgressions that Catholics had been taught condemned them to hell—eating meat on Fridays, touching the host—were sins no longer. "Instead of being priest-centered, the church became parishioner-centered," said Kelley. The largely passive laity was suddenly expected to become active, to leave their pews and take part in their faith and liturgy.

Catholic laity, particularly those involved in the Catholic Action movements in the 1950s, had been pressing for relaxation of the dogmatic, autocratic authority of the pre-Vatican Church, seeking an enhanced role for lay Catholics and a revision of the rules on contraception. Many among the clergy supported them. To them, the council wrought welcome developments.

Soon after Vatican II threw open the dark and creaky stained glass windows and let air and light into American Catholicism, Pope Paul VI slammed them shut. Ignoring "the recommendation of his own birth control commission," he declared in a 1968 encyclical, *Humanae Vitae,* that artificial contraception was contrary to natural and Church law.

The laity decided that they had a right to follow their own consciences when it came to contraception, according to sociologist Andrew Greeley, and that the Church no longer had the right to lay down certain rules. Weekly Mass attendance dropped from 65 percent in 1968 to 55 percent in 1973. Belief in papal infallibility declined.

Catholic laity, with the support of the lower clergy, decided it was not wrong to be "Catholic on their own terms."

The interior psyche and atmosphere of the Church had changed. The council had shown that Vatican teachings were mutable, and Catholics felt that unmarried bishops of Rome were wrong—and not just on the matter of natural law.

Before the papal encyclical, "29 percent of Catholics supported the idea of women priests," according to Garry Wills. "A month after the declaration became known in the United States, the approval was at 31 percent; three weeks later, 36 percent; two weeks later, 41 percent. . . . It has been going up ever since. By the 1980s, it was over 66 percent."

The role of women

The volatile issue of admitting women to the priesthood erupted in 1994, when the Vatican declared "definitively" in an apostolic letter that the Church could not and would not ordain women, and in fact did not have the authority to do so. Underscoring the emphatic missive was a declaration—characteristic of the ironhanded ideology and instinct of John Paul II's regime—that the subject of women in the priesthood was no longer open to discussion among the faithful.

In November of the following year, the Vatican retroactively declared the ban on the ordination of women to be an infallible teaching—"a fundamental doctrine of the faith, a Truth guaranteed by divine revelation and the workings of the Holy Spirit."

The Vatican's arguments were absurd. Wills, once again, puts it succinctly, calling it "biblical fundamentalism of the most simple-minded sort. The twelve apostles were men so priests must be men. But [eleven of] the twelve apostles were married, and the church authorities decided they could change that. . . . Are we to say that all priests must be converted Jews? The twelve were. Are they all to speak Aramaic?"

As with so many proclamations from Rome on sex, gender, and authority in the last two papacies, some American Catholics accepted the ruling and many more rejected it, albeit to varying degrees.

"You can't talk about it. Imagine that!" said Sister Sheila Lyne with a dismissive laugh.

————

Some of the Church's most vociferous and visible critics have been Irish Catholic women—from radical feminist theologian Mary Daly, who engaged in a protracted dispute with university officials over her refusal to teach men in her classes at Boston College, to the chameleon-like rebel and pop singer Sinead O'Connor.

Many women have left the Church largely because of its relentless institutional misogyny. But Catholic women, like men, have become Catholic on their own terms. And many remain active within the Church.

At the turn of the twenty-first century, 80 percent of jobs in Catholic parishes are held by women, according to the Rev. Philip Murnion, director of the National Center for Pastoral Life in New York. Women also hold approximately half the diocesan, administrative, and professional posts in the American Catholic Church. All positions of authority, however—those that determine matters of faith and Church policy—are held by ordained clergy.

The majority of those who both manage and do the hands-on, day-to-day, nitty-gritty work of teaching and caretaking in graffiti-covered churches and schools with leaky roofs built for early generations of immigrants and ethnics are Catholic sisters and laywomen, a disproportionate number of them of Irish descent.

In higher education, "there has been an openness among Catholic women's colleges to new minorities," said Sister Karen Kennelly, whose own Mount Saint Mary's College in Los Angeles, founded by the Sisters of St. Joseph Carandelet in the Santa Monica foothills in 1925, has always been geared toward daughters of immigrants. For some time, graduation rosters were dominated by names like O'Brien and Schmidt. In the 1990s, the names were more likely to be Gomez or Lee.

Catholic women's colleges like Mount Saint Mary's, whose traditional enrollment bases eroded considerably as more women students chose coeducation, have been "pioneers" in opening up institutions to ethnic diversity, said Kennelly. Her institution added associate degree programs in liberal arts, nursing, business, and early childhood education and set up an "alternative access program" for students whose test scores or capabilities aren't up to those required to pursue a baccalaureate—often because their native language isn't English.

"The Vatican's insistence that only celibate males can become priests has not stopped Catholic women from feeling called to ordination," a 1999 survey conducted by the Women's Ordination Conference showed. The study of 265 Catholic women active in their religion found that 52 percent would like to be priests or deacons. "Women who experience a call to the priesthood in the Roman Catholic Church today are not radicals on the fringe of the institution. They are mature, well-educated, regular churchgoers, active in their faith communities."

It is difficult to say how many women would enter the priesthood if it were open to them. Interestingly, fewer than 10 percent of nuns indicated in a 1994 *Los Angeles Times* survey that they would definitely seek out ordination if the Church allowed women priests. The reason, National Opinion Research Center researchers Elizabeth Durkin and Julie Durkin Montague suggested in the Jesuit magazine *America,* is that the "vast majority of the women surveyed are very satisfied with their lives as nuns and unlikely to leave the sisterhood, even if offered the opportunity to become priests." The response is very likely influenced, too, by the graying of the sisterhood: The vast majority of nuns are over forty-five, and few people make major life and career changes in their autumn or winter years.

"A lot of nuns can develop community better as parish ministers, but there are really only a handful of priests who are at all collaborative, or who don't insist on taking all the credit," said Lyne. "There's still all this stuff about 'You're not a priest; you can't run a parish; it's bad enough you don't have sacred hands.' They think they're so important with this mystique of their ordination."

Lyne considers herself "blessed" to have spent her professional life in nursing, hospital administration, and public health, "and not in parishes."

As for nuns who work in suburban parishes, a number of them are frustrated "about how male-dominated a world it is. How oppressive. Some of those who've had that kind of experience aren't even going to church anymore. They have their own Eucharist, and their own liturgy, and it's really very meaningful," said Lyne, who attends mass daily.

As Alan Wolfe, political scientist and head of the Center for the Study of Religion and Society at Boston College, sees it, the changes that have taken place in the Catholic Church since the 1960s "are probably more dramatic than in any other single American institution. American Catholicism is a religion by itself. It sees the Vatican in an advisory capacity if any, and most Catholics simply lead their lives and make their own moral decisions. Their Catholicism is very important to them, but they don't accept the church's teachings."

Clerical tokens and totems

On a bright blue St. Patrick's Day in 1999, an Irish American priest watching the New York parade on the steps of St. Patrick's Cathedral glanced at his watch. He was due at Moran's, the New York steakhouse, where a group of politically connected and professional men and women—several would take the shuttle down to the White House St. Patrick's Day party later that day—were getting together for green cheer and lunch. He would probably be asked to say grace.

"It's like Waterford," he said with a perceptible sigh of resignation. "They think they need a priest."

Like many of the well-heeled swells he was meeting at Moran's, he was in his mid-forties—old enough to recall the days when the presence of a prelate at an Irish American get-together would be considered an honor and a blessing, rather than a kind of "symbolic ethnicity." Irish Catholics of baby boom age and older were raised to defer reverentially, even obsequiously, to clergy, who represented authority and omniscience and were the conduit between the Almighty and everyday Catholics at all key junctures of their lives.

The priest garnered the respect the Irish reflexively pay to the educated. He was thought to be wise in the ways of the world and all the more admirable because he had rejected the realm of the flesh to answer a call from God. He embodied the essence of successful Irish American assimilation: respectability, patriotism, faith, affability, and dedication to a greater good. Social workers in Roman collars whose bonhomie balanced the fact they were better people than the rest, Irish priests in the movies demystified Catholicism for the American masses.

In what seemed to be the time it takes to say, "How about a game of golf, Father?" everything changed. Reports of sexual abuse of children by priests began surfacing in the mid-1980s, and by the early '90s they had taken on what *New York Times* religion correspondent Peter Steinfels called the "dimensions of a biblical plague."

Case after case that came to public attention showed that heads of dioceses dealt with a priest accused of sexual misconduct by sending him off for a stay at a rehabilitation center and then reassigning him to another parish with a "stern warning." The pedophiles' victims, meanwhile, were treated as legal adversaries; families were given cash settlements to pay for psychotherapy or to stay quiet, or both. The Church, wrote Steinfels, failed to recognize "sexual abuse as a deep pathology rather than a moral failing and as something devastating to its victims."

In June 1993, Pope John Paul II wrote an open letter to American bishops expressing "sorrow for the harm inflicted on victims and for the shock and demoralization suffered by the whole church" in the wake of revelations of hundreds of incidents of child abuse by priests and of Church officials' inadequate, insensitive responses to those who sought redress. When lawsuits and media scrutiny made it impossible for them to ignore, "the bishops' unwillingness to take a national approach" had created a "crisis of confidence in church leadership," Steinfels wrote.

Much as Cardinal Cullen had blamed Irish alcoholism on freedom of the press, some bishops accused "the media" of perpetrating the sexual abuse problem by bringing it to public attention. (Had reporters not brought clerical child abuse to light, presumably, the cover-ups and exploitation could have continued, unnoticed by any but its victims and their families.) Other diocesan heads shirked responsibility for priests' behavior, calling it the province of the police and the courts. One diocese claimed it had no authority over priests because they were "independent contractors."

Like doctors who refuse to testify against doctors and police who insist against all evidence that another officer has done no wrong, priests rally around their own and do what they can to protect the name of their profession. Though conservative estimates in the early 1990s suggested that 375 children and adolescents had been abused by priests each year in the previous four decades, a 1994 *Los Angeles Times* survey of Catholic priests showed that only 10 percent thought sexual abuse a problem.

Meanwhile, liberals blamed the sexual abuse on clerical celibacy and the Church hierarchy, arguing that it showed a clear need for allowing priests to marry and women to be ordained. Conservatives insisted it confirmed the pope's warnings "about theological dissent and moral breakdown." Church observers on both sides worried aloud that the scandals had caused a crisis of faith and undermined Catholics' respect for the priesthood, providing another impetus for Catholics to leave the Church.

A *Boston Globe* survey of faithful Catholics showed they were not leaving the fold; nor had their anger and disapproval at pedophiles affected their opinions of priests in general. They were, however, disgusted with the behavior of the Church hierarchy and many said they were thinking of reducing their financial contributions.

The pedophilia scandals convinced many Catholics that the crisis of Church leadership that had long loomed had to be addressed, that there was a need for new and better priests. Like writer Paul Wilkes, who received a foundation grant to survey Catholic parishes around the country in the 1990s, many see too many clergymen who are "either tired—having seen their Vatican II desires quashed—simply incompetent, or too afraid of offending their ecclesiastical superiors."

Contemporary Catholics, complained Wilkes, have become accustomed to "lifeless liturgies, priests whose best answer is no (or that sure sign of morbidity: 'We've never done that before'), clueless, noteless sermons that appear to be warmed-over term paper memories from a poorly taught New Testament 101 class."

Catholic University sociologist Dean Hoge has estimated that eliminating the celibacy requirement would quadruple the number of men who would enter the priesthood. A majority of priests (63 percent) and nuns (70 percent) agree with the laity (75 percent) that priests should be able to marry.

Departures and divisions in the flock

The percentage of Americans who were raised Roman Catholic but left the Church was consistent throughout the twentieth century—approximately 11 percent—except in the case of Latinos, who have been defecting at rates of over 25 percent in recent years, according to Andrew Greeley. "There is virtually no decline in belief by Catholics in major tenets of their faith. Their problems with the leadership are almost entirely in the areas of sex, gender, and authority."

Those are broad areas—and flash points in disagreements among American Catholics.

Conservatives represent a small portion of the nation's sixty million Roman Catholics, according to Philip Murnion of the National Center for Pastoral Life. Their number is probably balanced by a comparable proportion of extremely liberal churchgoing Catholics: members of groups like Dignity, the organization for gay and lesbian Catholics, and Catholics who worship in what Murnion calls "Our Lady of Rescue" parishes—churches like St. Francis Xavier in Manhattan and the Paulist Center in Boston that are short on traditional organization and authority and long on social justice and human services missions.

The Catholic League, whose members ascribe to a sort of Cliff Notes version of Catholicism that opens automatically to Church teachings on sex and is missing pages on Christian tolerance, is but a segment of a conservative subset. And while Greeley, for one, maintains that "the Catholic League represent no one but themselves—and Cardinal O'Connor," the organization has become a relentless and reliable source of inflammatory sound bites spewing intolerance while purporting to represent American Catholicism.

The Manhattan-based Catholic League, led by William Donahue, racked up a record of dubious achievement in its ardent attacks on real and imagined insults to the Church in the 1990s. For simplemindedness though, few matched its assault on the television series *Nothing Sacred*. Written by Jesuit Bill Cain based on his experiences at the Church of St. Francis Xavier in New York City, the briefly lived 1997–98 ABC-TV show presented one of the most sympathetic, realistic portrayals of a cleric to flicker across American screens in decades.

Overworked, underappreciated, and utterly human, Father Ray, played by Kevin Anderson, was a pastor to the poor and dispossessed, a man who questioned celibacy, his own belief in dogma, and institutional Church authority. Because of his deep faith in the fundamental work and teachings of Jesus Christ, he remained a priest. Father Ray's faith and doubts reflected those of many intelligent, committed Catholics, and his work showed the Church's ongoing commitment to one of its noble and least often recognized missions.

As far as Donahue and the League were concerned, good Catholics, priests in particular, don't ask questions, especially about sex. The League claimed credit, only partially deserved, for ABC's decision to cancel the show. And far more Americans read about Donahue's circumscribed views of sacrilege on *Nothing Sacred* than would ever see Cain's rendering of a priest's experience of Catholic liberal mission.

Intolerance tends to run amok in atmospheres of self-righteous religiosity, and an unmistakable streak of anti-Semitism—a disgrace to the American Irish Catholic legacy—runs through Catholic "defense" campaigns. Much of the hate mail Cain received when *Nothing Sacred* was airing complained about the Jewish writers and producers involved in the show. Though he originally wrote scripts for the show under an assumed name (Paul Leland), because "I didn't want anyone to mistake that as an official voice of the Catholic Church," Cain decided to put his own name on the series because Donahue questioned "the right of David Manson and Richard

Kramer to work on the show because they were Jewish, and a smear that then appeared in the *New York Post* calling both of them atheists."

Anti-Semitism surfaced at least twice in conservative campaigns against "anti-Catholic" art exhibits in the fall of 1999. The League followed New York Mayor Rudy Giuliani's lead in protesting the Brooklyn Museum's art exhibition "Sensation," now infamous for the controversy over its dung-dotted Madonna, and League members were among those who added their voices to the cacophony over the fact the director of the museum and the collector of the work on exhibition were Jewish.

A similar incident that took place just weeks after the sensation over "Sensation" added an Irish dimension to the fray. The Boston-based Catholic Action League demanded that Boston College close down an exhibition of contemporary work by Irish artists at the university's art museum. Protesters, few of whom had seen the exhibition, which was hardly iconoclastic by standards of much contemporary art, were outraged by reports that a self-portrait by Dublin artist Billy Quinn showed him nude, wearing a condom, and standing against a gold-leaf background inscribed with the words "AIDS pushed me. . . . It pushes all of us . . . into the realization of our own mortality."

When Boston College refused to censor the show, the university was peppered with protests, many expressing anti-Semitism of some sort. BC museum director Nancy Netzer received hate mail, threatening phone calls, and anti-Semitic death threats. The assumption that Jewish influence was somehow to blame for "anti-Catholicism" in an exhibition of work by Irish artists at a Jesuit university speaks volumes about the narrow-minded bigotry of the pious and censorious concerned.

Protesters were particularly peeved that the exhibit was of Irish art. League director C. J. Doyle charged that the BC exhibit amounted to "a celebration of Ireland's defection from Catholic culture."

A twenty-first-century Irish Church

Many in today's Ireland have defected from a Catholic culture infected with what the Rev. Liam Ryan, a prominent sociologist, called the "four deadly sins of Irish Catholicism: an obsession with sexual morality, clerical authoritarianism, anti-intellectualism or at best non-intellectualism, and the creation of a ghetto mentality."

That very small country was shaken to its core in the 1990s by a series of scandals involving Catholic clergy. In 1992, it was revealed that Bishop Eamonn Casey of Galway had fathered a child and supported him with Church funds. Two years later, when the Rev. Brendan Smyth was convicted of sexually abusing children, it became clear that he had been doing so for forty years and that Church authorities had known it. The political fallout over that incident helped bring down an Irish government.

The revelations discredited an Irish Church that, in Greeley's estimation, "tried to hold onto power too long." And while diminishment of Church authority was celebrated by a number of younger people, who saw it as long overdue and part of a happy new era of peace, prosperity, and secularism, it was deeply disturbing to many. Though increasingly secular, Ireland is still a country in which more than 80 percent of the public go to Mass each week.

Meanwhile in the 1990s, the younger clergy became more radical and antiauthoritarian than many would have imagined possible. "The extraordinary missionary tradition which sent thousands of Irish priests and nuns to a 'spiritual empire' in Africa, Asia, and Latin America has, in a sense, reversed itself, with returned missionaries supporting the ideas of liberation theology," wrote Fintan O'Toole, "ideas which threaten rather than reinforce the Church's place within Irish power structures."

Noting a "quiet spread of feminism" within the Church, even among nuns, O'Toole quoted Father Ryan, who observed that the Church leaders who treat women as second-class citizens would do well to bear in mind that "male geriatric dictatorship may well have been what finally toppled Communism in Eastern Europe."

The American clergy might look to Mother Ireland.

"I think the next pope is going to have to face up to the question of married clergy and possibly women priests," said Greeley. "The iron law of constitutional elections is that the next one will be unlike this one. How he'll be different remains to be seen."

––––––––

Americans of Irish descent are outnumbered by Hispanics in today's Church, though the Irish are still running things: They make up approximately 15 percent of the Catholic population but account for an estimated one-third of priests and half the bishops.

Irish Catholics are still more likely than other Catholics to participate in their church and call themselves devout. But Catholicism is no longer culture, nationality, and religion. Now that the Irish have "made it" in America, they expect their Church to be more egalitarian and demo-cratic—more in the secular Irish and American tradition.

There has been a recent ripple of interest in the early Irish Church among Catholics on this side of the Atlantic, who are drawn to its egali-tarian traditions and spirituality, not to mention the turn-of-the-millen-nium fad for all things Irish.

The pre-devotional Irish Church never existed here, so there are no roots to revive. However, the Celtic heritage has helped inspire one of the more vital Catholic communities in the country at Old St. Patrick's Church in Chicago, on West Adams Street, a short walk from the Loop. The city's oldest Catholic church is a testament to the vitality of Irish Catholic culture and community, traditional and new.

In early February 1999, the Chicago archdiocese launched a radio campaign inviting Catholics to "come with us on a spiritual journey." Weekly Mass attendance had dropped to a low of 25 percent (about what it was in pre-Famine Ireland). Yet on the Sunday before the announce-ment, Old St. Pat's Church was packed at every morning Mass.

One of the few buildings to survive Chicago's Great Fire of 1871, Old St. Pat's was the boyhood parish of Finley Peter Dunne, creator of the consummate turn-of-the-twentieth-century Irish American character Mr. Dooley. The parish in its early days lives on in Dooley's tales. ("They had Roddy's Hybernyun band playin' on th' cor-rner an' th' basemint iv th' church was packed. In th' ba-ack they had a shootin' gall'ry where ye got five shots f'r tin cints. . . . Th' booths was something iligant. Mrs. Dorsey had th' first wan where she sold mottoes an' babies' clothes.")

The church is a showpiece of Celtic Revival art, a creation of Chicago artist Thomas A. O'Shaughnessey, who between 1912 and 1922 designed windows, wall stencils, and light fixtures based on sketches he had made in Dublin of *The Book of Kells*. (See photo, page 164.)

O'Shaughnessey's windows tell stories of Irish Christianity and his-tory. Sanctuary windows show St. Patrick arriving at Tara; St. Columba, the sixth-century poet; St. Brigid; and St. Brendan. The east wall of the church is dominated by a twenty-five-foot-tall window dedicated to "the Glory of God and the honor of [Irish patriot] Terence MacSwiney and those men and women who have served and suffered for the freedom of Ireland." The stained glass panels incorporate the imagery and the abstract, lineal spirals and whorls of Celtic art.

Most stained glass church windows are painted in dark, rich tones. O'Shaughnessey's are made of colored opalescent glass (the kind used in Tiffany lamps) in striking pastel hues of blue, rose, cream, green, and orange that allow sunlight to radiate through. The walls and ceilings of St. Patrick's are painted in light colors and stenciled with multicolored designs. Unlike most cathedrals built in the nineteenth century, which are dark and imposing, this one is light-suffused and soothing.

Long in decline and surrounded by "the last vestiges of Skid Row," the parish had four registered members in 1983, when the Rev. Jack Wall was appointed its pastor. Today it is a vital, diverse urban Catholic community center. Sunday morning Masses draw young professionals, seniors, and young families, many of them Latino, who live nearby, and suburbanites willing to make the drive into the city because the Masses are much more inspiring than so many others.

At Old St. Pat's on the last January Sunday in 1999, the Rev. Gene Smith, invoking his "regular guy priest" persona, told Mass goers he'd keep the homily short because it was Super Bowl Sunday. He then preached a lively, articulate sermon on January, or Janus-like people— Gandhi, Elizabeth Seton, Martin Luther King—who looked forward as well as backward in their lives.

Old St. Pat's deliberately established itself as an alternative to parochial parishes, according to Wall. It is laity-centered, geared to young adults—who have a tendency to drift away from organized religion—and linked to Chicago's business, social action, and Irish communities. The church calendar lists regular meetings of a variety of groups—one for "devotion to Our Lady," one offering divorce support, a Jewish-Catholic couples group, and a Bible study meeting, along with choir practice, community outreach, and liturgy meetings. Coming up the following month were a Valentine's Day Mass, a civic forum on art as an expression of the sacred, a reading group meeting (*Portrait of the Artist as a Young Man*), and a Celtic St. Patrick's Day Mass followed by an Irish breakfast, a Mass featuring Irish musicians, and Siamsa na Gael: a celebration of the Celtic arts at Chicago Symphony Center.

Keeping a parish vital is no small challenge.

"I do six different liturgies for six communities to lay out an interpretation of life everyone can buy into. I have to," said Monsignor Kelley of Sacred Heart in Roslindale, Massachusetts. He added, "This is the hardest thing I have ever done."

In the American Church over the last thirty years, "there's been a massive change in psychology from priest-centered to people. Where's the center of Catholicism today? It isn't the clergy. It isn't the bishops. It's the educated Catholic laity, the bulk of whom are in the suburbs. The laity is getting stronger and stronger and is going to take over."

Catholics have "an ecclesiastical faith—a shared faith—that rubs against the American grain. The American perception of faith is that it's something personal and private. We have stuff we believe together: that human life is sacred; that people have a right to work; that there are rights and responsibilities to take care of those in need.

"This is the largest religious body in the country and it hasn't got a vision. If you want to change who gets ordained, why don't all the women stop working for the church one day?"

One of the unfortunate legacies of the Irish Catholic Church in the United States at the parish level is that when there's disagreement, "we want to pick a fight. We want there to be right and wrong," Kelley said. At Sacred Heart, "the Irish and Italians fought for sixty years. The Italians felt put down by the Irish; the Irish thought the Italians were too loud." Few people developed the "emotional and psychological skills to build community.

"There's still a lot of 'I'm healthy; you're sick.' We still want to pick a fight with authority. There's a lot of yes or no. Why not yes *and* no?"

It may be that the challenge to contemporary Catholics is to return to the deepest roots of Irish Catholicism and "learn how to build community."

CHAPTER EIGHT

Sea Changes: The New Irish in Ireland and America

You're not Irish, you can't be Irish
You don't know "Danny Boy,"
Or "Too-ra-loo-ra-loo-ral"
Or even "Irish Eyes,"
You've got a hell of a nerve
To say you come from Ireland
So cut out all this nonsense
And sing "McNamara's Band."

Folk singer Robbie O'Connell and friends perform this dismissive little ditty to much laughter and applause at Irish fairs and traditional music festivals in the United States. The lyrics are an anthem of the sort of amazement and irritation the Irish-born feel for Americans' fervid attachment to things Irish—or things they think are Irish. The sentimental Yank calling for "traditional" songs that were written on Tin Pan Alley, the rabble-rousing fireside republican on vacation, the deracinated American dressed in pants the color of Astro-Turf combing the Irish countryside for family connections are stereotypes the native Irish are brought up to look down on. And indeed they do.

"They were loud and exuberant and self-confident and bold, these great-grandsons and -granddaughters of the poor Irish emigrants who had fled the West of Ireland to escape famine and misery and death," wrote journalist and novelist Joe O'Connor, who encountered Yanks as a child while on vacation with his family in Connemara. "They were big spenders and big tippers. They drank a lot and talked a lot, they knew all the words of the more sentimental Irish songs, the ones with Irish place-

names in their titles. 'Galway Bay.' 'Fare Thee Well, Enniskillen, Fare Thee Well for a While.' . . . As the night wore on, the songs the Americans sang would become more pugnacious. They would start into rebel songs like 'O'Donnell Abu' or 'The Rising of the Moon.' "

The Irish in Ireland and Irish America might be described as two grand people separated by notions of a singular culture. But that would assume that the former think the latter can lay claim to a common heritage at all. The premise in Eire, as Medb Ruane wrote in the *Irish Times,* has long been that "we owned Irishness, not them." Irish Americans aren't Irish; they're Yanks, "no more than tourists" in what the native Irish know "to be 'our' culture, never mind having one of their own."

It almost goes without saying that the Irish in the United States have bowdlerized and hyperdramatized their heritage. Witness the phenomenon of Michael Flatley, dance lord out of Chicago, a consummate example of Irish Americanism in overdrive. He brought to an Irish folk art the utterly American conviction that bigger, faster, and flashier is better—and revitalized a genre and made a fortune in the bargain. With his dyed hair, faux brogue, razzle-dazzle, and Disneyfied renditions of Irish dance, he is emblematic of much that the native Irish both loathe and begrudgingly admire in their embarrassing cousins.

But as the increasing size of appreciative audiences at Robbie O'Connell's American gigs in recent years attest, some new sensibility is evolving—and not just because Americans have learned to love Irish folk music and look down on "Bing Crosby Irish." Ireland, quite famously, went through a metamorphosis in the last decade of the twentieth century; what is recognized less often, observed Niall O'Dowd, founding publisher of the *Irish Voice* newspaper and *Irish America* magazine, is that "Irish America has reinvented itself as well."

The emigration in the 1980s and 1990s of tens of thousands who would come to be called the "New Irish," while barely a blip in the American demographic, reinvigorated what had become a dormant, unappealing identity for many who feel an affinity with Eire. Coming as it did when the influence of the Catholic Church was waning, the world was shrinking, and Ireland was on the brink of prosperity, peace (one hopes), and a cultural renaissance, the influx of the New Irish set off a sequence of change that has been profound.

A New Irish spring

At some point in the mid-to-late 1980s, it was difficult not to notice a proliferation of Irish accents among nannies watching small children in playgrounds; at Irish pubs; and on building sites in San Francisco, Boston, and New York. The Irish economy was in the doldrums; America's was booming. Young Irish men and women came in droves to study, for vacation, or to visit relatives, and stayed.

Estimates on how many Irish took up residence in the United States in the last two decades of the last century are notoriously unreliable, largely because so many of the New Irish were "undocumented"—a euphemism for "illegal"—and reluctant to call attention to themselves when they first arrived.

Because they were white, usually polite, and spoke with those delightful brogues, they had less trouble than some other immigrants finding work. Irish American construction company owners in particular were willing to "forget" to ask for their green cards; two-career couples were happy to pay English-speaking babysitters off the books.

In old Irish urban neighborhoods like Dorchester in Boston and Sunnyside in Queens, New York, New Irish communities sprang up around extended families, immigration organizations, and pubs that were more than neighborhood bars with shamrocks in the windows. They were centers of communities, said contractor Paul McGonagle, who moved to Boston in the late 1980s to work for a while in the building trade. "People say Irish people spend a lot of time in bars—the bar was an employment agency, a bank, a social place. If you needed your car fixed, it was where you found a mechanic. It was a place to meet people." Like his wife.

The migration comprised what seemed to be a disproportionate share of entrepreneurs and creative types, whose presence was palpable: New newspapers and magazines appeared; seisun music wafted out of pub windows; theater companies and culture festivals started springing up. The Irish became ubiquitous—and successful—in the building business. "Don't think they don't use that charm," said an Italian American contractor, only half joking.

Nonetheless, the lives of any number of immigrants in the 1980s were markedly similar to those of the Irish who were new to America a century before: They lived in overcrowded apartments and worked as domestics or laborers. Worse, they were at the mercy of the Immigration and Naturalization Service or anyone who called the INS, which often meant "a life of concocted or 'borrowed' social security numbers, sometimes even fake U.S. birth certificates, made-up names, a good story, and always, always an eye on the door or over the shoulder," as Ray O'Hanlon describes the situation in *The New Irish Americans.*

Fortunately, the plight of Irish illegals made for both good news copy and a good cause. Irish Americans are well represented in the managerial ranks of print and electronic media, and editors and producers gave the situation prominent and sympathetic play. Successful entrepreneurs like Chuck Feeney and Massachusetts real estate mogul Thomas Flatley bankrolled immigrant support organizations, and Irish American congressional representatives Brian Donnelly, Bruce Morrison, and Joe Moakley and Senator Ted Kennedy pushed and prodded immigration legislation in Congress that resulted in the issuing of some seventy thousand visas to undocumented Irish (see Notes, pages 242–243).

A different wave

These were not your grandmother's Irish immigrants.

Each of the waves of immigration that came in the wake of the tidal wave out of Ireland in the late nineteenth and early twentieth centuries has had a distinct influence, O'Dowd explained. "In the '20s, you had a huge immigration that included many . . . from the Irish civil war. Then in the '50s, you had an economic immigration, mainly the sons and daughters of small farmers in rural areas. Their politics tended to be more rural, west of Ireland, very Catholic. They were a conservative influence on Irish America. Then in the '80s, you had the next generation, who were younger and better educated."

Having grown up in the television era and come of age as Ireland was starting to think of itself as a modern European nation, the New Irish were more cosmopolitan than their predecessors—a worldliness that at times seemed strikingly at odds with traditional Irish America.

Psychologist J. Kevin Nugent recalled being taken aback when he had been living in Boston for a matter of months and an Irish American man, hearing the rounded cadences of his Westmeath accent, "asked me with great earnestness and sincerity had I ever heard Dennis Day sing 'When Irish Eyes Are Smiling.' " New to the States, Nugent had yet to encounter American exuberance for muddled notions of Irishness—or learn the polite if patronizing posture his compatriots assume for such encounters. "He hadn't a clue about Irish music or Irish culture. At the time," he recalled, "I was astonished."

When Ireland's president Mary Robinson was vowing to lead a country that was open, tolerant, and inclusive, organizers of the New York St. Patrick's Day parade were busy barring Irish lesbian and gay groups from their line of march. Gay floats had been winning prizes for two years in St. Patrick's Day parades in Ireland in 1994, when organizers of the Boston St. Patrick's Day parade won a Supreme Court ruling allowing them to ban lesbian, gay, and bisexual marchers.

Independent filmmaker and curator Marie Jackson "couldn't *believe* the little green leprechauns all over the place and [the logos for the] Boston Celtics and the Fightin' Irish," and not just because the images are tacky. "Those were so deeply offensive to the Irish in Ireland when they first came out of England. They're based on old Punch cartoons where the Irish were treated as chimpanzees in the period of Darwin!"

She was put off, too, by assumptions Americans make about contemporary Ireland, such as "the idea that because I was a Catholic from

Northern Ireland, I would automatically be an IRA supporter. That is anathema to me." For a while, she and a friend "ran a film series at Boston College. We'd show one feature and a short from Ireland, and we would all hang out and have coffee and cookies afterwards. And a number of people came who had American accents but who called themselves Irish, and the first thing they would ask you was were you Catholic or Protestant, which I always find very offensive. And then they started talking about Gerry Adams. And when I said I didn't support Gerry Adams, it was like, 'Oh, we didn't know.' And they would butt right off. I wanted to say 'Wise up.' And in fact I would, I mean it wouldn't be as rude as that, but I'd tell them it was a bit more complicated than that."

Traditional Irish American organizations and entities tended to be part of established, ethnically homogeneous Church, civic, and social orders. Some of the '80s arrivals, by contrast, identified proudly and publicly with "the other" in American life: Sister Lena Deevy, founder of Boston's Irish Immigration Center, deliberately linked concerns of the city's Irish and Afro-Caribbean immigrants, sponsoring events like an annual Black-Green St. Patrick's Day gathering celebrating the relationship between Ireland and Montserrat in Boston, for example.

The New York Irish American band Black 47 began bringing its mix of Celtic music, rock, and hip-hop about a much different way of "Livin' in America" to Irish bars and festivals:

> *Workin' with the black man, Dominican and Greek*
> *In the snow days of January and drenchin' August heat*
> *No sick days or benefits and for Christ sakes don't get hurt*
> *The quacks over here won't patch you up unless they see the bucks*
>   *upfront.*

"When we got here, we found that there was nothing that represented us as Irish people," said Conor Howard, owner of Anna Livia Books in San Francisco, taking a lunch break with Eddie Stack, head of San Francisco's Irish Arts Center, while planning the 1999 Celtic Music Festival. "There weren't any real Irish artists, or real musicians. At the outset, Irish American culture was an offshoot. There was defensiveness about it. It was self-referential, and never really connected with Ireland."

Much of that has changed. The peace process in Ireland "has been a huge cultural dividend," as he sees it. "So much of the energy in Irish America has been taken up by Irish nationalism. Culture has opened avenues to an Irish American identity that barely existed before." In his estimation, "there's a new interest in the fusion of Irish and Irish American culture—a cross-fertilization" that is flourishing at a time in the assimilation process in which "a lot of people have reached a stage of wanting to figure out who they are."

Men in big green suits

Dormant for decades, American interest in Northern Ireland was revived with the outbreak of "the Troubles." In 1968, the year of Martin Luther King's assassination and just months after Chicago police beat protesters outside the Democratic National Convention while the whole world was watching, civil rights riots erupted in Derry. American television networks showed footage of members of the Royal Ulster Constabulary "wading into peaceful civil rights protestors, cracking heads with their batons and blasting others with high-powered water cannon. Major newspapers carried front page headlines describing the riots in detail and outlining incidents of police savagery."

"There was a sense, all of the sudden, a sense of 'Look what they're doing to *us*,' " recalled *Philadelphia Daily News* reporter and Irish American community activist Frank Dougherty.

Americans in general are not noted for their sophisticated grasp of international politics. When the Troubles broke out in 1969, "Irish Americans tended to think of it as the final act of the drama which began in 1916. There was an instinctive desire to rally behind the Irish, kick the British out, and reunite the country," William Shannon wrote in 1977.

The Catholic struggle in Northern Ireland was initially portrayed in the American media as analogous to the American civil rights movement, which had inspired leaders like John Hume. As Britain's involvement in Northern Ireland continued in the early 1970s, it increasingly was compared to America's in Vietnam. Much to the dismay of government officials and others in Eire who were up close and personal with the IRA's armed struggle, getting behind the Catholic cause was a no-brainer for liberal Irish American Democrats like Tip O'Neill, who was raised on republicanism in a working-class neighborhood in Cambridge, Massachusetts.

In 1969, when the Provisional IRA sought American support for its "armed struggle" to unite Ireland, it tapped Michael Flannery to lead the effort. A native of Tipperary, Flannery had joined the Irish Volunteers at fourteen and fought on the anti-treaty side in the civil war. Captured, imprisoned, and released by Free State forces, he left Ireland in 1927 for New York, where he was a daily communicant, held down an office job at the Metropolitan Life Insurance Company, and spent his life working with organizations like the Tipperary Men's Association and the Gaelic Athletic Association, and took a leadership position in what remained of Clan-na-Gael.

Men like Flannery—a small cadre of Irish civil war veterans and members of fraternal organizations like the Ancient Order of Hibernians, and Irish county organizations—had kept the republican cause alive in the United States and were gung-ho to get behind civil rights activism in Northern Ireland. Up to a point.

Articulate and outspoken, Northern Ireland civil rights activist Bernadette Devlin made a media-saturated foray to the United States in 1969 that provides a primer on the state of Irish American nationalism at the time.

Ardent supporters though they were of minorities in Ulster, the American nationalists were unsympathetic to the civil rights of black Americans, as Devlin was dismayed to discover when Irish American groups heckled her speeches in which she drew parallels between African American and Irish civil rights. To the horror of Hibernians, who until quite recently required that their members be practicing Catholics, Devlin criticized the Church and what in those days was known as "the establishment" and espoused socialism.

For her part, Devlin was disenchanted at the American notion of a free Ireland. "All the men in the big green suits cheered and roared when I mentioned James Connolly, until I started quoting what he actually said," she told the *Irish Times*.

The views from here

Contentious and controversial though it is, Irish republican activism in the United States has never been as pervasive as many in Ireland perceive.

In his comprehensive account *Irish America and the Ulster Conflict, 1968–1995,* Andrew J. Wilson stresses that "those who became involved in the Ulster conflict were only a very small minority. . . . The majority of Irish Americans remained apathetic and largely uninterested in Northern Ireland. Those with an opinion generally tended to endorse the goals of constitutional nationalism and condemn IRA violence."

Historians who have told the story of Irish American nationalism point out consistently that its key agitators have nearly always been more radical (and romantic) than nationalist leaders in Erin. They have also been far more adamant about Irish independence and republicanism than most Irish Americans. Time after time when given a choice, "the man who spoke for Ireland was the voice to which Irish Americans responded," according to historian Thomas Fleming. Much of the nationalist feeling in this country has had as much to do with the social and political standing of the Irish in America as anything.

Notably, the first major disagreement between the American diaspora and an Irish political leader was over slavery. Americans in the 1830s sent thousands of dollars to Daniel O'Connell, "the Liberator," whose massive political organizing led to passage of the Catholic Emancipation Act and who was pressing for repeal of the Act of Union, which abolished the Irish Parliament in 1801. O'Connell saw parallels between enslaved blacks and the colonized, destitute Irish—as would the abolitionist Frederick Douglass, who toured famine-stricken Ireland in 1845–46 and "heard in the 'wailing notes' of Irish songs echoes of the 'wild notes' " of the sorrowful songs he had heard in slavery. In 1842, seventy thousand Irish signed an antislavery petition, calling on Irish Americans to "cling by the abolitionists" and "treat the colored people as your equals, as brethren." Fleming writes that "Irish Americans were appalled." They were loyal Democrats, opposed to abolitionism, and afraid that freed slaves would compete with them for low-level jobs. Support for O'Connell's repeal effort fell apart immediately.

The Great Famine "rekindled, unified, and impassioned Irish American nationalism." Memories of the Famine and a fury at being forced into exile in an unwelcoming land trained Irish hatred on the British and fueled a desire for revenge. Crowded together in tenements, laboring on docks and scrubbing kitchens, caricatured as apes by cartoonists and loathed for their Catholicism, the Irish in America reconstructed their memories of the land they had left. The sense that they had been forced out of a place of extraordinary splendor (see Chapter 1) fostered "a belligerent nationalism," in Wilson's words.

Irish American nationalism took many forms. When the Prince of Wales (the future Edward VII) visited Manhattan, Colonel Michael Corcoran, commander of the 69th Regiment of the New York Militia, refuses to lead his regiment in a march to honor the man the Irish call "the Famine prince."

In 1866, the Irish American Fenian Brotherhood, a counterpart to the Irish Revolutionary Brotherhood, amassed a force of five thousand veterans of the Union and Confederate armies at the Canadian border, planning to take the British dominion hostage and declare an Irish Republic. According to Fleming, the Fenians were a formidable force, and "would have pulled it off" if the American government had not intervened, putting gunboats in the Niagara River, and marooning half the army in Canada.

Alexander Sullivan of Chicago, who led a powerful faction of Clan-na-Gael, which became the main representative of Irish American republicanism in the 1870s, exploded bombs in trains, subways, and government buildings in England in the early 1880s.

But most Irish Americans rallied to the more moderate causes of land reform and home rule in Ireland, which was led by Charles Stewart Parnell. Parnell had launched a concerted campaign for home rule in Ireland when revelations that he'd had a long affair with Kitty O'Shea, a married woman, brought his momentous political career to an end.

To second- and third-generation Irish Americans, an independent Ireland was less important as a political aim than as a symbol of American social equality, according to the historian Thomas N. Brown. Many saw British subjugation of Ireland as an emblem of powerlessness and inferiority that provided Anglo-America a rationale for ill treatment of the Irish here. Self-government would remove that stigma, fulfilling a psychological and social need for respectability that had long eluded the upwardly mobile Irish in America.

———

In the first two decades of the twentieth century, much of the money and support for Ireland's struggle for independence came from Irish America. United in their anger at ruthless reprisals against the men who led the Easter Rebellion in 1916, Irish Americans tried to capitalize on public awareness and criticism of British brutality in Ireland.

True to tradition, they backed Eamon De Valera when he visited the United States in 1919 in what turned out to be a watershed in the American nationalist movement. Sharing neither the absolute Anglophobia of Irish Americans nor the "passion for absolute republican independence" of American leaders of the Friends of Irish Freedom, De Valera formed the American Association for the Recognition of the Irish Republic. The organization recruited 750,000 members in short order, rendering the Friends of Irish Freedom obsolete.

Americans would give De Valera more than $10 million to support the IRA's military operations in the war of independence. They would ignore the Irish leader three years later, after Ireland had won its independence, when a civil war broke out over the treaty partitioning Ireland and creating the Irish Free State. The treaty was signed by Irish Republican Army commander Michael Collins and Sinn Fein founder Arthur Griffith. De Valera was outraged at the compromise and was backed by much of the IRA. The fighting that ensued was vicious and bloody, and Americans were disillusioned. When De Valera issued an "urgent call to Irish Americans to save the republic from the Free State," he received virtually no response.

De Valera's side lost the civil war, and a number of IRA men fled to America, where they kept the republican cause alive. "Dev" returned to power as prime minister in 1932 and gradually did away with tenets of the Free State treaty. Ireland officially became a republic in 1949. De Valera would periodically try to drum up American support to end the partition of Northern Ireland, but he inflicted fatal damage to his own cause when he not only remained neutral during World War II but complained about the American and British military presence in Northern Ireland and sent an emissary to express his sympathies to the German ambassador in Dublin when Hitler died.

As historian Lawrence J. McCaffrey explains it, most Irish Americans supported a form of home rule and thought that "the Free State was a reasonable response to the Irish demand for freedom," that Ireland's sovereignty would evolve. By insisting that Ireland must be "Gaelic as well as free," post-treaty Irish nationalism became "parochial, exclusive, isolationist, and irrelevant to the Irish of the diaspora making their way in the urban industrial centers of the English-speaking world."

De Valera's famous, if frequently misquoted, 1927 St. Patrick's Day Address, for example, extolled the virtues of "a land whose countryside would be bright with cozy homesteads, whose fields and villages would be joyous with the sounds of industry, with the rompings of sturdy children, the contests of athletic youths and the laughter of comely maidens, whose firesides would be forums for the wisdom of serene old age."

Funds for "freedom fighters"

When Michael Flannery announced the formation of Noraid at a New York press conference in 1970, he insisted that the funds it collected would go not to buy weapons but to support the families of imprisoned IRA members and other "humanitarian relief." His much-disputed claim was belied by many episodes, among them his arrest in 1981 for IRA gunrunning, and his penchant for observations like "an IRA soldier freed from financial worries for his family is a much better fighter," which supported his critics' contentions.

At a time when a majority of Irish Catholics had long since left the old urban neighborhoods and were, in fact, the country's second most prosperous and liberal-minded ethnic group, Noraid's base of support was made up largely of blue-collar, staunchly Catholic social conservatives. Many failed to see not only the parallels between the political and socioeconomic repression of Catholics in Northern Ireland and African Americans in the United States but the avowed Marxism of IRA leaders and the fatal repercussions of their terrorism on innocent people.

South Boston, where working-class Irish Americans chanted slogans like "Niggers out of Boston, Brits out of Belfast" during Boston's desegregation crisis in the mid-1970s, was a Noraid stronghold. So is the New York St. Patrick's Day parade, whose organizers drew—and ignored—vociferous criticism in 1983, when they chose Flannery as grand marshal.

Support for the IRA grew among middle-class Irish Americans when Britain and the Stormont government, in an effort to curb IRA bombing campaigns, started interning republican suspects in Northern Ireland in 1971. Reports of flagrant human rights abuses, including torture and forced confession, later confirmed by independent inquiries, started appearing in the mainstream press.

Stateside backing for republicans surged after Bloody Sunday, January 30, 1972, when British paratroopers shot and killed thirteen Catholic civil rights demonstrators in Derry. The next day, British Home Secretary Reginald Maudling announced a judicial inquiry into the episode and defended the paratroopers' action. In Dublin on February 2, a crowd estimated at 25,000 burned down the British embassy.

Britain's actions, excoriated around the world, were a flash point in Irish America. Senator Ted Kennedy, who had previously caused controversy in Washington by calling for British withdrawal from Northern Ireland, declared in testimony before Congress that "just as Ulster is Britain's Vietnam, so Bloody Sunday is Britain's My Lai." Masses were held for Bloody Sunday victims around the country, and Roman Catholic church leaders, who had to that point refrained from much comment on Ulster, spoke out. New York's Terence Cardinal Cooke issued a statement read from pulpits in his diocese calling on parishioners to "pray for those who have been imprisoned in Ulster, for civil rights reforms, and for new and far-reaching initiatives," Andrew Wilson recounts.

Three thousand people gathered at St. Patrick's Cathedral in New York for a Bloody Sunday service at which the Rev. Robert Gannon, former president of Fordham University, called the Bloody Sunday killings vicious and unprovoked: "Only stupid soldiers and stupid politicians would attempt the pacification of a country in 1972 by imprisonment without trial, torture of prisoners for information, and by hysterical shooting of innocent citizens who dared to march in their own ghetto."

Noraid's coffers swelled in the wake of the introduction of internment and Bloody Sunday. Documents the organization was required to file with the Foreign Agents Registration Act show that in the first six months of 1971, the group sent $11,500 to Belfast. Between January and July 29, 1972, Noraid "spent $25,440 on its U.S. operations and sent $312,000 to Ireland."

A different way

There was a tendency in Irish America to see the conflict in Northern Ireland "very simply, as almost a morality play where cruel British victimized the Irish and there was no nuance, no shading in between," recalled Ireland's ambassador to the United States Sean O'Huiginn, a former consul general to New York and a key diplomatic negotiator in Anglo-Irish relations.

Political leaders in the Irish Republic were dismayed that an organization that was wreaking havoc and brutality in Britain and Ireland was being portrayed as a band of romantic freedom fighters in America. Of greater concern to Irish officials than obnoxious American republican demonstrators was the seeming lack of opposition to IRA tactics among Kennedy and other political leaders.

John Hume of the Social Democratic and Labour Party lobbied Kennedy, and Hume, Kennedy, and the Irish diplomatic corps were successful in convincing House Speaker Tip O'Neill, Senator Daniel Patrick Moynihan, and New York Governor Hugh Carey to support "constructive dialogue between nationalists and unionists" and condemn American support for the violent tactics of the IRA. On March 16, 1977, the "Four Horsemen" of Irish American politics issued a joint appeal "to all those organizations engaged in violence to renounce their campaigns of death and destruction and return to the path of life and peace. And . . . to our fellow Americans to embrace this goal of peace and renounce any action that promotes the current violence."

Predictably, Noraid condemned the Four Horsemen, calling them lace curtain Irish sellouts and British lackeys. But alternatives to radical republicanism began to emerge.

In 1976, for example, Charles Daly, then head of the Joyce Foundation in Chicago; Tony O'Reilly, former Irish rugby star turned media magnate and president of H. J. Heinz Company; Dan Rooney, president of the Pittsburgh Steelers; and the Rev. Theodore Hesburgh, president of the University of Notre Dame, formed the American Ireland Fund to raise money for peace, culture, and charitable ventures in Ireland.

Now a $100 million campaign, the Ireland Fund was established "for hyperactive Americans, who wanted to find some way to give money to Ireland without doing harm," said Daly, now the retired head of the John F. Kennedy Library Foundation. "The problem with Noraid was that in some places it was the only game in town."

The organization had to disabuse some cherished notions, said Daly, recalling a "classic example of what we were up against." At an early Ireland Fund dinner, a prominent Irish American philanthropist became nonplussed as he listened to a then twenty-six-year-old unknown lawyer named Mary Robinson. "The fact there was a young woman from Ireland speaking about anything was a little surprising to him to begin with. She started talking about the position of the women in the family. It wasn't a feminist speech or anything; there were other aspects to it. And she mentioned divorce and he turned to me and said, 'She's not Irish!'" said Daly, laughing. "Divorce isn't Irish."

Ireland Fund dinners are black-tie, lavish affairs that raise more than $1 million in an evening. Their success reflects the Irish rise in corporate America in the last third of the twentieth century. The Ireland Fund's donor base quintupled between 1995 and 2000, according to the organization's executive director Kingsley Aikens. He attributes the surge to the "new glamour" of Ireland, Irish music, and Irish products, which has brought DCPs—"Deep Closet Paddys"—"out of the closet" about their Irish roots. Americans love a winner, he points out. And Ireland is a winner these days.

———

Until the late 1980s, Americans who cared about Ireland felt they had two choices: "If rich enough, they could don black tie and go to an Ireland Fund dinner. Or they could grab a placard and march with Noraid outside the British consulate," said publisher and editor Niall O'Dowd.

The Irish Immigration Reform Movement, founded in 1987 to lobby and provide other support for the New Irish, gave Americans with an affinity for their Irish heritage a chance to get behind a cause that wasn't exclusive or overtly political. That, in turn, led to constructive American involvement in the peace process in Northern Ireland, which "forced a rethinking and reevaluation" of stereotypes and received wisdom about the Irish on both sides of the Atlantic, O'Dowd said.

As Conor O'Clery, former Washington correspondent for the *Irish Times,* makes clear in his book *Daring Diplomacy: Clinton's Secret Search for Peace in Northern Ireland,* O'Dowd was instrumental in securing the support of Irish American businessmen and philanthropists Chuck Feeney and Mutual of America chairman Bill Flynn as peace envoys to Northern Ireland in the 1990s. Influential Irish American "support for unarmed strategy" encouraged the Clinton administration's unprecedented involvement in Northern Ireland, which many observers credit with moving the peace process closer to resolution than combined efforts had accomplished in decades.

"Before the peace process, the republican movement's top level contact in the United States had been Martin Galvin of Noraid; now it included important representatives of American business, politics, and trade unions, and could go all the way to the President of the United States," writes O'Clery. The informal network of peacemakers "helped win the visa for Gerry Adams and had opened up lines to the White House. They represented a crucial point of reference in the broadening of the nationalist debate."

American involvement "helped achieve more in the last five years of the peace process than in the seventy years before it," said O'Dowd. It changed Irish Americans' understanding of Ireland and "changed the dynamic of how Irish people view the Irish Americans as well." The breakdown of "stereotypes on both sides of the Atlantic has been dramatic." There is new understanding and appreciation in Eire for that elusive American quality, "can-do."

Ambassador O'Huiginn agreed: "The dialogue changed. There were Irish Americans who simplified the complexities of the situation in Ireland. There were also many people in Ireland who underestimated the sophistication of the Irish Americans. They simply took one or two egregious instances of stereotyping and simplification and said 'That's the whole thing.'"

Quite in contrast to American teenagers wandering through Belfast wearing T-shirts emblazoned with anti-British slogans or tourists who decide after too many rounds of Guinness and "Kevin Barry" that they'll go straighten out the misguided men guarding Northern Ireland's border, "the likes of the Kennedys, [Senator] Chris Dodd, Hugh Carey in New York at the time showed people at home that there were actually extremely thoughtful people with a very important contribution to make," O'Huiginn said.

"And, of course, President Clinton was, if you like, the culmination of that when he went to Ireland. The British media were gleefully expecting that he would crash all over like a bull in a china shop and in fact he put all of the prior politicians to shame with the incredible skill with which he picked his way through that mine field and said important things, but in a way that did not alienate or offend any constituency."

A subtle shift

For a long time, Marie Jackson "thought that the Irish were Irish, and that Irish Americans were something else." President Mary Robinson's speech in February 1995, "Cherishing the Irish Diaspora," encouraged her to see things differently. So did her encounters with people like an elderly couple she met while teaching at an Elderhostel in Indiana.

"He wore an Ireland sweater, and a green tam-o'-shanter with an orange bauble on top, and green checked pants. And I just *cringed* every time I came in the door. It was an ostentatious show of 'I'm Irish'—as if anybody in Ireland ever wore green checked pants," she recalled.

"He was really pro-IRA. He didn't want to know anything about the north, because as far as he was concerned, it was very cut and dried: the Brits were doing all these things on the Catholics, and they had to be got out. I had my hackles up against him, because he was everything in my concept of an Irish American that I couldn't stand."

Much to her dismay, she ended up in the same car with the professional Irishman on a class trip. During the ride, "I found out that he and his wife had raised fourteen children on a farm in southern New Jersey. He had put them all through college, and now they and their grandkids were all doing fine. And he told me that he and his wife had gone on a trip to Ireland and rented a car. And he said, 'A lot of people hitchhike in Ireland.' I said Yes, I know. And he said, 'So we turned in our car, and we hitchhiked.'

"And the idea of the two of them with their tam-o'-shanters and their attitude, hitchhiking with their suitcases—I suddenly stopped hating them, and I just loved them! I adored that they had done that."

Innovation, individuality, exuberance, and a glibness that comes of a tradition of free speech are very American values, quite distinct from the reticent, humble, communal traditions of Eire.

The world, of course, is smaller, and "the interaction between two sides of the Atlantic is much more immediate today," said O'Huiginn. "I think it's become a much more stable and productive relationship. There has been a sense in Ireland that we owned the Irish heritage and that it was up to us to say what was good and what was bad, what you're allowed to do and what you aren't. I think one of the things you realize when you come to the States is that Irish heritage is not a monopoly we have in Ireland that we allow the Irish Americans to borrow or share in the flavor of from time to time. That in fact the Irish Americans may have created a lot of it. I think we need to be understanding that Irish America is a culture with its own entitlements."

Americans' can-do instincts and diplomatically skilled negotiations in the peace process forced a reevaluation of the cultural cluelessness of Yanks in Ireland.

For decades, Irish Americans traversed Ireland in tour buses, longing for an illusory place. The Irish have shown a talent for giving them what they want—a quaint culture park experience is readily available at distances closer to Shannon Airport than many Americans would drive to get to a shopping mall: Bunratty Castle, where a "medieval" experience comes replete with sing-alongs of "Toora-Lural-Lura"; restaurants, gift shops, and three-star hotels under thatched roofs in Ireland's "tidy towns"; a new Celtic Theme Park in Limerick, for those who want a little "authenticity" without driving out to the Dingle Peninsula.

"People on both sides of the Atlantic have been guilty of perpetuating that 'shamrocks and leprechauns' syndrome—and my own theory is that was due to a sort of 'mutual disrespect,' if you like," said Helena Mulkerns, a writer who was at the center of the New York New Irish arts scene until she decamped to Managua, then Africa, where she works for the United Nations.

"The Americans wanted to go 'home' to Ireland and find the simple, happy bog-trotters of their dreams, and we saw them as fat-wallet here-they-come Yanks that we could make some money off!"

Indeed, "Most of us as young people learned to despise" the loud, proud people wearing "plaid trousers who had forgotten their origins and believed they had nothing to learn," said Kevin Nugent. Those negative images of Yanks would develop into full-blown, lurid impressions of Americans as "bullies and intimidators" during the Vietnam era and the Reagan-Thatcher years—representations that were reinforced by photos beamed around the world of whites beating up on blacks in the name of Irish pride during Boston's busing conflict.

But what the native Irish are often eager to dismiss as cultural imperialism or cluelessness is far more complex. As Nugent spent time in the United States, he came "to terms with America" and realized that, along with foreign policy he might oppose and expressions of powerlessness like those shouted from the rooftops and streets of South Boston during busing, there is a "commitment to civil rights" in America, "a genuine aspiration that people from different cultures be equal in society." He began to develop a "deep appreciation of the Irish American struggle—the people who came to work in subways and as domestic servants."

The man who so loved Dennis Day, Nugent realized, "was imprisoned in a culture that gave him no avenue beyond the green beer and parades and leprechauns. He was making a clumsy, uninformed effort to try to reconnect. There are no avenues to Irish culture; there's no sense of Irish American history. It is not regarded as a culture to be explored. People can now dress up in bow ties and go to *Riverdance,* but there's nothing coherent, no continuity to the Irish American experience. There's nowhere to fit it. There's much more need for rituals and reflection on what it means to be Irish American."

In aesthetic realms, as Fintan O'Toole points out, "U.S. culture is in part an Irish invention. And Irish culture is inconceivable without America." Traditional Irish music, for example, traveled to Appalachia, went back to Ireland in the form of country and western music, mixed it up with rock and roll, and spawned offshoots, including the crossover Celtic rock bands like Black 47. "If you want to know how Irish country fiddling acquired the speed, variety, and individuality that we now associate with a master like Martin Hayes, you have to look to the cities of the U.S.," O'Toole said. Sligo-born immigrants like Michael Coleman, Paddy Killoran, and James Morrison developed a twentieth-century style for Irish music. That sound, in turn, shaped the traditional music revival in Ireland from the 1970s onward.

"Irish movies owe far more to Hollywood than to the European cinema. The high flyers of Irish poetry have always acknowledged the immense influence of Robert Frost and Robert Lowell."

Like many Americans, Jane Duffin, editor of the *Irish Edition* in

Philadelphia, was blithely unaware when she was growing up that she had an ethnic identity, even when she began teaching the sociology of ethnic groups. "Then I traveled to Ireland," she said, "and I felt I was home. I felt as if everyone I saw was related to me. That we were from the same socioeconomic background, had the same values, the same norms and ways of addressing things.

"The younger Irish have added something wonderful in the last twenty years," said Duffin. Partly because of their influence, Irish America is also beginning to realize "it exists as a viable ethnic group. It is one way of being American. It provides richness to one's life—a connection with the past and something wonderful to pass on to children. Both cultures are changing, and they're changing one another."

———

In the mid-1990s, for the first time in its history, Irish immigration trends reversed. Many who had left Ireland out of economic necessity were returning home, lured by the healthy growl of the "Celtic Tiger."

Booming Ireland seemed to offer the best of both worlds. But many men and women had started businesses and families in the United States, and weren't as ready to leave as they might have thought. "I think everyone who comes here thinks they're going to go back," said contractor Paul McGonagle. "And now Ireland's changed, it's more European, there's more affluence, there's a lot of opportunity. I would go if the conditions were right. But even if it were a good opportunity for me, it might not be a good opportunity for my wife. I'm from the top of Ireland—Malin, in Donegal—and she's from five hours away in Tipperary."

What's more, "Irish life is different now. There were no drugs when we left. That was one reason people wanted to get their kids home. There are drugs here, sure, but at least they address the issue."

Nugent, who leads support groups at Boston's Irish Pastoral Center for native Irish families living in the States, noted that some are "petrified their children are going to act like spoiled brats." American "spunkiness and brashness do not work in an Irish setting that values the quiet, the understated, and the sweet."

But American brashness and "flexibility" are among the reasons Kevin Treanor, who owns three popular pub-restaurant-nightspots in

Greater Boston, thinks he will continue to bring up his young family in America. It is those traits that make "people open to so many things here. It is not bullshit—you really can be anything you want to be here. At home, it's a much narrower tunnel," he said.

As a father of "kids who are going to be Irish American," Treanor said he grows impatient with native Irish chauvinism about the heritage to which Americans also lay claim. "Irish Americans try really hard to be Irish. They emphasize that they've been to Ireland, and they feel proud of it when they talk to us. And Irish people are always telling them they're not Irish.

"I don't think they realize what Irish Americans have done. Some of the stuff boggles the mind. These guys get off the boat fighting. They're treated like dirt, they get into politics, and they change it completely. They go into business. And they paved the way for us. Take the visas. Why should Donnelly or Morrison or Ted Kennedy care about us? But they did."

He gestured at the dining room of An Tua Nua, one of his pub-restaurants, which is popular in Boston for its music, food, and authentic Irish atmosphere, and added: "Let's get real. I wouldn't be here if they didn't."

CHAPTER NINE

Irish America Coming into Clover

How drunk was Scott Fitzgerald when he said that there were no second acts in American lives?

—Martin Amis

On March 17, 1997, the New York St. Patrick's Day parade paused for a moment of silence to honor the memory of those who died during Ireland's Great Famine. For the first time on record, the oldest, largest Irish American ritual paid homage to the disaster in which one-quarter of Ireland's population died from starvation, disease, or neglect, and more than one million fled for their lives. The following day, the *New York Times* reported the unprecedented demonstration in a story headlined: THE IRISH FINALLY STOP TO REMEMBER.

The recognition of an Gorta Mor, the Great Hunger, in New York and elsewhere was a signal event in Irish America. An awareness of an unsentimental past added an explanatory preface and new depth and dimension to the standard-issue story of the Irish in America so many were raised on: a tale of heroes and heroics; of grand, gregarious men in the parish and around the precinct; and the long march to the White House from Tammany Hall. Loud, proud, and wildly sentimental, that ever-so-popular account has been eerily silent about the horrors that drove so many Irish to this country, the squalor and shame so many suffered, and

about how it is the Irish who didn't become priests, policemen, or politicians—including most women—have lived their lives.

When Boston's Súgán Theatre staged Tom Murphy's harrowing play *Famine,* it quickly became clear to Súgán artistic director Carmel O'Reilly that "this was a story that had not been told." The company mounted the production in 1995, two years before commemorations raised awareness of the cataclysm.

"People came in droves," recalled O'Reilly. "They came up from

Rhode Island, from as far away as New Jersey. The response was tremendous; we got cards and letters from Irish Americans who didn't really know what they'd come out of, thanking us. Knowing something about what had happened was a spiritual experience for some people, a way of reconnecting with this immigrant experience that left a lot of people rootless.

"We got negative reactions too. There were people who were bitterly angry that we had shown the Irish that way—poor and dirty and drunken; reduced to stealing turf. There is a shame about that, a feeling that Irish Americans spent all these years building themselves up, and we shouldn't be telling people about that."

"The déclassé part of the Irish experience was never spoken of until recently," said film director Jim Sheridan, who ran the Irish Arts Center in New York in the 1980s before he began making hit movies with Daniel Day Lewis. "The origin of *Angela's Ashes* was a play that Frank and Malachy McCourt did, *A Couple of Blaguards.* It ran for years, and no one paid attention. That wasn't a legitimate field. Until the influx of the immigrants in the 1980s, Irish American audiences were very conservative.

"But now there's a distance. There's been a shift of wealth, and Irish culture is for sale. There hasn't been much to buy besides Waterford in the Aer Lingus catalogue. Now you can go to *Riverdance.* You can look at *Angela's Ashes* or *My Left Foot.* And you can say, 'Look at how far we've come.' "

———

In the 1990s, every green-tinged book, movie, music act, and stage show seemed to turn red hot. Retirees who had hardly given thought to their ancestry started tracing their genealogies in Ireland. Third- and fourth-generation Americans signed up for Irish language classes, and sat in on traditional music sessions in Irish pubs.

Applications for Irish citizenship doubled in the United States. Tourist travel to Ireland grew exponentially. Wealthy Irish Americans bankrolled immigration assistance efforts; organized peace initiatives; funded Irish studies and cultural centers; launched economic exchanges. Young people in particular became enthralled with a new sense of Irish inheritance that was more pagan than pious, unconventional instead of circumscribed, and authentic rather than synthetic. Hipsters and historians hailed the arrival of a "new Irish identity" at the turn of the century.

By some lights, the "new Irish" identity in the United States is a newer, hipper version of what the sociologist Herbert Gans calls "symbolic ethnicity"—the tendency among latter-generation white ethnics in the United States to pick and choose among the more appealing aspects of their heritage, to identify themselves as Irish on St. Patrick's Day or Italian while vacationing in Tuscany, but American and middle-class at work. Symbolic ethnicity is little more than spice sprinkled on a bland American culture of telecommuting, suburban sprawl, and shopping malls.

Like any American enthusiasm, new Irishness has a hefty share of hokum to it—enough to set Andrew O'Hehir railing against the "blessings and divinations," the "keening New Age Goddesses," and "myth-informed Driveldance spectaculars" in *Salon*. Synthetic Irishry for the cyberage, he wrote, made him long for a "chorus of drunken cops singing 'Danny Boy.'" Almost.

And there has been some resistance in traditional Irish American quarters, like Ancient Order of Hibernians chapters that teach classes in Irish culture, to a more nuanced version of Irish American history, according to Kevin Whelan, director of Notre Dame's Irish Studies program in Dublin. There is some resentment in those circles of FBIs—a term used to describe "foreign-born Irish" and the American academics and culturati who embrace the values redolent in the peaceful, secular, and prosperous Ireland of today.

But there are two ways of approaching the Famine, said Whelan. "One is to see it as emblematic of the great disadvantage the Irish had to overcome in order to take their place in the American dream. The other is to see it as an example of the kind of man-made disaster with which the peoples of colonized countries are regularly afflicted to this day and to see parallels between it and the political and economic disasters which drive millions of immigrants to Europe and the U.S."

The latter approach involves "taking Irish studies out of the ghetto. It is not just ethnic massaging, it can offer to other people a paradigm for the immigrant experience."

———

How much the new Irish American identity will mix it up with others—or with its own unromantic past—remains to be seen.

As Patrick Goggins, a San Francisco Democratic Party political ac-tivist and president of the Irish Literary and Historical Society in the Bay Area, sees it, "You have to try to reach out. If you don't, you become in-ward, and in a multicultural area, you become part of the bigotry." Irish organizations have been part of it in the past, forgetting their own past, he said. "There are traditional Irish here who still resent Filipinos getting jobs at City Hall; people to the left on Sinn Fein who use the n-word.

"There are probably two hundred and fifty Irish organizations in San Francisco now. There might have been a hundred and twenty in 1980," said Goggins. They are in a range—from the American Ireland Fund, which throws tony parties in Pacific Heights, to the Irish Cultural Center built by the Carpenters Union, to music groups, and soccer clubs, he noted, sitting in O'Reilly's Irish Pub & Restaurant on Green Street. Adorned with hand-carved wood and murals depicting a pantheon of Ireland's scribes, O'Reilly's is at the center of New Irish culture in the Bay area. Owner Myles O'Reilly throws an Oyster and Beer Festival to celebrate the feast of Ireland's patron saint "and the integration of the Irish into San Francisco's multiracial community" on St. Patrick's Day each year.

Goggins has cofounded the Irish-Mexican Association, whose mem-bers celebrate St. Patrick's Day and Cinco de Mayo together each year. The two groups have more in common, he noted, than many might think: paganism, Catholicism, post-Colonialism, and emigration, to name three.

Rainbow's end

In the spring of 2000, a group of producers in Los Angeles discovered they could not raise the capital they needed to mount a production of *Finian's Rainbow,* a musical about dancing sharecroppers, Irish rogues, and leprechauns. Instead, they presented a production that they touted as a different sort of Irish experience: a low-key, quirky musical based on James Joyce's *The Dead,* which had enjoyed a successful run on Broad-way the winter before, despite mixed reviews.

The Great White Way is among the New York City institutions of which Irish Americans can truthfully say: "We built the place." The orig-inal American song and dance man, George M. Cohan, gave light and Eu-gene O'Neill lent shade to the twentieth-century American theater. Plays by George Bernard Shaw, Sean O'Casey, Samuel Beckett, Brendan Behan, Tom Murphy, and Brian Friel preceded more recent productions of London hits by young Irish writers Martin McDonagh and Conor McPherson to Broadway.

What was unusual about *The Dead* (leaving aside the fact that it is James Joyce put to music) was that its Broadway run overlapped not only with *Riverdance,* but also with a revival of O'Neill's *A Moon for the Misbegotten.* This was an eclectic trio of Irish shows.

In theater, music, literature, and art, "Irish culture has gone from monophonic to stereophonic," as *Philadelphia Daily News* reporter Frank Dougherty put it. From theater, to Celtic music festivals, to Irish fairs, to Bloomsday readings, to rock music, there are more routes to Irish culture and more complex renderings of it at the outset of the twenty-first century than there were even ten years before, when the biggest Irish gatherings in most places were St. Patrick's Day parades.

Calvin Trillin once compared New York's Columbus Day parade with the city's annual St. Patrick's Day pageant. "In selecting their grand marshals, the Italians go straight for glory, no questions asked. In 1979, when the grand marshal of the St. Patrick's Day parade was John Sweeney, then president of a union local that represented building cleaners, the grand marshal of the Columbus Day parade was Frank Sinatra. In 1980, the Irish had William Burke, a Transit Authority employee who had been executive secretary of the parade for many years; the Italians had Luciano Pavarotti. The Columbus Day parade is regularly led up Fifth Avenue by such celebrated Italian Americans as Yogi Berra and Lee Iacocca." In the late 1980s, while the Ancient Order of Hibernians were locked in fierce battle against the threatening forces of change that would eventually allow Dorothy Hayden Cuddahy, a pillar of the organized Irish American community, to become the first woman to lead the parade, Sophia Loren was grand marshal one year for the Italians.

Relentlessly anachronistic, the New York pageant remains pious, proper, dour, and defensive while Irish culture on both sides of the Atlantic goes through remarkable flux.

The "New Irish" influence has lent great vitality to Irish American culture (see Chapter 8). In the eighties and nineties New York bars and cafes "like Sin-e and An Beal Bocht became amazingly rich centers for young Irish people," said writer Helena Mulkerns. "The sheer numbers of New Irish in America—not just in New York and Boston, but in San Francisco, Chicago, New Orleans, Philadelphia, Miami, and Los Angeles—made it hard for them not to have some kind of impact. In places outside the bigger cities, sleepy local Irish bars and Irish festivals were suddenly being shaken up by this new generation of emigrants," whose influence has been diverse. There is, for instance, "a full-blown, all-Irish motorcycle club in Chicago called Na Fíanna"—after the warriors of the ancient Celtic Sagas. So if you're driving in and around Chicago, you might see a flock of fine Celtic knot logos flying along the freeway—on the backs of black leather jackets!

In mainstream American popular culture, "you still have the leprechaun mugs and the shamrock dish-cloths, but on the other hand, you have original crafts, and new ways of using the images," she continued. There has also been a tremendous "crossover influence: People from both backgrounds were able to create new work taking aspects from both cultures," from the band Black 47, formed by Wexford-born Larry Kirwan and New York police officer Chris Byrne, to *Riverdance*, " which came together as a result of collaboration between Irish American dancers and an Irish composer and producers."

And unlike some native Irish, who would dismiss such a notion, Mulkerns noted that "Irish America has its own separate culture, that native Irish may not always like, but it should be respected," said Mulkerns. "People hate Irish Spring soap commercials, but if that bothers you, go read Mary Gordon, William Kennedy, Alice McDermott, Michael Stephens, or see a play by Eugene O'Neill or a film by John Ford."

Irish ambassador to the United States Sean O'Huiginn sees culture as the sustaining link between Ireland and Irish America as well. In Irish county societies that were gathering places for many who immigrated in the 1950s, "you'd get a cross-section of professionals, surgeons, executives, financial people, and so on and we certainly had a strong sense that in that room was a constituency for all of the things we were trying to do in Ireland. And yet the problem was that most of the surgeons and high-status people were there for mom and pop, and when one's mom and pop passed away, their connection with the traditional society would then cease.

"The traditional county societies were very strong bonds for as long as the people who came from Ireland were alive, for as long as there were political links. But what is left when those people pass away is essentially a cultural affinity with Ireland, using culture in the widest sense, not just with the upper-case C. I think that the health of the relationship between Ireland and Irish America will depend to a very large extent on mobilizing that cultural interest, which is the successor to the personal relationship."

Remembering, forgetting

The urge to put an upbeat spin on the Irish past and resistance to those who do not runs deep in Irish America, even in efforts to memorialize experience.

Take Boston's Famine Memorial. A figurative work in bronze, the execution of which might politely be called unimpressive, the monument, according to its official description, consists of "two life-size sculptures, one depicting a family leaving Ireland's shores, impoverished and desperate, and another depicting a family arriving in Boston, filled with hope and determination."

Critics of the memorial were, predictably, accused of "elitism"—even anti-Irish bias. The sculpture is not a populist tribute. It is a sentimental if not ridiculous rendering of what happened to the starving, diseased, and destitute refugees who had the misfortune to make their way to Boston following their nightmarish journey out of Ireland in the mid-nineteenth century. As even a glancing knowledge of Boston history makes clear, it would be quite some time after the Famine Irish settled in Boston that their descendants would have reason to brim with hope and determination (see Chapter 2).

The two blockbusters of the late-nineties Irish arts boom caught the ambivalence in the American embrace of things Irish quite clearly: There was *Riverdance,* an upbeat muddle of quasi-Celtic folk art, multiculti fuzziness, and feel-good American showbiz; and the bleak, blackly humorous memoir *Angela's Ashes.*

As millions now know, McCourt's Ireland is no place to take Kathleen. His Irish eyes aren't smiling, and his recollections of Irish life in the old days in New York and the Emerald Isle are wholly unsentimental, starting from the first page: "Worse than the ordinary miserable childhood is the miserable Irish childhood, and worse yet is the miserable Irish Catholic childhood. . . . the poverty; the shiftless loquacious father; the pious defeated mother moaning by the fire."

A vocal sector of Irish Americans was ill at ease with McCourt's book from the get-go. Some insisted it was self-pitying—a damning indictment in a subculture in which it is considered a sign of character to grit one's teeth and get on with it (whatever "it" may be). There were objections to the author's candid portrayal of Ireland, the Catholic Church, and his family; contentions that he brought shame on others by making the Irish look bad.

The Irish have a well-earned reputation as begrudgers, and the longer *Angela's Ashes* stayed on the bestseller list, the more people attacked it. To hear some of the writer's more vehement detractors tell it, Limerick in the 1940s bore a remarkable resemblance to Shangri-La.

Fans of the book far outnumbered naysayers, though, and McCourt became a celebrity (a sure sign of success in America). People surrounded him at readings and public appearances. Strangers stopped him on the street, in airports, at White House receptions to congratulate him, thank him, or tell him: "That's my mother's story," or "That's my grandfather's story," or "I always thought my family was completely dysfunctional, now I know they were just Irish."

Angela's Ashes is an Irish American saga, the likes of which few had heard told before. It evokes the Ireland so many Americans' parents and grandparents left and never talked about; the sad places behind the picture postcard set of John Ford's *The Quiet Man*. It helps explain the lineage of dour censoriousness of the Church; the nastiness of overburdened, underappreciated women; the humor that makes getting through it possible.

Many Irish immigrants in America put the past entirely behind them; in that peculiarly Irish way, they coped with pain and hurt and bad memory by refusing to talk about it. For every grandfather with splendid stories and songs about Ireland's heroic past, there are many more grandmothers, uncles, and aunts who were grimly silent about the money they sent back to Cork; who didn't want to remember the family farm lost in Kerry.

Stoicism and denial take their toll. "On the intensely personal level, every Irish family knows what it is to feel a shadow falling across what should have been a happy table, the father's fist banging down, the bottle upended once too often, the mother rolling her eyes in a silent offering for the poor souls somewhere else," James Carroll has written. "What about the poor souls here?

"The Irish learned not to know what happened to them," writes Carroll. "In their determination to put the savage experience behind them, the survivors of the Famine denied its relevance. Those who emigrated began thinking of Ireland as a mythic place, and their children and grandchildren learned to think of it as a kind of lost paradise. Blarney-struck American entertainers and politicians exploited the fantasy."

But just when a legacy seemed largely reduced to Eiresatz, an excuse to draw ideological lines in the shifting sands of the culture wars, a new sense of what it means to be Irish in America began to emerge.

Much of the interest in contemporary Irish American culture is driven by those who rue the fact that their grandparents never talked about Ireland or had no interest in going back there. And those who are seeking alternatives to the Oirishry honed by their forebears. The waning influence of the Catholic Church, the vibrancy of today's Ireland, and the sophistication, self-awareness, and self-absorption of Americans born after World War II have all fueled the energetic interest in things Irish in recent years.

———

It is truth as well as cliché to observe that the Irish have been storytellers since the time of the Celts. The Irish American saga told most often is a tale of laughter and forgetting. It is suffused with sentimentality, that cloying sensation that is neither thought nor feeling, and selective in what it recalls.

Irish America's is a story of many splendors. It is also a parable of shame about the past, of secrets kept to endure and deny that shame, and of a sometimes sad singularity of vision. It is a tale of generosity and self-limitation; a people with a remarkable instinct for survival and a culturally inbred mistrust of their own success; a gregarious people who shrink from talk about themselves.

It is time to remember; to recognize; to render.

Notes

Chapter One

Interviews contributing to this chapter:
Thomas N. Brown, November 18, 1998, Cambridge, Massachusetts
Timothy Meagher, January 12, 1999, by telephone from Washington, D.C.
Garrett O'Connor, March 8, 1997, by telephone from New York
Niall O'Dowd, October 13, 1999, New York City

Major written sources consulted for this chapter:
Beatty, *The Rascal King*
Brown, *Irish-American Nationalism*
Callahan, *The Big Book of American Irish Culture*
Callahan, "The Joys of Being Irish"
Clark, *Hibernia America*
Curran, *Hibernian Green on the Silver Screen*
Curtis, *Apes and Angels*
Fanning, *The Irish Voice in America*
Glazier, *The Encyclopedia of the Irish in America*
Golway, *Irish Rebel*
Goodwin, *The Fitzgeralds and the Kennedys*
Hayden, *Irish Hunger*
Kahn, *The Merry Partners*
Moynihan, "The Irish"
O'Connor, *The Last Hurrah*
Quinn, *Banished Children of Eve*
Shannon, *The American Irish*
Williams, *'Twas Only an Irishman's Dream*
Woodham-Smith, *The Great Hunger*

Pages 15–18

The Leo Burnett ads were part of a March 1978 ad campaign for Schlitz, according to the Hartman Center for Sales, Advertising, and Marketing History, Duke University.

For a description of the Ancient Order of Hibernians and the Abbey Theatre, see Shannon, *The American Irish*, 264.

On the arrival of the Famine Irish in the new world, see Shannon, *The American Irish*, 27–41, and Clark, *Hibernia America.*

A stage Irish story, pages 18–21

Thomas Nast on the "politicized Celt as a menace" is from Curtis, *Apes and Angels*, 65; the "cross between a professional boxer and an orangutan" is from 58.

For descriptions of Irish minstrelsy, see Williams, *'Twas Only an Irishman's Dream*, 65–66; Callahan, *The Big Book of American Irish Culture*, 17, 25; and Peter Quinn's novel of Civil War–era New York, *Banished Children of Eve.*

Williams writes about Paddy Power in *'Twas Only an Irishman's Dream*, 66–68; Paddy and Sambo, 83–85; and vaudeville, 120.

The description of the New York St. Patrick's Day parade in the 1850s is from John Ridge, a historian of the group, "The Long and Winding Road: Two Centuries of Parades," *New York Post*, March 16, 1999.

"The Celt [as] a being spiritually superior" is from Brown, *Irish-American Nationalism*, 132.

The "fighting Irish" caricature is from Shannon, *The American Irish*, 144.

For descriptions of late-nineteenth-century theater, see John P. Harrington, "Irish in Theater," in Glazier, *The Encyclopedia of the Irish in America*, and Kahn, *The Merry Partners.*

On Boucicault, see Kahn, *The Merry Partners*, 66–67, and Williams, *'Twas Only an Irishman's Dream*, 98–100. The Henry James quote is from Harrington, *The Irish in Theatre*, 901. Williams discusses Harrigan and Hart on 158–68; Dan Mulligan's lament appears on 168. Callahan traces the trajectory of nineteenth-century entertainers through vaudeville, silent movies, and musicals in both the *Big Book of American Irish Culture* and "The Joys of Being Irish."

Defining sentimental style, pages 21–24

The account of Rose Kennedy at the Boston opening of *Playboy* is in Goodwin, *The Fitzgeralds and the Kennedys*, 239–42.

Devoy's reaction to Synge is in Golway, *Irish Rebel*, 185–86.

Carroll on the Famine immigrants' memory of Ireland is from Hayden, *Irish Hunger*, 205–11.

The description of Olcott draws on Williams, *'Twas Only an Irishman's Dream*, 213–16, and Fielder, "Chauncey Olcott."

Step dancing across the silver screen, pages 24–27

On urban Irish American characteristics, see Quinn, "Looking for Jimmy," and Moynihan, "The Irish," 245–50.

Curran's *Hibernian Green* considers movie priests. Charles R. Morris discusses Catholics, movie priests, and Hollywood in *American Catholic*, 196–209.

Assimilation Valhalla, pages 27–29
"Transmuted the dab of bad in Skeffington" is from Beatty, *The Rascal King*, 516.
What's Irish? pages 29–32
O'Neill is quoted in Shannon, *The American Irish*, 278; Wilson on Fitzgerald, 235.
"Derision of the hifalutin" is from Moynihan, "The Irish," 247–48.
Fanning on Mary Gordon is from Bayor and Meagher, *The New York Irish*, 509–10.
The description of Farrell's, Breslin's, Gordon's, and Quindlen's work as "disturbing, openly hostile, or decidedly ambiguous" is from Coffey, *The Irish in America*, 215.
Renderings dark, but not deep, pages 32–33
Three Screenplays by Edward Burns, p. 6
Sean Kelly and Rosemary Rogers, *How to Be Irish (Even If You Already Are)* (New York: Villard, 1999).
The description of the Dublin St. Patrick's Day parade is from Kevin Cullen, "Irish Make Holiday Green Again: Dublin Reinvents St. Patrick's Day," *Boston Globe*, March 17, 1998.

Chapter Two
Interviews contributing to this chapter:
Thomas N. Brown, November 18, 1998, Cambridge, Massachusetts
Edward Burke, December 1, 1998, Chicago
Danny Cassidy, February 15, 1999, San Francisco
Frank Dougherty, July 17, 1999, by telephone from Philadelphia
Jane Duffin, July 19, 1999, Philadelphia
Jack and Kathleen Flynn, May 20, 1999, New Jersey
Bob Gessler, July 23, 1999, by telephone from Philadelphia
Marty Gleason, February 2, 1999, Chicago
Patrick Goggins, February 18, 1999, San Francisco
Dan Hardin, February 2, 1999, Chicago
Edward Harrington, February 16, 1999, San Francisco
Conor Howard, Eddie Stack, February 17, 1999, San Francisco
James McBride, February 17, 1999, San Francisco
Lawrence J. McCaffrey, December 2, 1998, Evanston, Illinois
Eoin McKiernan, January 13, 1999, by telephone from St. Paul
Kevin Mullen, Michael Lennon, Maureen Lennon, February 17, 1999, San Francisco
Thomas O'Gorman, December 1, 1998, Chicago
Sean Prendeville, February 18, 1999, San Francisco
Peter Quinn, October 1998, by telephone from New York City

Matthew V. Storin, December 22, 1998, Boston
Major written sources consulted for this chapter:
Amory, *The Proper Bostonians*
Barnes, *Irish-American Landmarks*
Bayor, Ronald H., and Timothy J. Meagher, eds., *The New York Irish*
Beatty, *The Rascal King*
Birmingham, *Real Lace: America's Irish Rich*
Blessing, "Irish"
Brown, *Irish-American Nationalism*
Burchell, *The San Francisco Irish*
Clark, *Hibernia America*
Dowling, *California*
Emmons, *The Butte Irish*
Fisher, *Dr. America*
Glazier, *The Encyclopedia of the Irish in America*
Goodwin, *The Fitzgeralds and the Kennedys*
Greeley, *That Most Distressful Nation*
———, *The Irish Americans*
Harrington, *Fragments of the Century*
McCaffrey, *The Irish Catholic Diaspora in America*
———, *Textures of Irish America*
——— et al., *The Irish in Chicago*
Miller, *Emigrants and Exiles*
Morris, *American Catholic*
Moynihan, "The Irish"
O'Connor, *The Boston Irish*
O'Connor, *The Last Hurrah*
O'Gorman, "The Chicago Irish"
O'Hanlon, *The New Irish Americans*
Padden and Sullivan, *May the Road Rise to Meet You*
Shannon, *The American Irish*

Pages 37–41

The "tidbits" are culled from Barnes, *Irish-American Landmarks;* Glazier, *The Encyclopedia of the Irish in America;* and Coffey and Golway, *The Irish in America.* The Harrington quotes and the biographical information are from his *Fragments of the Century,* 3–17.

The Dooley description is from Fisher, *Dr. America.*

Data on westward migration are taken from Blessing, "Irish"; Greeley, *The American Irish,* 131–48; and interviews with McCaffrey and Brown. Urban population figures are from 1990 U.S. census, cited in the Associated Press.

The observations on the Boston Irish are based on my twenty years as a reporter in

Boston. Being female, I was not at the Clover Club gathering, but two men who attended confirmed the discussions of the *Boston Globe* and Bulger's crack about the Irish consul.

Gold Coast greenery, pages 41–45

Retired San Francisco police officers and amateur historians Kevin Mullen and Michael Lennon and librarian Maureen Lennon gave me a tour of Irish San Francisco on February 17, 1999. Sean Prendeville, Danny Cassidy, and Patrick Goggins were also helpful in orienting me in the Bay Area.

San Francisco history is drawn from Shannon, *The American Irish;* Burchell, *The San Francisco Irish;* Barnes, *Irish-American Landmarks;* and Birmingham, *Real Lace.*

Statistics on immigration to San Francisco are from Burchell and the 1990 U.S. census.

Information on Butte is from an interview with Ed Harrington; Emmons, *The Butte Irish;* Emmons's entry on Montana in Glazier, *Encyclopedia of the Irish in America,* 625–28; and a telephone interview with Peter Quinn.

Icons and other influences, pages 45–48

This section draws heavily on Barnes, *Irish-American Landmarks,* and Padden and Sullivan, *May the Road Rise to Meet You.*

Fintan O'Toole's "The Many Stories of Billy the Kid" appeared in *The New Yorker,* December 28, 1998, and January 4, 1999. Lawrence McCaffrey and Patrick Goggins, cofounders of the Irish-Mexican Association, filled me in on the legacy of the San Patricios.

Northern Territories, pages 48–50

Information on the Civil War veterans in the West is primarily from Glazier, *Encyclopedia of the Irish in America.* Meagher's plan is suggested in Emmons, *The Butte Irish.* The account of John Ireland's attempted resettlement of Connemarans is primarily from Morris, *American Catholic.*

For the history of St. Paul and Minneapolis, see James Silas Rogers's entry on St. Paul and Minneapolis in Glazier, *Encyclopedia of the Irish in America,* 822–24.

Tales of two cities, pages 50–56

The quote from *The Proper Bostonians* is on page 1 of Amory's book.

For Chicago history, I relied on conversations with Edward Burke and Thomas O'Gorman over a two-day period in December 1998; the McCaffrey interview and e-mails from McCaffrey; and McCaffrey et al., *The Irish in Chicago.*

I spent the weekend of November 20–22, 1998, in and around Notre Dame, where I spoke with faculty, administrators, and subway alumni and a few university officials. I spent the day at the Catholic Super Bowl between BC and Notre Dame on the BC campus, November 7, 1998. The BC data are from the Alumni Office. For the record, I am a graduate of Boston College.

The history of Boston draws primarily on Shannon, *The American Irish;* Beatty, *The*

Rascal King; Goodwin, *The Fitzgeralds and the Kennedys;* and O'Connor, *The Boston Irish.*

The *Harper's* quote is in Beatty, *Rascal King,* 260.

Background on the Kennedys is from Goodwin, *The Fitzgeralds and the Kennedys,* and Birmingham, *Real Lace.*

In "the city" and its environs, pages 56–60

Jack Flynn gave me a tour of Irish New York. The New York section draws heavily on John Ridge, "New York City," in Glazier, *Encyclopedia of the Irish in America,* 678–86; on Bayor and Meagher, *The New York Irish,* particularly "An End and a Beginning" by David M. Reims, 419–38. Statistics are on 421.

Moynihan, "The Irish," 217–87.

Census figures are from Bayor and Meagher, *The New York Irish,* 421.

Music and more, pages 60–62

For this section, I relied on Glazier, *Encyclopedia of the Irish in America,* 761–66; David Montgomery, "The Labor Movement," in Glazier, 525–31; Kevin Kenny, "The Molly Maguires," in Glazier, 623–24; and Joseph J. Kelly, "Pennsylvania," 761–67.

It's a great day—almost everywhere, pages 62–63

For Boston's St. Patrick's Day parade, see "In Southie, Record Crowd Loves a Parade," *Boston Globe,* March 15, 1999. The Savannah, Georgia, Chamber of Commerce tracks comparative St. Patrick's Day parade statistics; the New Orleans parade description is from Padden and Sullivan, *May the Road Rise to Meet You.*

John J. ("Wacko") Hurley and the South Boston Allied War Veterans Council appealed a 1994 Massachusetts Supreme Judicial Court ruling requiring them to include the Irish-American Gay, Lesbian, and Bisexual Group of Boston in their parade. In a decision written by Justice David Souter, the federal appeals court ruled that "the issue in this case is whether Massachusetts may require private citizens who organize a parade to include among the marchers a group imparting a message the organizers do not wish to convey. We hold that such a mandate violates the First Amendment."

Chapter Three

Interviews contributing to this chapter:

Marjorie Farrell, March 4, 1999, Cambridge, Massachusetts
Jerome Frese, November 21, 1998, South Bend, Indiana
Nora Gainer, January 30, 1999, Chicago
Mary Jo George, February 1, 1999, Chicago
Andrew Greeley, December 2, 1999, Boston
Tom Hayden, February 20, 1999, Los Angeles
Matthew Lennon, February 7, 1999, by telephone from Seattle
Michael Lennon, February 17, 1999, San Francisco

Timothy Lennon, February 2, 1999, Chicago

Lawrence J. McCaffrey, December 2, 1998, Evanston, Illinois

Monica McGoldrick, December 21, 1998, by telephone from New Brunswick, New Jersey

Rosemary McGrath, March 16, 1999, New York City

David McLaughlin, January 5, 1999, by telephone from Los Angeles

Jonathan Mooney, May 7, 1999, by telephone from Providence, Rhode Island

Kathleen O'Toole, January 11, 1999, Newton, Massachusetts

Tim Phillips, February 7, 1999, Boston, Massachusetts

John and Marge Scanlon, December 3, 1998, Chicago

John Shea, January 26, 1999, New York City

Matthew V. Storin, December 22, 1998, Boston

Major written sources consulted for this chapter:

Greeley, *The Irish Americans*

———, *That Most Distressful Nation*

Greeley and McCready, "The Transmission of Cultural Heritages"

McGoldrick, "Irish Families"

Miller, *Emigrants and Exiles*

Sheed, Wilfrid, *The Morning After*

Waters, *Ethnic Options*

Pages 65–69

Alice McDermott's acceptance remarks quoted in the *Boston Globe* and *New York Times,* November 19, 1998.

Nancy McMillan Gaines, my editor at *Boston Business* magazine, coined the term CWASP when she and I were debating shorthand terms to describe upper-middle-class Irish Catholics, the subject of an article I wrote for the spring 1986 issue of the magazine. We pronounced it "quasp."

Andrew Greeley did pioneering surveys at the National Opinion Research Center (NORC) at the University of Chicago in the 1970s that showed that, "in terms of education, income, and occupational achievement, Irish Catholics are the most successful gentile group in American Society." NORC data from the 1996 General Social Survey (GSS) show that, in average years of education completed among white ethnics, Jews ranked highest, with 15.37 years, followed by WASPs (13.93) and Irish Catholics (13.88). The University of Michigan's 1996 National Election Study (NES) showed Jews with the highest education level followed by Irish Catholics and then WASPs.

The GSS data show Jews with the highest median household incomes ($61,250), followed by Irish Catholics and Italian Catholics ($45,000), WASPs ($37,500), and Irish non-Catholics ($32,500). The NES data essentially concur, though

Italian Catholics rank slightly higher. The occupational prestige ranking put Jews first, followed by WASPs, Italian Catholics, Irish non-Catholics, and Irish Catholics.

NES data show that 27.3 percent of Irish Catholics who responded to the survey held executive/managerial jobs and that Irish Catholics are overrepresented in that job category. In addition, 22 percent of Irish Catholics held professional/specialty occupations and were tied with WASPs for second (after Jews) in that category.

Murphy quote is from *Irish America* magazine, November 1995.

So many shades of green, pages 69–71

Dennis Duggan said this when I met him while he was covering the St. Patrick's Day festivities in New York City for *Newsday,* March 17, 1999.

Look both ways, pages 71–75

McGoldrick's comments are from McGoldrick, "Irish Families," 545–46.

Anna Quindlen's comments are from the *New York Times,* March 14, 1991.

Mary Gordon's comments are from my telephone interview with her for a story I wrote for the *Boston Globe,* March 12, 1997.

Unlikely endurance, pages 75–77

O'Connor, *The Boston Irish,* xvii.

Miller, *Emigrants and Exiles,* 498.

Dunne, *Harp,* 27.

Lack of passion play, pages 77–79

Accounts of the Boston College–Margaret Thatcher flap are based on reports by Kevin Cullen in the *Boston Globe* in March 1995, background conversations with officials and former officials of Boston College, and conversations with BC alumni (of which I am one).

Wilfrid Sheed, *The Morning After: Essays and Reviews* (New York: Farrar, Straus & Giroux, 1971), 129.

Going along, getting along, all the way, pages 79–80

The discussion of Irish occupations is based on Moynihan, "The Irish"; surveys in *Irish America* magazine; and various interviews.

The quotation about banking is from Moynihan, "The Irish," 255.

Tom Wolfe, *Bonfire of the Vanities.*

And who would you be? pages 80–83

Pete Hamill's comments are from my telephone interview with him for a story I wrote for the *Boston Globe,* March 12, 1997, and from his *A Drinking Life.*

Dennis Clark's comment appears in various places, including Bayor and Meagher, *The New York Irish,* 533.

Statistics on Irish Americans in college are from the General Social Survey and the National Election Study. See note at the beginning of this chapter.

Paradox lost, and found, pages 84–85

Demographic data are from the General Social Survey and the National Election Study. See note at the beginning of this chapter.

Michael Hout was cited in my interview with Andrew Greeley, December 2, 1999; Glazier, *Encyclopedia of the Irish in America,* 3; Paul Green quote appeared in Dirk Johnson, "In Illinois, It's the Political Life for Riley, Gilhooley, et al.," *New York Times Week in Review,* March 14, 1999, 2.

Chapter Four

Interviews contributing to this chapter:

Thomas N. Brown, November 18, 1998, Cambridge, Massachusetts

Danny Cassidy, February 15, 1999, San Francisco

James T. Fisher, February 9, 1999, by telephone from St. Louis

Nora Gainer, January 31, 1999, Chicago

Mary Jo George, February 1, 1999, Chicago

Karen Kennelly, CSJ, July 23, 1999, by telephone from Los Angeles

Matthew Lennon, February 7, 1999, by telephone from Seattle

Monica McGoldrick, December 21, 1998, by telephone from New Brunswick, New Jersey

Janet Nolan, January 27, 1999, by telephone from Chicago

Mary Pat O'Connor, January 31, 1999, Chicago

Joan O'Donnell, July 21, 1999, Pound Ridge, New York

Catherine Early O'Neill, May 20, 1999, Montville, New Jersey

Kathleen O'Toole, January 11, 1999, Newton, Massachusetts

Beatrice Higgins Quinn, May 20, 1999, Far Rockaway, New York

Peter Quinn, October 12, 1999, New York City

Marge Scanlon, December 3, 1998, Chicago

Robert White, March 16, 1999, New York City

Reference works consulted for this chapter:

Notable American Women: The Modern Period, edited by Barbara Sicherman et al. (Cambridge: Harvard University Press, Belknap Press, 1980)

Famous American Women: A Biographical Dictionary from Colonial Times to the Present, edited by Robert McHenry (New York: Dover, 1983)

Mary Kenney O'Sullivan Papers

Leonora O'Reilly Papers

Women's Trade League Union Papers

Major written sources consulted for this chapter:

Bayor and Meagher, *The New York Irish*

Blessing, "Irish"

Cullinan, *House of Gold*

Diner, *Erin's Daughters*

Fanning, *The Irish Voice in America*

Farrell, *Studs Lonigan*

Fielder, "Chauncey Olcott"

Gordon, *Final Payments*

Greeley, *The Irish Americans*

———, *That Most Distressful Nation*

Howard, *Bridgeport Bus*

Kennedy, *Ironweed*

———, *Very Old Bones*

McCourt, *The Irish . . . and how they got that way*

McDermott, *Charming Billy*

———, *At Weddings and Wakes*

McGoldrick, "Irish Families"

Quinn, *An Irish Wake*

Takaki, *A Different Mirror*

Williams, *'Twas Only an Irishman's Dream*

Pages 87–90

I overheard this conversation about Irish women at a preview performance of Frank McCourt's *The Irish . . . and how they got that way* at the Wilbur Theatre, Boston, March 29, 1998.

For a discussion of Chauncey Olcott and Irish music on Tin Pan Alley, see Williams, *'Twas Only an Irishman's Dream,* and Fielder, "Chauncey Olcott."

For Irish American mothers, see Greeley, *That Most Distressful Nation* and *The Irish Americans;* Diner, *Erin's Daughters in America;* Fanning, *The Irish Voice in America;* and McGoldrick, "Irish Families."

For academics' lack of attention to Irish American women, see Weaver, "Who Can Find a Valiant Woman?" and Hoy, "Walking Nuns."

Rediscovering Bridget, pages 90–92

I attended the inaugural Brigid Award luncheon at the Four Seasons Hotel in Chicago, February 1, 1999.

The discussion of Irish servant girls draws primarily from Diner, *Erin's Daughters;* Blessing, "The Irish," 531; Takaki, *A Different Mirror,* 154—60. I have read and heard a few versions of the Bridget and the dust story. Frank McCourt told this one at the cast party following opening night of *The Irish . . . and how they got that way* in Boston, April 1, 1998.

Census and demographic data are quoted in Meagher, "Sweet Good Mothers." Statistic on domestic servants in New York is from Blessing, "The Irish." Statistic about domestic service in 1900 is from Diner, *Erin's Daughters,* 89. McCaffrey's comments on "sober and responsible" Irish women are in Bayor and Meagher, *The New York Irish,* 216.

Taking leave, pages 92–94

For women in nineteenth-century Ireland, see Meagher, "Sweet Good Mothers"; Diner, *Erin's Daughters;* Owens, *Smashing Times;* and Gibbons, *Critical Conditions.*

The account of Amelia Dunne Hookaway is from Janet Nolan, in Skerrett, *At the Crossroads.*

Rabble-rousing toward respectability, pages 95–98

Biographical information about Mother Jones is from *Autobiography of Mother Jones,* excerpted in Kearns, *Motherland.* On Irish women as union organizers, see Diner, *Erin's Daughters,* 99–105; David Montgomery, "The Labor Movement," in Glazier, *The Encyclopedia of the Irish in America,* 525–31; and the Mary Kenney O'Sullivan and Leonora O'Reilly Papers.

The description of the activities of Irish Catholic nuns is from Diner, *Erin's Daughters,* 130–37.

For discussions of women's suffragist activities and their role in the nationalist movement in Ireland, see Kiberd, *Inventing Ireland,* 395–410, and Owens, *Smashing Times.* The description of the New York Women Pickets and nationalism is based entirely on Joe Doyle, "Striking for Ireland on the New York Docks," in Bayor and Meagher, *The New York Irish,* 357–73.

Women's work, pages 98–100

My discussion of Irish American women and suffrage is based on interviews with Janet Nolan and Lawrence McCaffrey and on Diner, *Erin's Daughters;* Weaver, "Who Can Find a Valiant Woman?"; Mary Kenney O'Sullivan Papers; and Leonora O'Reilly Papers.

John Boyle O'Reilly quotations are from the Boston *Pilot,* January 14, 1871, 3, cited in Diner, *Erin's Daughters.*

Cahill, *How the Irish Saved Civilization:* on Medb, 71–78, 97; on Brigid, 175.

Gibbons, *Critical Conditions,* 118.

The ascent of the sainted mother, pages 101–8

Miller, *Emigrants and Exiles,* 482.

For widowhood and Irish life expectancy in the late nineteenth century, see Blessing, "Irish"; Diner, *Erin's Daughters.*

Diner, *Erin's Daughters;* Fanning, *The Irish Voice in America;* Kiberd, *Inventing Ireland;* and Greeley, *That Most Distressful Nation* discuss spheres of authority.

"The Kitchen Prayer" as quoted here appears in Marina Warner, *Alone of All Her Sex* (New York: Vintage, 1983).

MacDonald, *All Souls*, 1818.
The lace curtain rises, pages 108–12
On lace curtain values, see Shannon, *The American Irish*, 142.
Fanning discusses the "distorting obsessions" of motherhood and respectability
in *The Irish Voice in America*, 271–76; his analysis of *House of Gold* is on
335–41.
On the power of Irish women in the family, see Greeley, *That Most Distressful Nation*, 110; the unflattering comparison of Irish and Jewish mothers is on 135.
See Kiberd, *Inventing Ireland*, "Mothers and Daughters," 395–410, and "Fathers
and Sons," 380–94.
The Irish demographic data are from Blessing, "Irish."
Recording a legacy, pages 112–14
Kennedy family history is from Goodwin, *The Fitzgeralds and the Kennedys:* on Bridget Murphy Kennedy, 68–69; on Rose Kennedy and Wellesley, 153–55. The
quotes from books on Kennedy women—*Jacqueline Kennedy Onassis: A Portrait
of Her Private Years;* Jerry Oppenheimer, *The Other Mrs. Kennedy, Ethel Skakel
Kennedy: An American Drama of Power, Privilege, and American Politics,* and
Laurence Leamer, *The Kennedy Women: A Saga of An American Family*—are
from a review of those books, "Great Hair, Great Teeth, Great Public Relations,"
by Maureen Dowd, *New York Times Book Review,* October 9, 1994.
"The Spirit of Irish Women" by Jean Kennedy Smith appeared on the *Boston Globe*
op-ed page, March 17, 1998; Kevin Cullen, *Boston Globe,* July 2, 1998.

Chapter Five
Interviews contributing to this chapter:
Kathleen Corrigan (pseudonym)
Pete Hamill, March 1997, by telephone from New York City
Frank Malley (pseudonym)
Garrett O'Connor, March 8, 1997, by telephone from New York City
Joan O'Donnell, July 21, 1999, Pound Ridge, New York
Bill Regan, July 12, 1999, by telephone from Malden, Massachusetts
Dermot Walsh, December 17, 1999, by telephone from Dublin

Major written sources consulted for this chapter:
Curtis, *Apes and Angels*
Greeley, *That Most Distressful Nation*
———, *The Rise to Money and Power*
Hamill, *A Drinking Life*
Kahn, *The Merry Partners*

Kiberd, *Inventing Ireland*

McGoldrick, "Irish Families"

Moynihan, "The Irish"

Shannon, *The American Irish*

Stivers, *A Hair of the Dog*

Vaillant, *The Natural History of Alcoholism Revisited*

Walsh, "Alcohol and Ireland"

Walsh, "The Kennedy Way of Grief"

Woodham-Smith, *The Great Hunger*

Zola, "Culture and Symptoms"

"Alcohol and Society: How Culture Influences the Way People Drink." Stanton Peele Addiction Web site. <http://www.peele.net/lib/sociocul.html>.

Corrigan, Eileen M., and Shane Butler. "Irish Alcoholic Women in Treatment: Early Findings." *The International Journal of the Addictions* 26:3 (1991): 281–92.

Donovan, James M. "An Etiologic Model of Alcoholism." *American Journal of Psychiatry* 143 (1986): 1–11.

Greenslade, Liam, Maggie Pearson, and Moss Madden. "A Good Man's Fault: Alcohol and Irish People at Home and Abroad." *Alcohol & Alcoholism* 30:4 (1995): 407–17.

O'Connor, Garrett, M.D. "Alcoholism in American Irish Catholics: Cultural Stereotype vs. Clinical Reality." *American Academy of Addiction Psychiatry* 5:2 (Spring 1996).

———. "Recognising and Healing Malignant Shame: A Statement about the Urgent Need for Psychological and Spiritual Recovery from the Effects of Colonialism in Ireland," unpublished manuscript, June 6, 1995.

Orsi, Robert A. " 'Mildred, Is It Fun to Be a Cripple?' The Culture of Suffering in Mid-Twentieth Century American Catholicism." *The South Atlantic Quarterly* 93:3 (Summer 1994).

Pages 117–19

The researchers' quote is from B. Roberts and J. K. Myers, "Religion, National Origin, Immigration and Mental Illness," *American Journal of Psychiatry* 110 (1954): 759–64, quoted in McGoldrick, "Irish Families," 55.

Ethnic drinking differences are from Greeley, *That Most Distressful Nation,* and Glazier, *The Encyclopedia of the Irish in America,* 3.

Pete Hamill's comments are from my telephone interview with him for a story I wrote for the *Boston Globe,* March 12, 1997.

O'Connor's comments on alcoholism as a public health problem are from O'Connor, "Alcoholism in American Irish Catholics." Comparable rates of native Irish and American Irish alcoholism are discussed in Stivers, *A Hair of the Dog,* and Walsh, "Alcohol and Ireland."

Vaillant's study and observations are in *The Natural History of Alcoholism Revisited,* 99, 46–119; see also "Alcohol and Society" Web site.

Traits and traditions, pages 119–24

European Economic Union figures, 1999.

The National Health and Lifestyle Surveys.

The post-Famine Irish experience is discussed in Stivers, *A Hair of the Dog;* Shannon, *The American Irish;* Moynihan, "The Irish"; Shannon, *The American Irish,* and other historical sources; and Callahan, *The Big Book of American Irish Culture* and "The Joys of Being Irish."

Silences and shame, pages 124–26

O'Connor's description of today's Irish Catholic alcoholics is from O'Connor, "Alcoholism in American Irish Catholics."

Suffering and swallowed words, pages 126–30

Alice McDermott, *Charming Billy,* 196.

Walsh's discussion of stoicism and alcoholism is from "The Kennedy Way of Grief."

The Massachusetts Eye and Ear study is reported in Zola, "Culture and Symptoms."

Morrison is quoted in Bayor and Meagher, *The New York Irish,* 517.

Couch and Confessional, pages 130–32

Though the Freud observation is quoted in many places and by several reliable authors, including Anthony Burgess, Thomas Cahill, and Frank McCourt, I have not been able to find its original source; nor has my research assistant, Elizabeth Goodman, who combed the Freud concordance at Yale University and other references. She noted that the remark crops up repeatedly on Irish-related Web sites on the Internet, absent an original citation. Clearly, she noted, this is something Irish people like saying and repeating about themselves.

Speaking no praise, pages 132–34

The Irish Land League, led by Charles Stewart Parnell, devised a policy of leaving "severely alone" landlords and their agents who raised rents, and anyone who took over the land of an evicted tenant. A former British soldier who worked for an absentee landlord in County Mayo, Charles C. Boycott, became a test case for the Land League in 1880. Boycott found himself and his family quite severely alone, as servants and farmhands refused to work for him, merchants would not sell to him, and the mail carriers would not deliver his mail. The boycott quickly became a tactic used by Irish-led unions and others in the United States.

My discussion of Irish emotional silence and family patterns draws on works by Greeley, McGoldrick, and Garrett O'Connor and interviews with psychotherapists and alcoholism counselors.

Comments on Irish women drinking more than women from other ethnic groups are from McGoldrick, "Irish Families," and Vaillant, *The Natural History of Alcoholism Revisited.*

Stiletto smirks, emotional clubs, pages 134–37

Greeley's discussion of ridicule in *That Most Distressful Nation,* 108; I watched the Jesse Jackson episode on Martha's Vineyard, July, 1997.

I saw *Colin Quinn: An Irish Wake* at the Helen Hayes Theatre in New York, September 15, 1998.

God, but he was funny . . . , pages 137–39

The "response to the shibboleth" discussion is from Greenslade et al., "A Good Man's Fault."

I saw *Confessions of an Irish Rebel* at the Copley Square Theater, Boston, November 1, 1998.

Chapter Six

Interviews and discussions contributing to this chapter:
Anne McGlone Burke, January 25, 1999, by telephone from Chicago
Frank Butler, June 14, 1999, by telephone from Washington, D.C.
Charles Daly, November 24, 1998, Boston
Dr. Tom Durant, November 14, 1997, Boston
James T. Fisher, February 9, 1999, by telephone from St. Louis
Marianne Hughes, October 1, 1999, Cambridge, Massachusetts
Joe Leary, December 7, 1999, Newton, Massachusetts
Lawrence J. McCaffrey, December 2, 1998, Evanston, Illinois
Tim McCarthy, July 3, 2000, by telephone from Boston, Massachusetts
Mary Oates, June 23, 1999, by telephone from Weston, Massachusetts
Sean O'Huiginn, October 3, 1999, Boston
John Shea, January 28, 1999, New York City
Alan Wolfe, October 25, 1999, Chestnut Hill, Massachusetts

Major written sources consulted for this chapter:
Fisher, *Dr. America*
Ignatiev, *How the Irish Became White*
Moynihan, "The Irish"
Shannon, *The American Irish*

Pages 142–45

For information on native Irish generosity, see Donaghue et al., *Uncovering the Nonprofit Sector in Ireland;* Ruddle and Mulvihill, *Reaching Out;* and the government white paper cited in the text. Reports in recent years suggest giving has not kept pace with the expanding "Celtic Tiger" economy (see *Irish Times,* September 10, 1998).

A 1996 General Social Survey asked respondents if they had volunteered time in one of the following areas in the last month: health education; religious organizations; human services; environment; public/society benefit; recreation (adults); arts, culture and humanities; work-related organizations; political organizations or campaigns; youth development; private & community foundations; international/foreign; informal-alone-not for pay; other.

Among Irish Catholic, Irish non-Catholics, Jewish, WASP, and Italian Catholic respondents, Irish Catholics reported volunteering more than all others in four areas and more than most others in another five.

Among Irish Catholic, Irish non-Catholics, Jewish, WASP, and Italian Catholic respondents, the Irish Catholics surpassed all others in making contributions in four categories and were first or second in nine of the fifteen categories.

In terms of actual dollars contributed, Irish Catholics were not remarkable.

Pooled results from the General Social Surveys of 1988, 1989, 1990, 1991, 1993, 1994, analyzed by Boston College sociology department fellow Anthony Savoie show the following:

- that Irish Catholics are overrepresented in white-collar occupations (35.8 percent vs. 30.4 percent among other respondents) and in sales and clerical work (31.4 percent vs. 28.4 percent) and that they are underrepresented in blue-collar jobs (32.8 percent vs. 41.2 percent)
- that 7.2 percent of Irish Catholics worked in service (government, health care, clergy, psychologists, social workers, police, and firefighters), in contrast to 4.3 percent of respondents among Irish non-Catholics, Jews, WASPs, and Italian Catholics

Calvin Trillin's comments are from "American Chronicles: Democracy in Action," *New Yorker,* March 21, 1988.

Scoundrels, stereotypes, scapegoats, pages 145–48

I saw *Ragtime:* The Musical at the Colonial Theatre in Boston, January 21, 1999. The quotes are from press material handed out by SFX Theatricals/Broadway in Boston at the time of the run.

Accounts of the nascent labor movement and the Draft Riots are from Blessing, "Irish"; Morris, *American Catholic;* and Peter Quinn's review of Noel Ignatiev's *How the Irish Became White, America,* March 16, 1996.

Religion as race, religious racism, pages 148–50

The description of the Orange Riots is from Padden and Sullivan, *May the Road Rise to Meet You,* and Michael A. Gordon, "Orange Riots," in Glazier, *The Encyclopedia of the Irish in America,* 748–50.

Mooney's article appeared in *Boston Globe,* July 17, 1999.

For chronicles of busing in Boston, see Lukas, *Common Ground;* Lupo, *Liberty's Chosen Home;* and MacDonald, *All Souls.*

The description of the media presentation of Hicks is in Lukas, *Common Ground,* 136; the "family feud" discussion is on 246.

Dissonances among like voices, pages 150–51

McGreevy, *Parish Boundaries,* 134–36.

The account of Tammany Hall is from Shannon, *The American Irish;* Morris, *American Catholic;* and Edward T. O'Donnell, "Tammany Hall," in Glazier, *The Encyclopedia of the Irish in America,* 887–89.

For labor, see Morris, *American Catholic,* 209–21.

Weaving the safety net, pages 151–55

Frankel and Moynihan quotes are from Moynihan, "The Irish," 217–87; see also Blessing, "Irish."

Shannon's description of government is in *American Irish,* 60–67.

Brown and McKeown, *The Poor Belong to Us,* 1–12.

The number of non-Catholics enrolled in Roman Catholic schools grew from 2.7 percent in 1970 to 13.4 percent in 2000, according to a report in the August 6, 2000, *New York Times Education Life.* Background on inner-city Catholic schools today from the Inner City Scholarship Fund, Archdiocese of Boston.

Irish pagan babies, pious apostates, and presidents, pages 155–58

See Harrington's autobiography, *Fragments of the Century,* 4–13. The comment about Harrington's *The Other America* is from Victor Navasky's review of Maurice Isserman's biography *The Other American: The Life of Michael Harrington, New York Times Book Review,* May 28, 2000. See also Isserman biography.

The story of Dooley and the schoolchildren is in Fisher, *Dr. America,* 231–32. I also interviewed Fisher by telephone from St. Louis, February 9, 1999.

Moynihan's comment on Harvard and Fordham men is from Moynihan, "The Irish," 271.

O'Neill's reflections on Ronald Reagan are in O'Neill and Novak, *Man of the House,* 330–31.

Leaving the best unspoken, pages 158–61

On Kennedy and "archetypical attitudes," see Shannon, *The American Irish,* 225–30.

Chapter Seven

Interviews contributing to this chapter:

Edward Burke Jr., December 2, 1998, Chicago

Andrew Greeley, December 2, 1999, Boston

Monsignor Frank Kelley, November 11, 1999, Boston

Sister Karen Kennelly, July 23, 1999, by telephone from Los Angeles

Timothy Lennon, February 2, 1999, Chicago

Sheila Lyne, February 1, 1999, Chicago

Monsignor Philip Murnion, October 1, 1999, by telephone from New York City

Nancy Netzer, January 2000, by telephone from Chestnut Hill, Massachusetts

John Scanlon
Alan Wolfe, October 25, 1999, Chestnut Hill, Massachusetts

Major written sources consulted for this chapter:
Fisher, "Clearing the Streets"
Greeley, *Furthermore!*
McCaffrey, "Irish American Catholicism"
Morris, *American Catholic*
Wills, *Bare Ruined Choirs*
——, *Papal Sins.*

Pages 163–66

Introductory quote is from Morris, *American Catholic,* 321.

Survey data about Catholic attitudes are from Greeley, *Furthermore!,* 264, and University of Michigan Election Study, 1996. National Opinion Research Center and Gallup Poll data are cited in Ribadeneira, "Pope Likely to Challenge U.S."

Information on the decline in religious orders is from Morris, *American Catholic,* 292.

On the rebelliousness of current Irish Catholics, see McCaffrey, "Irish American Catholicism."

On "Catholic divorce," see Wills, *Papal Sins,* 171.

Homosexuality in the priesthood is discussed in Paulson, "Rector's Book on Clergy, Sex Is Bestseller."

Wills's statements about "the admission of married men" are from Wills, *Papal Sins,* 195.

My discussion of the popularity of theology on college campuses is based on interviews with administrators and faculty at Boston College, the University of Notre Dame, and St. Louis University. The statistics on "highly committed" Catholics is from Greeley, interview, December 2, 1999.

A devotion built on desperation, pages 166–69

The anachronistic view of Catholicism is from Morris, *American Catholic,* 40.

The "witches' brew" discussion is from Morris, 41.

The account of the devotional revolution in Ireland relies almost entirely on research and writing by Larkin, "The Devotional Revolution in Ireland." The description of Cullen is from Larkin and from Morris, *American Catholic,* 40–47.

The description of Irish puritanism is from McCaffrey, "Irish American Catholicism."

Mission to the new world, pages 169–71

Statistics on Irish seminarians is from Morris, *American Catholic,* 51.

The terms of "immigrant uplift" are in Morris, 111.

The account of New York archbishops is from McCaffrey, "Irish American Catholicism"; Morris; and Schemo, "Legacy of Leadership for Next Archbishop." Shelley is quoted in Schemo.

Rochester information is in Morris, 144.

Wills's quote about the "church-school complex" is in *Bare Ruined Choirs,* 24.

The village center, pages 171–74

McGreevy on Visitation is from *Parish Boundaries,* 94–97.

Fisher discusses the Irishization of the American Church in "Clearing the Streets."

The laity emerge, pages 174–76

On the Catholic response to *Humanae Vitae,* see Greeley, *Furthermore!,* 248. He also discussed the encyclical in an interview, December 2, 1999.

On growing support for women priests, see Wills, *Papal Sins,* 106.

The role of women, pages 176–78

For this section I relied on the *Frontline* program "The Catholic Church and Sex"; Greeley, *Furthermore!;* and Wills, *Papal Sins.*

Wills's comments on the Church's position on women's ordination are from *Papal Sins,* 104–5.

The survey on women's ordination is cited in Murphy, "Catholic Women Knock at a Closed Door."

Durkin and Montague's assertion is in their article "Surveying U.S. Nuns."

Clerical tokens and totems, pages 178–81

On sexual abuse within the Church, see Steinfels, "The Church Faces Trespasses of Priests."

John Paul's letter is quoted in Steinfels.

Greeley on pedophilia is in *Furthermore!,* 69–90.

Liberal versus conservative positions were expressed on the *Frontline* program "The Catholic Church and Sex."

The *Globe* survey is reported in Wilkes, "Must Catholics Settle for Less?"

Hoge is quoted in Morris, *American Catholic,* 317.

Departures and divisions in the flock, pages 181–83

The *Nothing Sacred* and "Sensation" discussions are based on Jurkowitz, "Nothing Sacred Boycott Gains Momentum"; Blaney, "Resurrecting Lost Episodes"; and Rich, "Pull the Plug on Brooklyn." The Cain quote on Donahue is in Tim Feran, "Greeley, Panel of Priests Say It's All Fine with Nothing Sacred," *Columbus Dispatch,* January 16, 1998.

C. J. Doyle's quote is from Lawrence, "Catholic Group Denounces Controversial BC Exhibit."

The discussion of the Boston College museum flap is based on my discussions with Nancy Netzer and BC faculty members familiar with the episode.

A twenty-first-century Irish Church, pages 183–87

The discussion of Hispanics in the Church is from McCaffrey, "Irish American Catholicism."

The Liam Ryan quote and other references to the Church in Ireland are from O'Toole, *The Lie of the Land,* 65–75, and Greeley, *Furthermore!*

The physical descriptions of Old St. Patrick's Church in Chicago are from Skerret, *At the Crossroads.* I spent the morning of January 31, 1999, at the church.

Chapter Eight

Interviews contributing to this chapter:

Thomas N. Brown, November 18, 1998, Cambridge, Massachusetts

Charles Daly, November 24, 1998, Boston

Frank Dougherty, July 14, 1999, by telephone from Philadelphia

Jane Duffin, July 19, 1999, Philadelphia

Conor Howard and Eddie Stack, February 17, 1999, San Francisco

Marie Jackson, January 27, 1999, Boston

Paul McGonagle, December 14, 1999, Boston

Helena Mulkerns, July 30, 2000, by e-mail

Kevin Nugent, July 12, 1999, Boston

Niall O'Dowd, October 13, 1999, New York City

Nuala O'Faoilain, January 31, 1999, Chicago

Sean O'Huiginn, October 3, 1999, Boston

Kevin Treanor, December 12, 1999, Boston

Pages 189–91

For Joseph O'Connor's recollections of Yanks in his youth, see the introduction to *Sweet Liberty,* 3–19.

Medb Ruane, "Greening of Irish Americans Finally in Place," *Irish Times,* September 7, 1998.

A New Irish spring, pages 191–92

For an extensive description of the "undocumented Irish" in the 1980s, see O'Hanlon, *The New Irish Americans,* 38–50.

The 1965 Immigration and Nationality Act limited immigration from Western Europe and established policies that would favor "family reunification." That put young Irish in the 1980s at a disadvantage, since few were children or siblings of people who had migrated in the most recent surge of Irish immigration in the 1950s.

The 1986 Immigration Reform and Control Act provided 40,000 Donnelly visas, named for Representative Brian Donnelly, a major sponsor of the bill. Although these visas were earmarked for the citizens of thirty-five European countries, the Irish snapped up 16,000 of them. The 1986 act provided amnesty for undocumented aliens who had come to the United States before January 1, 1982, but did not protect the many undocumented Irish who arrived after that year. It also increased the penalties for hiring undocumented aliens, making many of their lives more difficult.

In 1987, an undocumented construction worker, Patrick Hurley, founded the Irish Immigration Reform Movement, which would garner the support of many established Irish American organizations and the financial backing of such successful entrepreneurs as Chuck Feeney, Thomas Flatley, and Denis Kelleher. The IIRM was instrumental in pushing for reforms that resulted in the Immigration Amendments of 1988, a measure backed by Donnelly, Roman Mazzoli, and Representatives Charles Schumer and Howard Berman. Enacted just as the supply of Donnelly visas was running out, the amendments provided almost 30,000 green cards over two years plus a new 20,000-visa lottery system for 1990 and 1991 for which Ireland could qualify. (The visas from this law are called Berman visas.)

Representative Bruce Morrison, backed by the Irish government, forged the legislation that resulted in the Immigration Act of 1990, which provided 48,000 Morrison visas to immigrants from the Republic of Ireland. Morrison visas were later granted to immigrants from Northern Ireland as well.

Men in big green suits, pages 195–96

My primary written sources for the history of Irish American nationalism in this chapter are Brown, *Irish-American Nationalism;* Fleming, "The Green Flag in America"; Glazier, *The Encyclopedia of the Irish in America;* McCaffrey, *Textures of Irish America;* McCaffrey, *The Irish Catholic Diaspora in America;* O'Clery, *Daring Diplomacy;* and Wilson, *Irish America and the Ulster Conflict.*

The description of TV coverage of the Royal Ulster Constabulary is from Wilson, 21.

Shannon's comments on Irish Americans' attitudes toward the Troubles appear in Wilson, 139–40.

Details of Devlin's visit to the United States are from Wilson, 31–40.

The views from here, pages 196–200

The history of Irish American nationalism in the nineteenth century is from Wilson, *Irish America and the Ulster Conflict;* Fleming, "The Green Flag in America"; Glazier, *The Encyclopedia of the Irish in America;* and my interview with Thomas N. Brown.

McCaffrey's comments on Irish nationalism are from *Textures of Irish America,* 154.

Funds for "freedom fighters," pages 200–1

Flannery's comments are from Wilson, *Irish America and the Ulster Conflict,* 290. For a discussion of the class background of IRA supporters, see McCaffrey, *Textures of Irish America,* 155–63.

The account of Bloody Sunday and American reaction is primarily from Wilson,
51–75.

A different way, pages 201–5

Discussion of the Four Horsemen is based on Wilson, *Irish America and the Ulster
Conflict;* McCaffrey, *Textures of Irish America;* and interviews with Sean
O'Huiggin and Charles Daly.

Aikens's figures about the Ireland Fund are from a telephone discussion between
him and my research assistant, Elizabeth Goodman.

O'Dowd's "two choices" are quoted in O'Clery, *Daring Diplomacy,* 26. O'Dowd's
other comments are from my interview with him.

Comments on Martin Galvin are in O'Clery, 147–48.

A subtle shift, pages 205–9

O'Toole's comments on cultural crossover are from "The Irish American Cultural
Swap Shop," *Irish Times,* May 11, 2000.

According to the Irish Center for Migration Studies, immigration from Ireland to the
United States "abated and reversed itself" in 1995. Between that year and July
2000, some 118,000 American immigrants returned to Ireland. The hunger of
the "Celtic Tiger" economy created a labor shortage, and Ireland, for the first
time, was attracting immigrants looking for work in its thriving economy. For the
first time, too, the country has been experiencing the problems of in-migration—
prejudice, discrimination—that immigrants from Ireland have encountered in
other lands, according to news and anecdotal reports.

Chapter Nine

Interviews contributing to this chapter:

Frank Dougherty, July 17, 1999, by telephone from Philadelphia

Patrick Goggins, February 18, 1999, San Francisco

Helena Mulkerns, July 30, 2000, by e-mail

Sean O'Huiginn, October 3, 1999, Boston

Carmel O'Reilly, September 28, 1998, Cambridge, Massachusetts

Jim Sheridan, September 11, 1998, by telephone from Dublin

Pages 211–15

Martin Amis quote is from "Travolta's Second Act," *New Yorker,* February 20, 1995.

Clyde Haberman, "The Irish Finally Stop to Remember," *New York Times,* March
18, 1997.

Under Irish law, an American citizen who can prove that a grandparent was born in
Ireland is eligible for Irish citizenship. In 1989, 1,080 Americans applied for
"foreign birth registration"; in 1998, the number was 2,042, according to the
Irish embassy in Washington, D.C.

Andrew O'Hehir wrote on "New Irish" chic in the online magazine *Salon,* March 17,
1998 <http://www.salon.com/feature/1998/03/cov_17kitsch.html>.

Whelan quote is from Carol Coulter, "The Tiger and the Leprechaun: In the US, Irish Studies Is Now a Multimillion-dollar Industry, but How Should It Be Defined?" *Irish Times,* June 10, 1998.

Rainbow's end, pages 215–18

Trillin on Irish and Italian parades is in "American Chronicles: Democracy in Action," *New Yorker,* March 21, 1988.

Remembering, forgetting, pages 218–20

On the Boston Irish Famine Memorial, see Fintan O'Toole, "$1m Famine Memorial a Monument to Kitsch," *Irish Times,* July 3, 1998; Christine Temin, "The Public's Art?" *Boston Globe,* August 30, 1998; Jack Thomas, "Was Globe's Critic Too Hard on Irish Famine Memorial?" *Boston Globe,* September 21, 1998.

My account of the mixed response to *Angela's Ashes* is based on a telephone interview with Frank McCourt in February 1998; a conversation in Boston on April 1, 1998; and witnessing fans of the book that evening and on other occasions. See also Alex Beam, " 'Tis Rough for McCourt in Ireland," *Boston Globe,* November 11, 1999, and Kevin Cullen, "Limerick Rises from the Ashes," *Boston Globe,* January 17, 2000.

Bibliography

Books

Amory, Cleveland. *The Proper Bostonians.* New York: E. P. Dutton, 1947.

Barnes, John A. *Irish-American Landmarks: A Traveler's Guide.* Detroit: Gale Research, 1995.

Bayor, Ronald H., and Timothy J. Meagher, eds. *The New York Irish.* Baltimore: Johns Hopkins University Press, 1996.

Beatty, Jack. *The Rascal King: The Life and Times of James Michael Curley, 1874–1958.* Reading, Mass.: Addison-Wesley, 1992.

Birmingham, Stephen. *Real Lace: America's Irish Rich.* New York: Harper & Row, 1973.

Blessing, Patrick J. "Irish." In *The Harvard Encyclopedia of American Ethnic Groups,* edited by Stephan Thermstrom. Cambridge: Harvard University Press, Belknap Press, 1980.

Brown, Dorothy M., and Elizabeth McKeown. *The Poor Belong to Us: Catholic Charities and American Welfare.* Cambridge: Harvard University Press, 1997.

Brown, Thomas N. *Irish-American Nationalism.* New York: Greenwood, 1980.

Burchell, R. A. *The San Francisco Irish: 1848–1880.* Berkeley: University of California Press, 1980.

Cahill, Thomas. *How the Irish Saved Civilization.* New York: Doubleday, Anchor, 1996.

Callahan, Bob, ed. *The Big Book of American Irish Culture.* New York: Viking Penguin, 1987.

Carroll, James. *An American Requiem: God, My Father, and the War That Came Between Us.* Boston: Houghton Mifflin, 1996.

Casey, Marion R. *Ireland, New York, and the Irish Image in American Popular Culture, 1890–1960.* Doctoral dissertation. Ann Arbor: UMI Dissertation Services, 1998.

Clark, Dennis. *Hibernia America: The Irish and Regional Cultures.* Westport, Conn.: Greenwood Press, 1986.

Coffey, Michael, ed., and Terry Golway. *The Irish in America.* New York: Hyperion, 1997.

Cullinan, Elizabeth. *House of Gold.* Boston: Houghton Mifflin, 1969.

Curran, Joseph M. *Hibernian Green on the Silver Screen: The Irish and American Movies.* Westport, Conn.: Greenwood Press, 1989.

Curtis, L. Perry Jr. *Apes and Angels: The Irishman in Victorian Caricature.* Washington, D.C.: Smithsonian Institution Press, 1971.

Diner, Hasia. *Erin's Daughters in America.* Baltimore: Johns Hopkins University Press, 1983.

Donaghue, Freda, Helmut K. Anheier, and Lester M. Salamon. *Uncovering the Nonprofit Sector in Ireland: Its Economic Value and Significance.* Baltimore and Dublin: Johns Hopkins University Institute for Policy Studies, Center for Civil Society Studies, and the National College of Ireland, 1999.

Dowling, Patrick J. *California: The Irish Dream.* San Francisco: Golden Gate Publishers, 1989.

Emmons, David M. *The Butte Irish: Class and Ethnicity in an American Mining Town.* Chicago: University of Illinois Press, 1990.

Fanning, Charles. *The Irish Voice in America from the 1760s to the 1980s.* Lexington: University of Kentucky Press, 1990.

Farrell, James T. *Studs Lonigan: A Trilogy.* New York: Vanguard Press, 1978.

Fisher, James T. *Dr. America: The Lives of Thomas A. Dooley.* Amherst: University of Massachusetts Press, 1997.

Gibbons, Luke. *Critical Conditions: Transformations in Irish Culture.* South Bend: University of Notre Dame Press, 1997.

Glazier, Michael, ed. *The Encyclopedia of the Irish in America.* South Bend: University of Notre Dame Press, 1999.

Golway, Terry. *Irish Rebel: John Devoy and America's Fight for Irish Freedom.* New York: St. Martin's Press, 1998.

Goodwin, Doris Kearns. *The Fitzgeralds and the Kennedys.* New York: Simon & Schuster, 1987.

Gordon, Mary. *Good Boys and Dead Girls, and Other Essays.* New York: Viking, 1991.

———. *Final Payments.* New York: Ballantine, 1979.

Greeley, Andrew M. *Furthermore! Memories of a Parish Priest.* New York: Forge, 1999.

———. *The Irish Americans: The Rise to Money and Power.* New York: Harper & Row, 1981.

———. *That Most Distressful Nation: The Taming of the American Irish.* Chicago: Quadrangle Books, 1972.

Greeley, Andrew M. and William C. McCready. "The Transmission of Cultural Heritages: The Case of the Irish and the Italians." In *Ethnicity: Theory and Experience,* edited by Nathan Glazer and Daniel P. Moynihan, 209–35. Cambridge: Harvard University Press, 1975.

Hamill, Pete. *A Drinking Life.* Boston: Little, Brown, Back Bay Books, 1994.

Harrington, Michael. *Fragments of the Century.* New York: E. P. Dutton, Saturday Review Press, 1973.

Hayden,Tom, ed. *Irish Hunger: Personal Reflections on the Legacy of the Famine.* Boulder: Roberts Rinehart, 1997.

Howard, Maureen. *Bridgeport Bus.* New York: Penguin, 1980.

Hoy, Suellen. "Walking Nuns: Chicago's Irish Sisters of Mercy." In *At the Crossroads: Old St. Patrick's and the Chicago Irish,* edited by Ellen Skerret. Chicago: Loyola Press, Wild Onion Books, 1997.

Ignatiev, Noel. *How the Irish Became White.* New York: Routledge, 1995.

Kahn, E. J. Jr. *The Merry Partners: The Age and Stage of Harrigan and Hart.* New York: Random House, 1955.

———, ed. *Motherland: Writings by Irish-American Women about Mothers and Daughters.* New York: William Morrow, 1999.

Kennedy, William. *Ironweed.* New York: Viking Press, 1983.

———. *Very Old Bones.* New York: Viking Press, 1992.

Kiberd, Declan. *Inventing Ireland: The Literature of the Modern Nation.* Cambridge: Harvard University Press, 1995.

Lukas, J. Anthony. *Common Ground: A Turbulent Decade in the Lives of Three American Families.* New York: Knopf, 1985.

Lupo, Alan. *Liberty's Chosen Home: The Politics of Violence in Boston.* 2nd ed. Boston: Beacon Press, 1988.

MacDonald, Michael Patrick. *All Souls: A Family Memoir of Southie.* Boston: Beacon Press, 1999.

McCaffrey, Lawrence J. *The Irish Catholic Diaspora in America.* Washington, D.C.: Catholic University Press, 1997.

———. *Textures of Irish America.* Syracuse: Syracuse University Press, 1992.

———, et al. *The Irish in Chicago.* Urbana: University of Illinois Press, 1987.

———. "Irish American Catholicism." In *The Encyclopedia of the Irish in America,* edited by Michael Glazier, 128–37. South Bend: University of Notre Dame Press, 1999.

McCarthy, Abigail Quigley. *Private Faces, Public Places.* New York: Doubleday, 1972.

McCarthy, Imelda Cogan. "Out of Myth into History: A Hope for Irish Women in the 1990s." *Journal of Feminist Family Therapy* 4, no. 3/4 (1992).

McCourt, Frank. *Angela's Ashes.* New York: Scribner's, 1997.

———. *The Irish . . . and How They Got That Way.* Wilbur Theatre, Boston, March 29, 1998.

McDermott, Alice. *At Weddings and Wakes.* Boston: G. K. Hall, 1993.

———. *Charming Billy.* New York: Farrar, Straus & Giroux, 1998.

McGoldrick, Monica, "Irish Families." In *Ethnicity and Family Therapy,* edited by Monica McGoldrick et al. 2nd ed., 544–66. New York: Guilford Press, 1996.

McGreevy, John T. *Parish Boundaries: The Catholic Encounter with Race in the Twentieth Century Urban North.* Chicago: University of Chicago Press, 1998.

McHenry, Robert, ed. *Famous American Women: A Biographical Dictionary from Colonial Times to the Present.* New York: Dover, 1983.

Miller, Kerby A. *Emigrants and Exiles: Ireland and the Irish Exodus to North America.* New York: Oxford University Press, 1985.

Montgomery, David. "The Labor Movement." In *The Encyclopedia of the Irish in America,* edited by Michael Glazier, 525–31. South Bend: University of Notre Dame Press, 1999.

Morris, Charles R. *American Catholic: The Saints and Sinners Who Built America's Most Powerful Church.* New York: Random House, 1997.

Moynihan, Daniel Patrick. "The Irish." In *Beyond the Melting Pot: The Negroes, Puerto Ricans, Jews, Italians, and Irish of New York City,* by Nathan Glazer and Daniel Patrick Moynihan. 2nd ed. Cambridge: MIT Press, 1970.

O'Casey, Sean. *Three Plays: Juno and the Paycock; The Shadow of a Gunman; The Plough and the Stars.* London: Macmillan, 1964.

O'Clery, Conor. *Daring Diplomacy.* Boulder: Roberts Rinehart, 1997.

O'Connor, Edwin. *The Last Hurrah.* Boston: Little, Brown, 1956.

O'Connor, Joseph. *Sweet Liberty: Travels in Irish America.* Niwot, Colo.: Roberts Rinehart, 1997.

O'Connor, Thomas. *The Boston Irish: A Political History.* Boston: Northeastern University Press, 1995.

O'Dwyer, Paul. *Counsel for the Defense.* New York: Simon & Schuster, 1979.

O'Hanlon, Roy. *The New Irish Americans.* Niwot, Colo.: Roberts Rinehart, 1997.

O'Neill, Tip, with William Novak. *Man of the House: The Life and Political Memoirs of Speaker Tip O'Neill.* New York: Random House, 1987.

O'Toole, Fintan. *Ex-Isle of Erin: Images of a Global Ireland.* Dublin: New Island Books, 1997.

———. *The Lie of the Land: Irish Identities.* London: Verso, 1997.

Oates, Mary J. *The Catholic Philanthropic Tradition in America.* Bloomington: Indiana University Press, 1995.

Owens, Rosemary Cullen. *Smashing Times: A History of the Irish Women's Suffrage Movement, 1889–1922.* Dublin: Attic Press, 1984.

Padden, Michael, and Robert Sullivan. *May the Road Rise to Meet You: Everything You Need to Know about Irish American History.* New York: Plume, 1999.

Quinn, Colin. *An Irish Wake.* Helen Hayes Theatre, New York City, September 15, 1998.

Quinn, Peter. *Banished Children of Eve.* New York: Penguin, 1994.

Ruddle, Helen, and Ray Mulvihill. *Reaching Out: Charitable Giving and Volunteering in the Republic of Ireland.* 1994 Survey. Dublin: National College of Industrial Relations, 1994.

Shannon, William V. *The American Irish.* Amherst: University of Massachusetts Press, 1990.

Skerrett, Ellen, ed. *At the Crossroads: Old Saint Patrick's and the Chicago Irish.* Chicago: Loyola Press, Wild Onion Books, 1997.

Stivers, Richard. *A Hair of the Dog: Irish Drinking and American Stereotype.* University Park: Pennsylvania University Press, 1976.

Takaki, Ronald. *A Different Mirror: A History of Multi-Cultural America.* New York: Little, Brown, 1993.

Vaillant, George E. *The Natural History of Alcoholism Revisited.* Cambridge: Harvard University Press, 1995.

Waters, John. *An Intelligent Person's Guide to Contemporary Ireland.* London: Duckworth, 1997.

Waters, Mary C. *Ethnic Options: Choosing Identities in America.* Berkeley: University of California Press, 1990.

Weaver, Mary Jo. "Who Can Find a Valiant Woman? American Catholic Women in Historical Perspective." In *New Catholic Women: A Contemporary Challenge to Traditional Religious Authority,* 1–36. Bloomington: Indiana University Press, 1996.

Williams, William H. A. *'Twas Only an Irishman's Dream: The Image of Ireland and the Irish in Popular Song Lyrics, 1800–1920.* Urbana: University of Illinois Press, 1996.

Wills, Garry. *Bare Ruined Choirs: Doubt, Prophecy, and Radical Religion.* Garden City, N.Y.: Doubleday, 1972.

———. *Papal Sins: Structures of Deceit.* New York: Doubleday, 2000.

Wilson, Andrew J. *Irish America and the Ulster Conflict, 1968–1995.* Washington, D.C.: Catholic University Press of America, 1995.

Wolfe, Tom. *Bonfire of the Vanities.* New York: Farrar, Straus & Giroux, 1990.

Woodham-Smith, Cecil. *The Great Hunger: Ireland 1845–1849.* London: Hamish Hamilton, 1962; New York: Penguin, 1991.

Articles

Blaney, Rita. "Resurrecting Lost Episodes: Nothing Sacred." *National Catholic Reporter,* October 8, 1999.

Callahan, Bob. "The Joys of Being Irish." *Salon,* March 17, 1998. <http://www.salon.com/feature/1998/03/cov_17callahan.html>.

"Cheers: How the Irish Drink in the 1990s." *Irish Times,* December 28, 1998.

Donovan, James M. "An Etiologic Model of Alcoholism." *American Journal of Psychiatry* 143 (1986): 1–11.

Durkin, Elizabeth, and Julie Durkin Montague. "Surveying U.S. Nuns," *America,* February 11, 1995.

Fielder, Mari Kathleen. "Chauncey Olcott: Irish-American Mother Love, Romance, and Nationalism." *Eire-Ireland* 22:2 (1987): 4–26.

Fisher, James T. "Clearing the Streets of the Catholic Lost Generation." *South Atlantic Quarterly* (Summer 1994): 604–29.

Fleming, Thomas. "The Green Flag in America." *American Heritage,* June-July 1979, 50–63.

Greenslade, Liam, Maggie Pearson, and Moss Madden. "A Good Man's Fault: Alcohol and John, Irish People at Home and Abroad." *Alcohol & Alcoholism* (1995): 407–17.

Johnson, Dirk, "In Illinois, It's the Political Life for Riley, Gilhooley, et al." *New York Times Week in Review,* March 14, 1999.

Jurkowitz, Mark. "Nothing Sacred Boycott Gains Momentum." *Boston Globe,* October 1, 1997.

Larkin, Emmet. "The Devotional Revolution in Ireland, 1850–75." *The American Historical Review* (June 1972).

Lawrence, J. M. "Catholic Group Denounces Controversial BC Exhibit." *Boston Herald,* November 11, 1999.

Meagher, Timothy J. "Sweet Good Mothers and Young Women Out in the World: The Roles of Irish American Women in Late Nineteenth and Early Twentieth-Century Worcester, Massachusetts." Reprint from *U.S. Catholic Historian* 5 (1986).

Murphy, Carlyle. "Catholic Women Knock at a Closed Door." *Boston Globe,* September 19, 1999.

O'Gorman, Thomas J. "The Chicago Irish—The Greening of the Prairie." *World of Hibernia,* Spring 1996.

Paulson, Michael. "Rector's Book on Clergy, Sex Is Bestseller—Among Priests." *Boston Globe,* June 30, 2000.

Quinn, Peter. "Looking for Jimmy." *The World of Hibernia* (Spring 1999).

Ribadeneira, Diego. "Pope Likely to Challenge U.S." *Boston Globe,* January 26, 1999.

Rich, Frank. "Pull the Plug on Brooklyn." *New York Times,* October 19, 1999.

Schemo, Diana Jean. "Legacy of Leadership for Next Archbishop." *New York Times,* February 12, 2000, sec. A.

Smith, Jean Kennedy. "The Spirit of Irish Women." *Boston Globe,* March 17, 1998.

Steinfels, Peter. "The Church Faces Trespasses of Priests." *New York Times,* June 27, 1993.

Walsh, D. "Alcohol and Ireland." *British Journal of Addiction* 82 (1987): 118–20.

Walsh, Joan. "The Kennedy Way of Grief." *Salon,* July 22, 1999. <http://www.salon.com/news/feature/1999/07/22/grief/index1.html>.

Wilkes, Paul. "Must Catholics Settle for Less?" *Boston Globe,* December 19, 1999, sec. C.

Zola, Irving Kenneth. "Culture and Symptoms: An Analysis of Patients' Presenting Complaints." *American Sociological Review* (October 1966): 615-30.

Other sources

"The Catholic Church and Sex: A Roundtable Discussion." On "John Paul II: The Millennial Pope." *Frontline.* WGBH, Boston, November 16, 1999.

Leonora O'Reilly Papers, Mary Kenney O'Sullivan Papers, Women's Trade Union League Papers. Schlesinger Library, Radcliffe College, Cambridge, Mass.

Surveys of National Opinion Research Center Data. Commissioned by author, March 1999.

National Health and Lifestyle Surveys. Galway: Health Promotion Unit, Department of Health and Children, Dublin Centre for Health Promotion Studies, National University of Ireland, February 1999.

National Opinion Research Center General Social Survey. Chicago: National Opinion Research Center, University of Chicago, 1996.

1996 Michigan Election Survey.

Index

Page numbers of photographs appear in italics.